French Gastronomy *and*

the Magic of Americanism

In the series *Politics, History, and Social Change*, edited by John C. Torpey

ALSO IN THIS SERIES:

Donald Pitkin, *Four Germanys*

John Torpey and David Jacobson, *Transformations of Warfare in the Contemporary World*

Heribert Adam and Kogila Moodley, *Imagined Liberation: Xenophobia, Citizenship, and Identity in South Africa, Germany, and Canada*

Aidan McGarry and James Jasper, *The Identity Dilemma: Social Movements and Collective Identity*

Philipp H. Lepenies, *Art, Politics, and Development: How Linear Perspective Shaped Policies in the Western World*

Andrei S. Markovits and Emily Albertson, *Sportista: Female Fandom in the United States*

Nicholas Toloudis, *Teaching Marianne and Uncle Sam: Public Education, State Centralization, and Teacher Unionism in France and the United States*

Philip S. Gorski, *The Protestant Ethic Revisited*

Étienne Balibar, Sandro Mezzadra, and Ranabir Samaddar, eds., *The Borders of Justice*

Kenneth H. Tucker, Jr., *Workers of the World, Enjoy! Aesthetic Politics from Revolutionary Syndicalism to the Global Justice Movement*

Hans-Lukas Kieser, *Nearest East: American Millennialism and Mission to the Middle East*

Ernesto Verdeja, *Unchopping a Tree: Reconciliation in the Aftermath of Political Violence*

Rebecca Jean Emigh, *The Undevelopment of Capitalism: Sectors and Markets in Fifteenth-Century Tuscany*

Aristide R. Zolberg, *How Many Exceptionalisms? Explorations in Comparative Macroanalysis*

Thomas Brudholm, *Resentment's Virtue: Jean Améry and the Refusal to Forgive*

Patricia Hill Collins, *From Black Power to Hip Hop: Racism, Nationalism, and Feminism*

Daniel Levy and Natan Sznaider, translated by Assenka Oksiloff, *The Holocaust and Memory in the Global Age*

Brian A. Weiner, *Sins of the Parents: The Politics of National Apologies in the United States*

Heribert Adam and Kogila Moodley, *Seeking Mandela: Peacemaking between Israelis and Palestinians*

Marc Garcelon, *Revolutionary Passage: From Soviet to Post-Soviet Russia, 1985–2000*

Götz Aly and Karl Heinz Roth, translated by Assenka Oksiloff, *The Nazi Census: Identification and Control in the Third Reich*

Immanuel Wallerstein, *The Uncertainties of Knowledge*

Michael R. Marrus, *The Unwanted: European Refugees from the First World War through the Cold War*

RICK FANTASIA

French Gastronomy *and* *the* Magic of Americanism

TEMPLE UNIVERSITY PRESS
Philadelphia • Rome • Tokyo

TEMPLE UNIVERSITY PRESS
Philadelphia, Pennsylvania 19122
www.temple.edu/tempress

Library of Congress Cataloging-in-Publication Data

Names: Fantasia, Rick, author.
Title: French gastronomy and the magic of Americanism / Rick Fantasia.
Description: Philadelphia : Temple University Press, 2018. | Series:
    Politics, history, and social change | Includes bibliographical references
    and index. |
Identifiers: LCCN 2018021246 (print) | LCCN 2018024830 (ebook) | ISBN
    9781439912317 (E-book) | ISBN 9781439912294 (cloth: alk. paper) | ISBN
    9781439912300 (pbk. : alk. paper)
Subjects: LCSH: Gastronomy—France. | Popular culture—United States. |
    Globalization.
Classification: LCC TX637 (ebook) | LCC TX637 .F28 2018 (print) | DDC
    641.01/3—dc23
LC record available at https://lccn.loc.gov/2018021246

9 8 7 6 5 4 3 2 1

Dedicated to the memory of

RENÉ MÉTRAL (1935–2017),

who shared with me his knowledge and love
for French gastronomy,
and

PIERRE BOURDIEU (1930–2002)

whose advice and encouragement
made me think I might be able to make
analytical sense of it

Contents

Preface: Making Sense of both France and "France"   ix

Acknowledgments   xv

1 Who Killed Bernard Loiseau?   1

2 The Symbolic Economy of French Gastronomy   37

3 Fast Food in France: A Market for the Impossible   91

4 Industrial Cuisine and the "Magic" of Americanism   127

5 Conflicts of Interest: A Cultural Field in Transformation   167

Index   213

Preface

Making Sense of both France and "France"

S o who am I to be writing a book about France anyway? And a book about French gastronomy at that! After all, I am American and have been my entire life. For over half of it I've worked as an academic, teaching and writing about class, culture, and cities, mostly in the United States. Where, along this intellectual path, did France come from and why French gastronomy? Frankly, where did I get the chutzpah to think I could insinuate myself, intellectually, into the very heart of French society and begin rummaging around in its cultural imagination? In certain ways I was compelled to engage with "France" because it had always loomed large, symbolically, in my own cultural imagination. And this, before ever having visited the country or knowing very much about it. For me, "France" had always signified a particular expression of "Europe," in the sense of being a generic construction that seemed to represent and embody qualities of refinement, of venerability, of erudition, and of sophistication. Although not entirely absent from the world I knew, these tended to be rare qualities in my surroundings growing up. With this preface I'd like to provide a short "socio-self-analysis" by offering some reflections on my relationship with France as a place, and with "France" as a symbolic construction. In other words, I wish to identify the principal social determinants that compelled, or made possible, the work that produced this book. Although the form seems autobiographical, its objective is socioanalytic, with the aim of objectifying the experiences that produced this work.[1]

My first trip to France in 1970 was part of a dual escape strategy. One purpose was to take myself away from the lure of violent radicalism that had begun to bubble over among my fellow antiwar activists at a community college in upstate New York. Our group was largely made up of Vietnam War veterans, local working-class youths awaiting their fate in the impending draft lottery, and students from New York City who were seeking refuge upstate as part of their own escape plan. At the time the radicalism of our rhetoric seemed inadequate to counter the provocations of the Nixon administration, and so militant action was increasingly contemplated and quietly discussed (though in retrospect, it seems very possible that those doing the most to encourage violent actions were undercover provocateurs working for the government). In the context of this political turbulence, being a 19-year-old community college student seeing few clear routes ahead of me, I took the advice of a sympathetic instructor and made a plan to go to France to study.

The second motive for my escape strategy was to seek a kind of social refuge in France. In taking out a loan to study in Paris for a year, I was bankrolling a fantasy of social mobility (a student loan of $1,000 in 1970 somehow covered the cost of a one-way flight, all student fees, and several months of room and board!). By making my way to Paris, I imagined I was defying the probability of a conventional lower-middle-class life in upstate New York and avoiding the social fate of my father, a Willy Loman–like figure who was a white-collar salesman with a warm, generous, outsized personality but little self-worth. France was an opening to another world, as it has been to generations of idealistic young Americans chasing their bohemian escapade in Paris. For me, Paris was also a site of social levitation where, despite having arrived with few French language skills, I soaked in its cultural cornucopia and learned nearly every contour and cranny of the city by taking a different walking route home every night after the last metro, from the bars and cafés of the Latin Quarter to a dilapidated but magnificent little studio apartment in the north of the city. Although the Paris I inhabited was not the Paris of writers and artists and intellectuals that filled my cultural imagination, I could begin to imagine what inhabiting that Paris might be like.

---

1. In this I have been encouraged by Pierre Bourdieu's socioanalytical orientation in *Sketch for a Self-Analysis* (Chicago: University of Chicago Press, 2008).

Some years later, and after taking a rather long, meandering route through college, with stops both before and after for extended stints as a worker and labor organizer, I went to graduate school to study sociology. The combination of a less-than-privileged social background and several years of experience on the shop floor had given me confidence and motivation to challenge areas of sociological theory and research that concerned labor and the working class. By taking a critical stance in graduate school and beyond, I was in a somewhat oblique position in relation to mainstream sociology, with its strong currents of positivism and its quantitative imperative, and to the radical alternatives that had been spawned in reaction to it, particularly those weighted down by various inflections of Althusserian structuralism. It was in this intellectual context that I encountered the work of Pierre Bourdieu.

One advantage of having gone on to marry into a French family was that it occasioned regular visits to France during summer breaks and on sabbatical leaves. These visits were a vantage point from which I could observe the daily rhythm of life in a small village near the Alps and provided an opportunity to struggle with the French language skills that had always been so difficult to master. For an American academic increasingly interested in the sociology of France, such regular visits provided a valuable observation post. For an academic attempting to understand the social logic of French gastronomy, having a father-in-law with a lifetime of experience as a French chef and restaurant owner was a truly unique gift. He was more than willing to share the language, techniques, organization, and informal ways of the French restaurant, all of which had been practiced every day in his kitchen.

I was fortunate to have been introduced to Pierre Bourdieu in 1990, just as I was beginning a small research project to study the establishment of markets for American mass culture in France. I was particularly drawn to the processes of production, marketing, and consumption of fast food, blue jeans, Disneyland, Tupperware, and other iconic American mass cultural goods. To be able to read Bourdieu and then be able to discuss this work with him at various points was an extraordinary privilege that was critically important on several levels. One thing that I soon understood was that I would not be able to practice Bourdieu's analytical approach effectively if I were only focusing on the social world "out there" (i.e., the empirical world of American mass cultural goods in France), without, simultaneously, analyzing the social world "in here" (i.e., the conceptual universe of received categories operating inside of my own head). That is, Bourdieu's theoretical method required a thorough questioning of the internalized social world, a sort of mental and conceptual "housecleaning" through which the conventional categories of sociological analysis are critically reappraised. Fundamentally, this also required a reconsideration of the very object of my analysis, which meant (in this case) a thorough reexamination of what I had imagined would be a perfectly reasonable "cultural studies" approach to "Americanization" in France. This reappraisal prompted me to erase and to redraw the boundaries of the project several times. At the most basic level, it pushed me to relinquish a conceptual framework in which fast food (or "Americanization") could be understood as a thing-in-itself and to begin to consider ways in which Americanized mass culture and traditional (French) cultural forms had been constructed in relation to one another. Thus, despite the appearance of a relationship of mutual disdain at the symbolic level, what began to reveal itself was a relationship that was thoroughly interpenetrated at the institutional level and in completely counterintuitive ways.

In the summer of 1995, before arriving for one particular meeting with Bourdieu, I had expected that an early study of fast food in France would be completed upon the publication of a forthcoming article on the topic.[2] During the discussion, however, it became clear that the project was actually just getting started, for if I were serious about constructing a truly relational analysis it would require an understanding of the practices and institutions of haute cuisine, in relation to the practices (and practitioners) of fast-food production and consumption in France. This meant that on top of the research I had already completed on the latter I would have to begin collecting a sufficient quantity of empirical material to allow for a serious analysis of the former. My father-in-law proved to be extremely helpful in this regard by serving as an informal, but informed, informant on French gastronomy, as well as for making available to me a personal archive of trade magazines and journals from his participation in the chef profession. Starting with these sources I began to construct a database that had three elements: (1) biographic dossiers on 37 chefs who had received three-star ratings in the *Michelin Guide* during the decade of the 1990s; (2) a collection of the profiles of 244 other French chefs who had received recognition within the profession during that same decade, by virtue of having been the focus of at least one profile published by the main professional journal for chefs; (3) studying the career trajectories of less-consecrated chefs by examining the resumes of "culinary professionals" that included 792 chefs and

---

2. R. Fantasia, "Fast Food in France," *Theory and Society* 24 (1995).

640 culinary workers in secondary positions, in a directory put out by the publishers of an important French culinary guide.[3]

Such a newly reconfigured (and expanded) project would prove to be extremely time consuming, since much of the work could only be done during relatively short windows of time, but it was a thoroughly rewarding intellectual experience for it forced me to rethink almost everything. This included a long-standing intellectual commitment to a Marxist analysis that favored "production" over the cultural and symbolic dimensions of the social world. Critical to the process of rethinking, especially during its early stages, were the gestures of support and encouragement from Professor Bourdieu. Partly, they served to compensate for a relatively modest level of institutional consecration (an educational background outside of the most highly ranked centers of sociological training, and a somewhat modest position at an undergraduate college which, although somewhat elevated socially, stocks only a limited supply of scientific capital). And partly, encouragement from Bourdieu provided a strong source of motivation in a process of intellectual renovation that might otherwise have seemed too difficult, or too "impractical," or simply too unrewarding to a sustained investment of time in the middle of a busy academic career. To have felt oneself as part of Bourdieu's scientific project, if only for a few years, provided a powerful impetus. Since no one was as aware of the impact of the conditions of intellectual production on scientific work as Bourdieu, it is hard to believe that the demonstrations of generosity and attention that he extended were with no thought to their value as a source of symbolic capital. Moreover, in the process of rethinking, Bourdieu's analytical method represented a potent alternative source of intellectual/scientific authority, serving as counterweight to the residues of positivism in American sociology, as well as to both the preconstructed political requirements of cultural studies and the categorical imperatives of Marxist theory.

Perhaps most important, Bourdieu's encouragement provided crucial symbolic ballast for a project that, among other things, has sought to demystify a cultural domain whose value so many have seemed to have a stake in safeguarding. Whether fruitful or not at an analytical level, to the extent that this project disturbs the veil of belief surrounding French gastronomy, it can be viewed as a challenge to the stylistic pretensions of social and intellectual elites everywhere. Among many things, "Europe," "France," and

---

3. Les Éditions du Bottin Gourmand, *Les Étoiles de la gastronomie française 1998–1999* (Paris, 1998).

especially French gastronomy have served as symbolic resources furnishing endless opportunities for social elites to display their good taste and their cultural plumage to one another. Quite frankly, the prospect of helping to deflate such pretentions has probably helped me stay focused on this protracted project for far longer than I otherwise would have imagined.

Acknowledgments

Over the long life of this project there were many people who lent encouragement and criticism, in various forms, and I am extremely grateful to them all. They include Jérôme Bourdieu, Mary Ann Clawson, Catherine Eden, Priscilla Parkhurst Ferguson, Marita Flisback, Zoe Greenfield, Chaia Heller, Micah Kleit, Michèle Lamont, Vanina Leschziner, Emily Ruppel, and Loic Wacquant. In addition, I'd like to thank my hosts and audiences at a number of Sociology Departments, both in the United States and abroad, for kindly permitting me to present various parts of this work at various stages. While I take complete responsibility for all errors of logic and presentation, this book has benefited greatly from their ideas and insights.

Thanks to Mélusine Bonneau, Anna Marechal, Christiane Métral, and Nathalie Métral for their assistance with the research at various points, as well as Jamie Armstrong for her production work and Kate Weigand for developing the index. Throughout the life of this project I have enjoyed the support and goodwill of a wonderful group of colleagues in the Smith College Department of Sociology; and I am grateful to the Provost's office and the Committee on Faculty Compensation and Development at Smith for sabbatical support, travel grants, and other funding assistance that facilitated the research that has made this book possible. And many thanks to Ryan Mulligan, Nikki Miller, and the rest of the Temple University Press team for their work in bringing this book into being.

French Gastronomy *and*

the Magic of Americanism

1

Who Killed Bernard Loiseau?

A Preliminary Autopsy

It is not entirely clear why the sudden death of the *master chef* Bernard Loiseau caused such a stir in France. His wide notoriety surely played a role, as his beaming smile was displayed seemingly everywhere, on television screens and across the pages of all the major mass-market magazines.[1] It may also have been the sheer incongruity between the brutal way that he died and the grandeur and elegance of the world that he left behind. Or perhaps it was that, after having occupied such a central place in such a revered domain, it was simply impossible for most people to imagine haute cuisine without the presence of Bernard Loiseau, who was among the grandest of the grand chefs of France when, on the afternoon of February 24, 2003, at the age of fifty-two, he retired to his bedroom with his hunting rifle and took the hard way out. While a medical autopsy left no doubt that it was he who had pulled the trigger, the absence of a suicide note left family, the media, colleagues in the culinary profession, and most everyone else searching for a motive.

---

1. A poll published by the trade magazine *L'Hôtellerie* indicated that almost nine out of ten French people recognized the face of Bernard Loiseau, making him perhaps the most widely recognized of all the chefs in France, according to William Echikson, in "Death of a Chef," *New Yorker*, May 12, 2003, p. 61.

Almost immediately, speculation centered on the downgrading of Loiseau's la Côte d'Or restaurant by the *Gault&Millau* guide, which had recently lowered his rating from nineteen to seventeen, out of a possible twenty points. Paul Bocuse, Loiseau's longtime friend and probably the most venerated of the grand chefs of France, bitterly declared "Bravo, *Gault-Millau*, you have won," noting that "*Gault-Millau* took away two points, and, along with two or three press articles, that is what killed Bernard."[2] Jacques Pourcel, renowned chef and president of the Chambre Syndicale de la haute cuisine française, circulated a letter to his colleagues blaming "terrible media pressure" for the death of Loiseau; while François Simon, food critic for the newspaper *Le Figaro*, suggested that Loiseau's la Côte d'Or might have been in danger of losing its third star in the all-important *Michelin Guide*.[3]

The entire French culinary profession seemed to engage in a long moment of introspection following Loiseau's demise, with the outsized influence of the gastronomic guides as a central focus of culpability. Within months of the tragedy a survey of head chefs was commissioned by a restaurant industry trade magazine that posed the question unambiguously: "The tragic disappearance of Bernard Loiseau, last February 24th has revived a lively polemic on gastronomic guides and critiques. What is your opinion of the latter?"[4] The chef/respondents were offered several structured answers to choose from, but overall their survey responses were quite muted. Only 10.5 percent of the chefs agreed with the statement that the gastronomic guides "create an impossible level of stress"; while an even smaller percentage (7.7 percent) indicated that they had themselves been judged "wrongly" by the guides (37.5 percent thought that food critics failed to visit their restaurants regularly enough to make an informed critique). It probably should not be surprising that just a small percentage of chefs were willing to express enmity or resentment with respect to gastronomic guides since,

---

2. Craig S. Smith, "Bitterness Follows French Chef's Death," *New York Times*, February 26, 2003, p. A3. Two days earlier, after having spoken with Loiseau by telephone and finding him depressed, Bocuse had sent him a photo of the two of them on which he had written, "Bernard, life is beautiful" ("La Disparition tragique du chef Bernard Loiseau," *Le Monde*, February 25, 2003).

3. See Echikson, "Death of a Chef," pp. 61–62.

4. The survey, by *Néorestauration* magazine, was conducted by fax on a sample of 3,920 head chefs in a wide variety of restaurants and kitchens (commercial, institutional, independent, and chain establishments) and had a 9.92 percent (389) response rate. See Patrice Cecconello, "Les Guides gastronomiques: Un baromètre indispensible," *Néorestauration*, no. 400, July/August 2003, p. 36.

as a group of "believers," these practitioners of the gastronomic faith could not be expected to easily or simply reject the system of belief that governed their professional lives.

In response to the death of Loiseau, a representative of the *Gault&Millau* guide immediately rushed to deny culpability. Its head, Patrick Mayenobe, reportedly asserted, "It's not a bad score or one less star that killed him. . . . This great chef must have had other worries," adding "on the contrary, he said in 2000 that if he passed from 19 to 17 out of 20 [rating points], that it would be a formidable challenge for him to return to the top"; while a spokesperson for *Michelin* reportedly "would only express sadness for Loiseau's death and confirm that his stars were safe—for this year at least."[5] While the loss of a *Michelin* star could have a seriously damaging effect on the career of a chef, including on their position and reputation within the profession, and therefore in French society, not to mention the economic viability of their restaurant, the power of the *Gault&Millau* rating was much less significant at the time of Loiseau's death. I show in this book that not only was its power of consecration always a distant second to the power of the *Michelin Guide* but whatever influence it once wielded has diminished in recent years, thereby complicating any clear understanding of his reaction. After all, at the time Loiseau took his life he still held the highest rating in the more important *Michelin Guide*.[6]

Of course it was also possible that Loiseau harbored a "fear of falling," or an anxiety about *losing* a *Michelin* star. Indeed, several months prior he had attended a meeting at *Michelin* headquarters in Paris, where—after having been gently warned, "stay in your kitchen and don't do too much business"—he is said to have confided to Paul Bocuse that "he would kill himself if he lost a star."[7] Later, *Michelin*'s director of publications, Derek Brown, with whom Loiseau had met, denied the significance of the meeting, noting that "Bernard was his usual charming, warm, dynamic self. . . . We didn't and never would threaten to take away a star, and we did not advise him what to do. We are not a consultancy, after all."[8]

---

5. Quoted in J. B. "Disparition tragique"; and Amanda Ripley, "Fallen Star," *TIME Europe*, vol. 161, no. 10, March 10, 2003, p. 47.

6. At the time of his suicide he knew that he had retained his three stars because while the annual *Michelin* ratings are typically released in March, they happened to have been released in early February in 2003 (as they were again in 2004), several weeks before his suicide. Smith, "Bitterness Follows," p. A3.

7. Smith, p. A3, and see Echikson, "Death of a Chef," p. 67.

8. Echikson, "Death of a Chef," p. 67.

Apart from the explicit reactions by the gastronomic guides, defense of the system of gastronomic criticism was mounted by the press on both sides of the Atlantic. One, issued by the former restaurant editor of the *New York Times*, seemed calculated to deflect criticism of the guides by underscoring the relative insignificance of *Gault&Millau*, pointing to its "precipitous decline" in recent years and its low standing in relation to the importance of *Michelin* stars, while noting that "if Mr. Loiseau was distraught, it probably wasn't over stars," adding (adamantly, but somewhat incongruously): "I don't believe for a minute that the press killed the chef. To the contrary, Bernard Loiseau benefited mightily from press laurels. In 1986, he rose to prominence when a popular French magazine named him an up-and-coming culinary genius. The magazine was *Gault&Millau*."[9]

In the issue that followed his suicide, the weekly *Paris Match* displayed the photo of a bright, smiling Loiseau on its cover and an eight-page photo spread of the chef inside that presented him interacting happily with his family and colleagues, at work and at play, and included one photo of him out hunting, with a rifle slung over his shoulder. The accompanying article surveyed the various theories of his suicide, playing down the issue of the guides, while emphasizing instead his powerful hunger for cultural recognition ("It was my goal to be huge as a chef, like one of the greatest of soccer stars" p. 40) as well as the financial pressures he faced that threatened to mire him in debt until the year 2010.[10] It is quite true that after being granted his third star in the all-important *Michelin Guide* in 1991, Loiseau embarked on an ambitious and expensive series of renovations and additions to his la Côte d'Or restaurant; he also purchased three bistros in Paris, creating a culinary edifice that made him the first grand chef to be listed on the Paris stock exchange.[11] But even though he had headed a substantial business operation, Loiseau's finance director rejected the idea that money was the cause of his death, suggesting a less rational motivation: "All of that is completely false. The restaurants were doing quite well"; he stressed

9. Whether or not Loiseau benefited is really beside the point, just as the suicide is really beside the point with respect to the influence of the guides on culinary practices. In fact, even more recently than 1986 Loiseau was named one of the "Best Eight Chefs of France" in the magazine, published every trimester. See Luc Dubanche, "Bernard Loiseau: La force du bâtisseur," *Gault&Millau*, no. 337, Winter 1999–2000, pp. 54–58.

10. "Bernard Loiseau: Une vie brisée," *Paris Match*, no. 2806, February 27–March 5, 2003, pp. 36–43.

11. The acquisition of three *Michelin* stars and its significance is detailed in William Echikson's remarkable profile of Bernard Loiseau, *Burgundy Stars: A Year in the Life of a Great French Restaurant* (Boston: Little, Brown, 1995).

that although "Bernard started to think that if he didn't change, next year he'd lose a star, then reservations would go down, debts would accrue, and he would go bankrupt," Loiseau had no pending financial troubles at the time of his suicide: "It would have taken a decade of losses before we were bankrupt."[12] If the problem was not financial, then what could it have been? Speculation turned to the effects of stress and overwork on Loiseau's mental and emotional state, a completely reasonable assumption in a profession where the top chefs are expected to maintain establishments that consistently perform at a level approaching perfection. In her article "A Chef Dies: How Many Stars Are Enough?" Patricia Wells, the influential food critic of the *International Herald Tribune*, recounted her final interaction with Loiseau: "The last time I spoke with Loiseau was in October 2000, at a *Michelin* luncheon to honor the world's three-star chefs. Then, the chef Michel Guerard told me that the challenge of maintaining three stars is 'like Michelin asking us to be Olympic champions every day.' Loiseau added, 'The toughest thing in life is to endure.'"[13]

It was Dominique Loiseau, Bernard's wife and collaborator, a former food writer and the second most conspicuous personality at la Côte d'Or, as the face that greeted customers at the entrance to the dining room, who openly raised the issue of Loiseau's mental state. "*Gault&Millau* didn't kill him" she told a journalist, recounting his periodic bouts of depression and chronic overwork.[14] Newly chosen to lead the ownership group of her husband's enterprises, and having served as codirector of Bernard Loiseau S.A. from the time of its initial listing on the stock exchange, Dominique Loiseau took firm control of the family business shortly after his death.[15] Although seemingly in the best position of all to assess her husband's mental state, as the new sole restaurant owner her primary goal was now to maintain the restaurant's three-star *Michelin* rating, so it also would have been exceedingly impolitic for her to join in the public criticism of the gastronomic guides.[16]

---

12. Bernard Favre, Loiseau's finance director is quoted in Ripley, "Fallen Star," p. 47, and in Echikson, "Death of a Chef," p. 67.

13. Patricia Wells, "A Chef Dies: How Many Stars Are Enough?" *International Herald Tribune*, February 26, 2003.

14. Echikson, "Death of a Chef," p. 62.

15. Patrice Cecconello, "Dominique Loiseau aux commandes du groupe Bernard Loiseau SA," *Néorestauration*, April 2003, p. 15n397.

16. Echikson noted of Dominique Loiseau ("Death of a Chef," p. 67) that "she was careful not to blame the guidebooks for the tragedy." Her determination to maintain a three-star rating was something that she was explicit about, and it was a goal that she shared with her

All of this suggests that a definitive answer to the question, "Who Killed Bernard Loiseau?" would remain elusive. Although a medical autopsy would surely verify that he had died of a gunshot wound, and a forensic analysis would have confirmed that it had indeed been Loiseau who pulled the trigger, thereby satisfying official medical or legal inquiries, and a psychoanalytic postmortem might have provided names for the psychic demons that tormented him, I propose that none of these would permit us to truly understand what caused Loiseau to take his own life. The standard measures remain incomplete, because to fully understand the nature of the pressures and forces bearing down on a human being requires attention to the logic of the social world that they inhabit and an analysis of their trajectory through it. In other words, more so than a medical autopsy or forensic psychology, what is needed is a "social autopsy."[17]

As with a medical autopsy, a social autopsy should avoid treating the event as a tragedy (however tragic it undoubtedly is when a person is driven to such despair), not only because we want to reduce the analytical distortions that sentimentality inevitably generates but because tragedy represents just one mode of expression through which social recognition is conferred, and the social construction of recognition is an important element of what we want to understand about French gastronomy, the social world inhabited by Bernard Loiseau. This is why, however counterintuitive it may seem, a social autopsy cannot be accurately performed if we primarily rely on the people closest to the subject for our evidence, since those most closely implicated in the subject's life may actually be deeply implicated in the social mechanisms we are trying to understand. For example, each of those surrounding Bernard Loiseau tended to shift culpability to the other, with the chefs blaming the guidebooks and the food writers, and pointing us away from the chef profession, while the guidebooks and the food writers denied culpability, pointing us toward his finances. His financial adviser denied that he had had money problems and implied that the chef may have had a shaky mental state, while his wife, who now owned and managed the money (and therefore remained in need of the blessing of the guidebooks

---

restaurant manager, Hubert Couilloud, and her new head chef, Patrick Bertron (who had been Loiseau's trusted "second" for two decades), according to Steven Greenhouse in "A Restaurant in Mourning Keeps Its Sights on Its Stars," *New York Times*, September 10, 2003, pp. D1 and D6.

17. This was the term employed by Eric Klinenberg in his dissection of the social, political, and institutional "organs" of the city of Chicago in his book, *Heat Wave: A Social Autopsy of Disaster in Chicago* (Chicago: University of Chicago Press, 2002).

and the food writers), pointed us toward the pressures of the profession as the cause of her husband's unsteady mental condition.

Culpability circulated in this way because everyone had a certain stake in the picture being sketched, with each seeking to protect his or her particular interests deriving from each one's position in relation to all of the others while, at the same time, upholding the integrity of the overall arrangement. Viewed together, those who surrounded Bernard Loiseau in life and who came forward to try and make narrative sense of his death resembled, in miniature form, the universe of French gastronomy itself. That is, it was a microscopic version of the French gastronomic "field," by which we mean a distinctive and relatively insulated domain of human activity, with its own history, its own rules and institutions, as well as its distinctive antagonisms, harmonies, resources, and rewards. The focus of our analysis is not Bernard Loiseau, or any of the other great chefs who have occupied dominant positions in the gastronomic field, but we must draw frequently on elements of their life (or death) to make sense of the social logic of the French gastronomic field.

The task is to uncover the social forces operating in and through this field of practices; a field in which there are no innocents among the inhabitants, since all participants have a stake in either maintaining or exposing its contradictions and its mysteries. These social forces may be both material and symbolic and will tend to be embodied in economic and cultural practices that are both established and emergent, and to which distinctive social groups are drawn, having been predisposed toward one or another pole of this field. Thus, the sort of social autopsy to be performed must comprise more than the factors that led to a biological death, but that requires analysis of a social life. This includes examination of the field(s) of practice in which social actors operate, the practical context of their practice.

In such an investigation our focus is drawn to the major fault lines running through French gastronomy, as these illuminate the social mechanisms of institutional hierarchy and symbolic authority that govern not only gastronomy but most other cultural fields as well. Within French gastronomy, one of oldest and most prominent fissures has been the tension between artisanal and industrial practices. That is, between those methods of culinary practice largely guided by the skills, experience, traditions, and artistry of grand chefs; and industrial practices principally organized around the deployment of machinery and other technological processes in the various stages of food production, preparation, and distribution. The analytical approach to be taken here is not a straightforward narrative history of French gastronomy, for it is my view that the trajectory of the field has been mainly shaped during a particular conjuncture in the history of the field. From the 1970s through the 1990s cracks appeared in the system of French gastronomy that expanded fairly widely and threatened to break apart the entire edifice. It is the social character of this break—what it demonstrated about French society and culture and the ways they have been held together—that is the primary object of our investigation. The cracks that opened at the center will be traced as they extend outward into areas of French society that may seem far afield from traditional gastronomic concerns. That is, not only are the shifting tectonic plates beneath the cultural edifice of French gastronomy a focus but also the reverberations of these shifts in such varied developments as the growth of commercial sprawl on the periphery of French cities in the 1970s and the reconfiguration of French rural life and economy in the 1980s and 1990s. We are compelled to widen our analytical lens in this way because (a) the traditional boundaries of the field were themselves stretched and extended during this period, thereby becoming less recognizable than before, the distortion compounded by the addition of new institutional entries into the field; and (b) the simultaneity of changes across widely disparate areas of French life make it nearly impossible to sustain a single, linear narrative to grasp it. Our analysis, therefore, proceeds through several stages in the development of the field, albeit not in linear fashion.

We begin below (in the current chapter) by briefly retracing the roots of the gastronomic field in its emergence as an expression of the French literary imagination and, subsequently, in its institutional expression with the invention of the restaurant in the period following the Revolution. We then advance well into the nineteenth century to track the process by which the gastronomic field acquired its characteristic forms and attained its relative autonomy from other cultural fields. The following chapter (Chapter 2, "The Symbolic Economy of French Gastronomy") demonstrates the structures of belief and the forms of social organization that sustained the relative autonomy of the gastronomic field through much of the twentieth century. With particular attention to the rules, the customary practices, the sources of value, and the rites of consecration that have organized the rarified world of grand chefs and great restaurants in France, we consider gastronomy as a primary source of cultural power for the French and for the rest of the world. The two chapters that comprise the following section represent an examination of the incursion of industrial processes and commercial marketing techniques that entered the gastronomic field in the 1970s, largely impelled by the corporate investments of American firms and their French cousins. The first, Chapter 3 ("Fast Food in France: A Market for the Impossible"), traces the development, in France, of a market for American-style fast food, emphasizing what fast food represented, in social, cultural, and economic terms for French employers, workers, and consumers, as well as for the contours of the wider gastronomic field. Subsequently, Chapter 4 ("Industrial Cuisine and the 'Magic' of Americanism") presents the wide range of institutions, practices, and practitioners occupying the industrial sector of the French gastronomic field. These include the industries of food processing, institutional catering, and chain restaurants. In taking measure of this sector we are better able to situate it in relation to the gastronomic field as a whole, whose symbolic features draw heavily from the aesthetic vocabulary of haute cuisine. The industrial regions of the field, on the other hand, have been the primary vehicle for introducing American forms of economic (neoliberal) ideas and practices into French society more generally.

As this book seeks to demonstrate, a tectonic shift occurring in the gastronomic field in France scraped the cultural bedrock and changed French society. The character and the dynamics of these transformations are documented in Chapter 5 ("Conflicts of Interest: A Cultural Field in Transformation") and illustrate the complex and contradictory ways that the major institutions and practitioners of French haute cuisine adapted to the changing configuration of the gastronomic field. The chapter extends the analysis to reveal the paradoxical mechanisms by which the cult of *le terroir* and the related fetishism of "the local" have been largely underwritten by the very forces of standardization, homogenization, and profit maximization that they were created to oppose.

The Foundations of the Field

With its roots tracing back to some of the earliest printed works, late fifteenth-century German and Italian "cookery books," the symbolic conditions for French gastronomic practice were seen as having been set out with the publication of La Varenne's *Le Cuisinier François* in 1651. It was a work that summarized the cooking practices of the French nobility and identified a distinctive French way of cooking that was differentiated from medieval foodways in its use of certain spices, flavors, and technical innovations in the food preparation process.[18] This line of demarcation was increasingly defined by a succession of similar works that were published over the following decades, each of which tended to assert proper culinary practices (through recipes and observations) while disapproving of others.[19] Such jostling served to establish a framework of both old and new within the culinary sphere, thereby setting out, in germinal form, the outline of a modern culinary aesthetic.

The genesis of a French gastronomic field was the product of more than these early published narratives and texts, however. While texts charted the symbolic parameters, practice also required an institutional mooring, and it was the French Revolution that created the conditions for the development of an institutional foundation for haute cuisine. The precise nature of the historical relationship between the Revolution and the restaurant is a subject of varying interpretation, however. The simplest line of explanation argued that the cooks who once worked in the kitchens of aristocratic households were forced to open restaurants when their employers either fled the country or were slain in the Revolution's aftermath. However, as Stephen Mennell and others have pointed out, "the first of a new form of eating-place open to the public—that which came to be known as the restaurant—made its appearance in Paris during the two decades *before* the Revolution."[20]

Probably the most persuasive narrative has argued that by rupturing the guild system the Revolution created the conditions for the transfer of the artisanal practices of haute cuisine from the court to the bourgeoisie via a

---

18. François Pierre de La Varenne, *La Varenne's Cookery: The French Cook; The French Pastry Chef; The French Confectioner*, trans. Terence Scully (London: Prospect Books, 2006). These methods included the use of bouillon or stock for various dishes, spicing with bouquet garni, the use of egg whites to clarify and fat and flour to thicken, the slow cooking of meats, and the use of a reduction process to concentrate flavor. These were not revolutionary innovations, as Stephen Mennell points out, for they had most likely been practiced for some time in various aristocratic kitchens (*All Manners of Food*, 2nd ed. [Chicago: University of Illinois Press, 1996], pp. 64–74).

19. Mennell, *All Manners of Food*, pp. 72–73, notes the vitriol in the reactions of successive authors to their predecessors. The key works were identified by Revel as including: Nicolas de Bonnefons's *Les Délices de la campagne* (1645); Pierre de Lune's *Le Cuisinier* (1656); Jean Ribou's *L'École parfaite des officiers de bouche* (1662); *L'Art de bien traiter* signed semianonymously by L.S.R. (1674); and Massialot's *Le Cuisinier royal et bourgeois*[sic] (1691) and *Instructions pour les confitures* (1692). See Jean-François Revel, *Un festin en paroles: Histoire littéraire de la sensibilité gastronomique de l'Antiquité à nos jours* (Paris: Plon, 1995), pp. 172–181.

20. Mennell, *All Manners of Food*, p. 136. Jean-Robert Pitte, "The Rise of the Restaurant," in *FOOD: A Culinary History from Antiquity to the Present*, ed. Jean-Louis Flandrin and Massimo Montanari (New York: Columbia University Press, 1999), p. 475, is one who has made this argument, offering several examples of chefs who had worked in royal households before opening their own establishments after the Revolution.

new institution, the restaurant.[21] The earliest restaurants were enterprises run by sellers of "restorative" bouillons or meat-based consommés (themselves often called "restaurants") that were ingested to "restore" health and strength.[22] In 1765 a Monsieur Boulanger (who was also known, variously, as Champ d'Oiseaux and Champoiseau), a purveyor of "restaurants," or bouillons, opened a Paris shop in which he sold (in addition to his restaurants) certain foodstuffs whose sale was restricted by the guild system, and specifically violated the established prerogatives of the *traiteurs* guild (comprising cooks and caterers).[23] The guild filed a suit against Boulanger but ultimately decided in his favor, thus signaling the approaching demise of the guild system and encouraging these new, generic establishments that sold cooked food, eaten in place.[24] Although it took several decades before the term "restaurant" would be officially recognized for what it was coming to represent, the new establishments flourished after the Revolution. Where there had been approximately one hundred restaurants in Paris prior to the Revolution, the number would rise to five hundred or six hundred under the empire and to some three thousand during the restoration of the monarchy (1814–1848).[25]

---

21. This is the view Jean-Robert Pitte expressed in *French Gastronomy: The History and Geography of a Passion*, trans. Jody Gladding (New York: Columbia University Press, 2002) and later summarized in his chapter, "The Rise of the Restaurant," Flandrin and Montanari, *FOOD: A Culinary History*, pp. 471–480.

22. Prior to the "restaurant" one purchased food in taverns, at inns, and at markets, all located outside of the city walls (beyond the sphere of taxation) or drank in a café, the first of which was opened in 1674 in Paris. One could also purchase foods prepared by *traiteurs*, *rôtisseurs*, or *charcutiers*, who, under guild statutes, held a monopoly over various forms of cooked meats. Rebecca L. Spang, *The Invention of the Restaurant: Paris and Modern Gastronomic Culture* (Cambridge, MA: Harvard University Press, 2000), pp. 7–11.

23. See Pitte, "The Rise of the Restaurant," in Flandrin and Montanari, *FOOD: A Culinary History*, pp. 474–476.

24. Various historical accounts of French gastronomy have reported the outcome of the "Boulanger affair" in this way, including Pitte, "The Rise of the Restaurant," Flandrin and Montanari, *FOOD: A Culinary History*, p. 474, and Mennell, *All Manners of Food*, p. 139. However, in her otherwise analytically rich analysis of the rise of the restaurant in France, Spang informs the reader, incongruously, that most accounts have the *traiteurs* winning their lawsuit, thus restricting Boulanger (and other "restaurateurs") from selling anything besides these consommés and asserting that "no evidence in the judicial, police, or corporate archives substantiates the story of Boulanger's *defeat* [my emphasis] at the hands of the litigious caterers." See Spang, *Invention of the Restaurant*, p. 9.

25. Pitte, "The Rise of the Restaurant," Flandrin and Montanari, *FOOD: A Culinary History*, p. 476; and see Theodore Zeldin, *France 1848–1945 Taste and Corruption* (New York: Oxford University Press, 1980) p. 391.

This can perhaps be seen as representing the triumph of Paris over the rest of France as much as it was the triumph of the revolution over the monarchy, for in resolving the division between Paris and Versailles the Revolution shifted the axes of politics, culture, and commerce to the capital as the undisputed center.[26] Moreover, while Paris was becoming renowned for its restaurants, the mystique of the restaurant was amplifying the symbolic construction of Paris, as Rebecca Spang has noted: "As the fame of the city's restaurants spread, so the myth was disseminated of Paris as the nation's *grand couvert*" (which translates to "big place setting").[27] Widely established in Paris, restaurants were soon spread throughout the country, as traditional cabarets and dance halls (*guinguettes*) changed themselves into restaurants and as a style of aristocratic grandeur and excess devolved from Paris to various provincial outposts, preserved in the aspic of haute cuisine. As one analyst has written:[28]

The refinement once associated with the old aristocratic households could be found in the deluxe restaurants of the *grands boulevards* of Paris (the Café Riche and the Café Anglais), on the Place Bellecour in Lyon, and in the back streets of Bordeaux. The great restaurants relied on recipes developed and written down by Antonin Carême, the chef who presided over the *extraordinaires* (official banquets for major state occasions of the Empire and Restoration) and by his successors, Dugléré, Urbain Dubois, and, last, but not least, Escoffier. Chefs prepared beautiful creations out of fish and shellfish, *foie gras* from Strasbourg (which became the very symbol of good dining in France), seasonal game, chicken, and sirloin, all buried beneath mountains of truffles and dripping with brown sauces thickened with cream or butter. Menus at these restaurants could be as long as the dinner menus for the great occasions of the Ancien Régime, but now, for reasons of convenience and price, customers picked and chose the dishes they wanted before the food was prepared and served.

---

26. See Priscilla Ferguson, "A Cultural Field in the Making: Gastronomy in Nineteenth Century France," in *FRENCH FOOD on the Table, on the Page, and in French Culture*, ed. Lawrence R. Schehr and Allen S. Weiss (New York: Routledge, 2001), p. 11.

27. Spang, *Invention of the Restaurant*, p. 235.

28. Pitte, "The Rise of the Restaurant," Flandrin and Montanari, *FOOD: A Culinary History*, p. 477.

It is this sort of cornucopian representation that has been a central part of the complicated illusion of the restaurant; the symbolic dimension that one historian has identified as the restaurant's mythic core—its legends and lore and mystique. More than mere embellishment, the production of the phantasmagoric has been viewed as a central part of the restaurant's function.[29] Not only did restaurants serve to locate Paris in the French cultural imagination, as we've indicated, but, as Rebecca Spang has shown, restaurants can be seen as having symbolically performed a wide variety of "social" tasks. For example, she indicates how on one level, restaurants enacted a distinctively modern and bourgeois sociability as "publicly private" spaces that allowed one to be alone in public, to ignore others while being among them. On another, the restaurant composed a theatrical spectacle calculated to conceal the hellish kitchen area, physically and symbolically separating it (backstage) from the opulence of the dining room "out front." Moreover, the restaurant provided its customers with an illusion of hospitality, welcome, and generosity that masked any pecuniary interests and, in the context of a bourgeois order that "implicitly required the presence of somebody outside," represented an institution of both exclusion and envy.[30]

In these ways the institution at the very center of French gastronomy, the restaurant, performed an extraordinary amount of symbolic labor, a point to be revisited in subsequent chapters. For the moment, however, it should be noted that in the establishment of French gastronomy a fair amount of the actual work of symbolic construction was performed by a new type of socioliterary persona, the gastronome, a figure who emerged as the product of the very gastronomic universe whose boundaries he was assigned to define and to police.

The term "gastronomy," meaning "the art and science of delicate eating," or of eating well, was sometimes used interchangeably with the word "gourmand," before the latter was increasingly employed as a pejorative term of excess and of greed, as in "glutton."[31] It was in the spirit of the earlier meaning that the notorious Alexandre-Balthazar-Laurent Grimod de la Reynière (1758–1838) published his annual *Almanach des gourmands* over the course of the first decade of the nineteenth century, chronicling the development of French gastronomy; and later, in 1825, Jean-Anthelme

---

29. Spang, *Invention of the Restaurant*, pp. 234–236.

30. See Spang, *Invention of the Restaurant*, pp. 86–87, 234, 236, 239–241, 245.

31. Mennell, *All Manners of Food*, pp. 266–267. The *Oxford English Dictionary* defines "gourmand" as both "one who is over-fond of eating, one who eats greedily or to excess, a glutton" and "one who is fond of delicate fare; a judge of good eating."

Brillat-Savarin (1755–1826) published his *Physiologie du goût* (Physiology of Taste) a book of "meditations" on taste, the senses, the preparation of meals, the social character of dining, and the philosophy and aesthetics of food, the table, and the body.

An important genre of gastronomic writing was established through these works, one that served both a devotional function with regard to food and eating and manners and also to render visible the gastronome/author as a social actor in the world that was being depicted and symbolically constructed. Thus Grimod de la Reynière not only told of restaurants visited and of meals eaten but often did so through descriptions of the weekly outings of his "*Jury de Dégustateurs*" (Taster's jury) and later, his "*Société des Mercredis*" (Wednesday Society).[32] These were groups composed of those sophisticated diners that Grimod assembled (and with whom he participated) who gathered together on a weekly basis to dine and to judge dishes and restaurants, thereby casting themselves as central players in the world that Grimod was depicting in his writings. Thus the gastronome-as-tastemaker was essentially brought into being by the gastronome-as-writer. In asserting their evaluative judgments in this way, gastronomic writers prefigured the role played by the gastronomic guides (such as the *Michelin* red guide) as institutional gatekeepers, and, by establishing themselves as arbiters of taste, gastronomes also represented a significant part of the restaurant "public" in this formative period.

In an analysis of the genesis of gastronomy as a cultural field in the nineteenth century, Priscilla Ferguson places gastronomic literature at its very foundation. She argues that through gastronomic writers (Grimod de la Reynière, Carême, Brillat-Savarin) as well as through dominant literary figures from other cultural domains who wrote about gastronomy (Balzac in literature and Fourier in philosophy) the emergent "gastronomic field" was able to receive symbolic fortification from more secure and established cultural fields. Thus as gastronomic writing was accepted as good literature the gastronomic field was afforded a measure of legitimacy, thereby aiding in its establishment and in its achievement of a certain level of autonomy.

According to Ferguson, Brillat-Savarin played a particularly important role in this process because, unlike most of the food writing done by journalists and chefs, his was a noninstrumental viewpoint and his writing had a quality that transcended the domain of gastronomy, placing it "within a larger intellectual and social universe": "For Brillat-Savarin, the text was its

---

32. See Mennell, *All Manners of Food*, pp. 267, 272.

own end, a status hardly altered by the few recipes included in the work. The often noted stylistic qualities of the *Physiology of Taste*—the anecdotal mode, the witty tone, the language play—give this work an almost palpable literary aura."[33]

An analytical focus on the importance of literature in the emergence of the gastronomic field is insightful, but two qualifications are in order. One has to do with the limits imposed on a social analysis of the gastronomic field by a focus on literary practices alone. While literature was undoubtedly crucial in the genesis of a gastronomic field in the way that Ferguson has shown, a fuller grasp of its social logic would seem to require that the means of its symbolic construction be conjoined to a broader range of social practices. A second hesitation has to do with the relations between fields, and in particular with the idea that the relative strength of a field (its "cultural resonance" and "cultural resistance" in Ferguson's terms) is a function of its dependence on its connections to other cultural fields (or in relation to the "larger society" in her words).[34] Despite the fact that it must be demonstrated empirically and not simply asserted, one would expect the strength of a field to rest not so much on its dependence on other fields as on the degree of relative autonomy it enjoys from other fields. In other words, its strength would seem to reside in its ability to operate in terms of its own proper rules and principles of regulation and on its own internal evaluative criteria, thus fortified against principles of evaluation and regulation introduced from other fields (as in the domain of cinema, for example, where the rules and principles governing the artistic field have been challenged, if not superseded by standards introduced from the economic field).[35]

While in the early stages of its formation, gastronomy may indeed have acquired a level of social prestige through the links it was able to forge with individuals and institutions in more established fields, like philosophy and literature; as it gained a certain autonomy (the phase of "consolidation" for Ferguson), it asserted itself as more than a branch of either, and therein lay its strength as a field. In other words, the strength of a field rests on its capacity to uphold and maintain its own rules and its own standards of

33. Quoted (pp. 616–617) in Priscilla Ferguson, "A Cultural Field in the Making: Gastronomy in 19th Century France," *American Journal of Sociology*, vol. 104, no. 3, November 1998, pp. 597–641.

34. Ferguson, "Cultural Field in the Making," p. 602.

35. See L. Creton, *Cinéma et marché* (Paris: Armand Colin/Masson, 1997); and J. Tunstall, *The Media Are American* (New York: Columbia University Press, 1977). Ferguson, "Cultural Field in the Making," p. 632.

evaluation, over and above those of competing or neighboring fields. Of course the independence of a field is always relative and a function of its historical trajectory, but achieving independence does not consign a field to "the cultural equivalent of solitary confinement" as Ferguson fears. To the contrary, it can be viewed as a measure of its maturation.

Moreover, however independent they may be at any given historical moment, the various fields of human activity that constitute a society are always structured, hierarchically, in relation to one another, even when the effects of dominance are sometimes expressed negatively, as in the case of the field of culture, which operates (or once did) according to principles directly opposed to those that govern the economic field.[36] The relations that prevail between different cultural fields (as well as between the cultural and the normally more powerful political and economic fields) reflect the relations of relative dominance and subordination of practices within the society, although they may be configured differently in different societies and in different historical periods. Thus just as a field can achieve a degree of independence, the autonomy of a social field may wane or be eroded over time and in relation to other fields in the society.

Over the first half of the nineteenth century, Brillat-Savarin's meditations on taste, the body, and the aesthetics of food, Grimod de la Reynière's symbolic construction of a French "public" for restaurants, and chef Antonin Carême's celebration of the culinary arts, taken together, can be seen as having symbolically constructed a certain design for living, the "art of eating well," whereby the act of properly nourishing the body simultaneously accomplishes the proper nourishment of the soul. It was a form of perception that, among other things, abandoned the traditional dietetic/medicinal principles of cooking that had governed culinary practice for several hundred years, in favor of a kind of pure gastronomic aesthetic, very much the equivalent of the stance of "art for art's sake" that emerged contemporaneously in fields of artistic practice.[37] It can be seen as having been one part

---

36. Pierre Bourdieu's writings on the relations between fields are widely spread across his huge corpus of work, but he provided a simple diagram to illustrate the relationship between the field of cultural production and the field of power in *The Field of Cultural Production* (New York: Columbia University Press, 1993), pp. 37–40. Bourdieu has shown that the disavowal of the economy is at the very heart of the functioning and transformation of the cultural field, and he therefore had good reason for entitling his analysis "The Field of Cultural Production, *or: The Economic World Reversed*" (my emphasis) in that same volume (pt. I, chap. 1, pp. 29–73). In the same volume, also see chap. 2, "Faith and Bad Faith," pp. 78–80.

37. See Pierre Bourdieu, *The Rules of Art: Genesis and Structure of the Literary Field* (Stanford, CA: Stanford University Press, 1996), especially pt. I, chap. 1, "The Conquest of Autonomy"

of a gradual process of symbolic labor through which the gastronome was distinguished from (and elevated above) the gourmand. Constructed as the discriminating connoisseur and raised to "the lofty position of high priest for this new cult," the gastronome was thereby discursively differentiated from the sinful and indulgent gourmand, the glutton who "only knows how to ingest."[38] The development of a pure gastronomic disposition was an expression of a distinctive "art of living," the basic inspiration for all acts of cultural distinction, and a (barely) misrecognized assertion of bourgeois dominance in the society. As Pierre Bourdieu put it, "At stake in every struggle over art there is also the imposition of an art of living, that is, the transmutation of an arbitrary way of living into the legitimate way of life which casts every other way of living into arbitrariness."[39]

The other purpose that the gastronomic literature served was a nationalizing one, symbolically cementing the distinctive and enduring association that has come to prevail between cuisine and France. Although the association had been recognized earlier, as the culinary practices of the French aristocracy had been exported to royal kitchens throughout Europe (much as the French language had been adopted as the lingua franca of European courts everywhere), the modern concept of the nation was only just emerging in early nineteenth-century France and thus the gastronomic literature inscribed grand cuisine and culinary practice in the national consciousness at a formative moment.[40] The authoritative writing style of the most influential gastronomes, combined with their vigorous and explicit declarations

(pp. 47–112), and see chap. 5, "Field of Power, Literary Field, and Habitus," in *The Field of Cultural Production: Essays on Art and Literature* (New York: Columbia University Press, 1993). Jean-Louis Flandrin points out that in the seventeenth century the fine arts borrowed the metaphor of *taste* from the culinary domain, where it had long been central to the dietetic principle, because taste is what determined the age and the toxicity of foodstuffs and served to match specific foods to the temperament and the body of the individual. See Jean-Louis Flandrin, "From Dietetics to Gastronomy," in Flandrin and Montanari, *FOOD: A Culinary History*.

38. Ferguson, "Cultural Field in the Making," pp. 608–609.

39. Pierre Bourdieu, *DISTINCTION: A Social Critique of the Judgement of Taste*, trans. Richard Nice (Cambridge, MA: Harvard University Press, 1984) [1979, Les Éditions de Minuit], p. 57. In this case "cuisine for cuisine's sake" is the expression of a "pure culinary aesthetic" upholding the sublime (in the act of consumption) alongside the artistry of human creation (in the act of production), against merely "cooking to eat" (as a basic practical and biological matter of necessity) or "cooking for sale" (as a commercial matter of business).

40. Priscilla Ferguson ("Cultural Field in the Making," p. 20) points out that while seventeenth-century cookbooks had asserted the "Frenchness" of their methods, this was a social reference to the French court and aristocracy and not to a geographic France, which did not yet exist.

of a French "culinary nationalism," helped to establish a firm link between Frenchness and the culinary arts.[41] Contributing to the strength of the association was the centralization that followed the Revolution and that placed Paris (and its restaurants) at the symbolic and institutional center of the nation; as well as the publication, in 1808, of the first of many gastronomic maps of France that redrew the map of the nation using culinary divisions instead of political or administrative boundaries, a visual innovation that was as much a contributor to the national myth-making apparatus as it was a product of it.[42]

The symbolic construction of the French nation entailed more than the elevation of a center, for the other side of the centrality of Paris was its periphery, located in newly created "*départements*," with all of the material and symbolic resources that they brought with them into the new nation. The problem of national sovereignty has been worked and reworked in a recurring symbolic project designed to sort out the relationship between the capital and the regions, Paris and the provinces, the center and the periphery. Just as a body of writing and a group of writers offered up a national culinary discourse that buttressed the nation as it "nationalized" its cuisine, writers and their writings also served to symbolically incorporate the regions into the nation by "nationalizing" regional cuisines.

A culinary provincialist literature emerged at the beginning of the nineteenth century that took the form of cookbooks focused on regional dishes and that codified traditional local recipes.[43] It was written by local dignitaries, scholars, and cooks; published by local publishers; and intended for local readers in places like Alsace, Gascogne, Languedoc, Provence, and elsewhere. However, after about 1900, regional culinary books were increas-

---

41. Priscilla Ferguson, "Cultural Field in the Making," pp. 620–622. While Ferguson makes a good case for the nationalizing tendencies of the gastronomic literature, she is mistaken when she minimizes the importance of regional cuisines (and their literatures) in the national project in order to strengthen the case for centralization. This is unfortunate, for it misses something analytically important about the relationship between the nation and the regions.

42. Grimod de la Reynière introduced "alimentary topography" as a necessary element of gastronomic education; while the *carte gastronomique* presented a cornucopian image of the French national landscape, symbolically representing France through a visualization of what is now termed its culinary patrimony. See Spang, *Invention of the Restaurant*, p. 169.

43. The most popular of these books, *La Cuisinière de la campagne et de la ville ou la nouvelle cuisine économique* by L. E. Audot, was reportedly reprinted forty-one times between 1833 and 1900; and Gérard's *Ancienne Alsace à table* (1862) and Tendret's *La Table au pays de Brillat-Savarin* (1882) are reportedly still in print today. See Julia Csergo, "The Emergence of Regional Cuisines," in Flandrin and Montanari, *FOOD: A Culinary History*, p. 505.

ingly published in Paris as part of a nationalizing impulse that celebrated "the culinary riches of France in all its regional and social diversity."[44] Some of these were compilations of local family recipes that sought to survey the breadth of French culinary practices, and others reflected royalist Catholic political sentiments, holding up traditional rural France against the degradations of modern urbanization (a perspective that, later on, would slide more or less easily into Vichy fascism), but together they reflected a general nostalgia for a rural way of life that was felt to be disintegrating in the swirl of modern industrial development. As Julia Csergo put it:

> Perpetuating the romantic conception of the local as a conservatory of the sensibility of the past, a new system of representations emerged in which regional cuisines became the embodiment of local agricultural traditions and rural allegiances, family and religious customs, and nostalgic longing for a pre-industrial, pre-urban past. . . . These reconstructed regional cuisines allowed modern urban society to resurrect its provincial roots by savoring dishes consecrated by memory. Peasants who went to Paris in search of employment frequently revived the atmosphere of the villages they left behind by choosing to live and associate with others from the same region.[45]

On one level, it is by now axiomatic that nostalgia for the regional and the traditional is a product of nationalizing/centralizing and modernizing forces, so that one is not only preconditioned by the other but actually mutually constitutive of one another. At the same time, however, to the extent that nationalism always represents a mythic social unity, we should keep in mind that the French nation was the assertion of a largely invented sociocultural homogenization.[46]

---

44. Csergo, "Emergence of Regional Cuisines," p. 506.

45. See Csergo ("Emergence of Regional Cuisines," pp. 507, 513n3), who also points to the rise of ethnology museums in the latter two decades of the nineteenth century as further expressions of this modernizing nostalgia.

46. This is a central point in Eugen Weber's classic study, *Peasants into Frenchmen*. In it he suggests that the public expression of a French national identity in the late nineteenth century covered over social heterogeneity and deep sociocultural divisions between city and country and that patriotic discourse betrayed a widespread practical ambivalence over the nation and the modern (Stanford, CA: Stanford University Press, 1976). See chap. 7, "France, One and Indivisible" and esp. pp. 112–114. This is a view that is not fundamentally at odds with the notion of nation as a social construct, such as that advanced by Greenfeld, for example, who has viewed the construction of French nationalism as a matter of the appropriation of the category "the people" by eighteenth-century French elites, who redefined citizenship to include

Culinary nationalism, then, can be seen as having served to reinforce French national consciousness, while firmly attaching to the French nation an association with cuisine. As Ferguson has shown, this was largely accomplished by a new genre of culinary literature that charted the contours of an emergent gastronomic field. However, culinary "nationalization" seems to have been less of a linear process of increasing centralization than it was a process of conquest, occurring over two stages. In the first, Paris conquered Versailles by the Revolution, asserting its political and cultural authority over the new nation, and this was reflected in the culinary domain by the invention and proliferation of restaurants, both by the rise of the gastronomes and their writings and by the ideological construction of a French culinary nationalism. In a second stage, the center asserted itself in relation to the periphery, and in the culinary domain this was expressed by the rise and representation of regional cuisine in the first half of the nineteenth century and its gradual appropriation by the gastronomic field in the latter decades of that century and the early decades of the twentieth century. This was not to be mistaken for a kind of oppositional version of regionalism (or whatever might have been the culinary equivalent of a rebellious Corsica or Vendée) but rather as a domesticated expression of provincial cultural pride.[47]

Within the culinary world itself, there was no more important player in establishing the legitimacy of regional cuisine than Maurice-Edmond Sailland, pseudonymously known as "Curnonsky." A chef and gastronome, Curnonsky famously traveled the length of France, in the years following World War I, with his friend and colleague Marcel Rouff, with whom he published twenty-four of his twenty-eight volumes of *La France gastronomique*. These were the first of what would become a rich genre of tourist guides concentrating specifically on regions and their dishes, wines, and restaurants, and in them, as well as in the other books produced by Curnonsky and his circle, culinary wonder was conjoined with tourism, firmly

themselves and swore loyalty to a state that was increasingly elevated to the level of the sacred in response to the waning of their influence and power. See Liah Greenfeld, *NATIONALISM: Five Roads to Modernity* (Cambridge, MA: Harvard University Press, 1992), pp. 154–155.

47. This was expressed in various initiatives, according to Csergo, including the founding of various ethnological museums and societies (like the Société des traditions populaires in 1886; the Société d'ethnologie nationale et d'art populaire in 1885; the first ethnographic museum, the Museon Arlaten in 1894; and the Société dauphinoise d'ethnologie et d'anthropologie in 1894) and the growth of "regionalist" gastronomic societies in Paris that were formed by provincial elites living in the capital to preserve regional cultural forms; an initiative often encouraged by political interests eager to cultivate agricultural interests with regional roots. Csergo, "Emergence of Regional Cuisines," pp. 507–508.

fixing the two realms together in the French national consciousness.[48] He was a powerful influence in establishing the legitimacy of regional cooking (in a universe dominated by Paris) and thus in shaping the terrain of French gastronomy at a crucial point in its development.[49] Curnonsky advanced a kind of culinary populism that advocated simplicity in presentation and technique and that eschewed stylistic deference to social elites; and he advocated a "gustatory pluralism" that emphasized the quality of raw materials and rejected doctrinaire cooking styles. For these reasons he has been likened to Gault and Millau, who would come to name and to promote nouvelle cuisine decades later.[50]

Curnonsky and his circle have sometimes been noted as having "invented" traditional French peasant cuisine by recovering it and recognizing (and thereby sanctifying) it as haute cuisine. However, as Mennell has pointed out, the peasant dishes that they gathered together in their writings tended to reflect the "festival dishes" that French peasants would have perhaps eaten on annual feast days or in very rare periods of plenty but that did not comprise their everyday diet.[51] For example, the dinner menu presented in a typical listing in their 1923 guide to La Savoie—soup, a plate of local ham and sausage, scallops in cream, green beans, sheep's leg, dessert and a local wine—would have likely represented a truly extraordinary and memorable feast for a typical Savoyard peasant of the time.[52]

---

48. See Csergo, "Emergence of Regional Cuisines," p. 510. As Stephen Mennell points out ("Food and Wine," in *French Culture Since 1945*, ed. M. Cook [London: Longman, 1993], p. 184), the linkage between tourism and gastronomy were quickly capitalized on by the tire companies, Michelin and Kléber-Colombes, who published guides to restaurants and hotels in France and stood to benefit substantially from the growth of auto tourism.

49. In a 1927 poll of its readers conducted by *Paris-Soir*, Curnonsky was elected "prince of the gastronomes," receiving 1,823 out of 3,388 votes cast. One historian of French gastronomy has noted that in the culinary world Curnonsky's judgments "were irrevocable" and "he was feared by food service figures and restaurant owners, whose fame and fortune he could establish." See Jean-Robert Pitte, *French Gastronomy: The History and Geography of a Passion* (New York: Columbia University Press, 2002), pp. 138–139.

50. Mennell offers this comparison in his depiction of Curnonsky ("Food and Wine," pp. 185–186).

51. Mennell, p. 187.

52. The menu cited was from l'Auberge du Bras de Fer in the town of Taninges in the French Alps, and one of many that Curnonsky and Marcel Rouff cite from local inns, restaurants, and hotels in their *La France gastronomique: La Savoie* (Paris: F. Rouff, 1923), p. 32. Until the middle of the twentieth century, the French peasant diet in traditional regions, as well as among workers who retained peasant traditions, was still mostly based on slowly boiled vegetables (soups) that were eaten at every meal of the day. In the wealthier peasant households, soup might be supplemented with cheese or eggs or charcuterie [various cold

It hardly mattered that regional dishes were not what peasants ate, for Curnonsky's writings were not intended as ethnological chronicles but were meant to legitimize and popularize regional culinary cultures in relation to Parisian grand cuisine. His guides and his writings were thus instrumental for "nationalizing" regional cuisine through acts of assertion (or representation), in the same way that Brillat-Savarin, Grimod de la Reynière, and Carême had been instrumental in establishing gastronomy as French a century earlier. Curnonsky's was a "domesticated" regionalism, easily digested into a gastronomic universe fully dominated by Paris and its restaurants and, once incorporated, this reconstituted universe could then be expanded outward from Paris to the rest of the world.

The Conquest of Autonomy

The development of the French gastronomic field has been characterized as a process of "consolidation" by Priscilla Ferguson: "The gastronomic field took shape in two major phases: emergence over the first half of the nineteenth century, consolidation thereafter."[53] "Yes" and "No," we must respond. "No" if the term "consolidation" refers to a linear movement toward a condition of internal cohesiveness and unification, for that characterization would tend to misunderstand one of the fundamental properties of a social field, that it is an arena of struggle and conflict. For as Pierre Bourdieu explained in terms of his own practical use of the concept, a field is a field of *force* operating on those within it and is equally a field of *struggles* through which social agents act to preserve or transform the distribution of forces within it.[54] What appears to be the consolidation of the field may therefore reflect a particular representation imposed by social actors with the power to impose their own vision (and division) of the social world. So, just as it was suggested that the process of culinary "nationalization" ought to be considered in terms of the relational tension between the regional and the national, we ought to remain open to the nonlinear trajectory of the

---

meats and sausages]. For most peasants, animal protein was too valuable to be consumed and had to be retained for sale at market, and so until the 1880s French peasants very rarely ate any meat at all; by 1900 they ate only a quarter of the average meat ration of a city dweller and just a fifth of what Parisians consumed, a division that continued up until World War II. See Weber, *Peasants into Frenchmen*, p. 142, and see Theodore Zeldin, *France 1848–1945 Taste and Corruption* (New York: Oxford University Press, 1980), p. 381.

53. Ferguson, "Cultural Field in the Making," p. 601.

54. See, for example, pp. 101–102 in Pierre Bourdieu and Loic J. D. Wacquant, *An Invitation to Reflexive Sociology* (Chicago: University of Chicago Press, 1992).

gastronomic field, paying attention to the internal schisms that propel it. If it at all resembles other cultural fields, the domain of culinary practices will be, among other things, a site of conflict over legitimacy and recognition and thereby a conflict over competing visions and divisions of the social world. At the same time, we readily respond with a "yes" to Ferguson's notion of consolidation of the gastronomic field, if by that is meant acts of consolidation by some social forces over and against others. Again, symbolic representations of unity and solidity may very well be an attempt by interested factions to make certain things happen with words; in effect, making a fait accompli by declaration. To avoid becoming an unwitting instrument of complicity in a process of ratification, then, our analytical task must be to understand, simultaneously, the social construction of the social world and the social construction of its representation.

As we demonstrate in subsequent chapters, the social life and logic of the gastronomic field has been characterized by an ongoing struggle to preserve its autonomy in relation to other fields and other logics. If the symbolic construction of autonomy took place over time in the ways that others have shown, the assembly of its material infrastructure has been more recent. The latter decades of the nineteenth century saw the development of a range of practical and technical innovations that, together, created the institutional infrastructure to support a self-regulating (and reproducing) gastronomic field in France. Advances in food production, processing, preservation, distribution, and storage were under way throughout Europe, compelled by the same kinds of forces that were driving industrial development more generally. However, Europe's rapid urbanization and population growth had generated enormous levels of food production requirements that could not be met by European agricultural capacity alone (while improvements in transportation made it possible to develop agricultural links to colonial and former colonial economies outside of Europe). Thus, while such ancient practices as bread making, wine making, and sausage making could be surprisingly responsive to industrial methods (mechanization, chemistry, temperature control, systems of storage, etc.), there were other traditional food production practices that were simply abandoned in the face of trade competition, as when American and Russian cereals were introduced in the 1880s and Europeans were forced to abandon certain traditional forms of grain cultivation.[55]

---

55. Giorgio Pedrocco, "The Food Industry and New Preservation Techniques," in Flandrin and Montanari, *FOOD: A Culinary History*, p. 482.

Although French scientists had earlier made crucial advances in food preservation techniques, including Louis Pasteur's discoveries of the scientific bases of food sterilization that served as its foundation, the practical roots of a food-processing industry were slower to develop in France than elsewhere.[56] Aided by innovations in refrigeration techniques, American firms successfully entered the European market during an agricultural depression in 1873, by exporting substantial quantities of fresh and processed foods to Europe. The mass production of preserved foods had already been well under way in the United States, where canning factories had expanded rapidly with the outbreak of the Civil War and where companies like Campbell, Heinz, and Borden had successfully experimented with advertising techniques that would later be employed in Europe.[57] As Europe's agricultural crisis lifted, the imposition of protectionist tariffs and the appearance of alternative markets permitted European agricultural interests to begin to compete again with U.S. industry. However, America's facility with commercial techniques in the food preservation industry, a facility that reflected its growing supremacy across all industrial sectors, meant that the presence of the "American model" would remain a permanent fixture in Europe, in French society, and in the domain of commercial foodways.

Virtually synonymous with the industrial logic of efficiency, high volume, and standardized practices, the very embodiment of industrial modernity itself, the "American model" has represented a form of socioeconomic practice that is always most visible when posed in relation to its opposite form. In other words, like all such cultural representations, the notion of "Americanism" has required a reciprocally defining "other," and that has been readily furnished by Europe and by France when they have been represented as old, traditional, cultivated, and refined. Such broad cultural categories and representations are almost always advanced to accomplish a symbolic goal of one kind or another, with effects both between and within

---

56. France was heavily agricultural, with southern growing seasons that were virtually year-round, and so a French food-processing industry was developed relatively late and in a small scale, especially relative to Germany. German firms developed earlier (in 1830s and 1840s) in Baltic port cities for both domestic consumption and for export to Russia and Scandinavia, thereby creating strong links between German agricultural practices and the food-processing industry. The industry was stimulated further with the discovery of methods to preserve condensed milk and with the development of a milk-based baby food by Henry Nestlé (a German scientist residing in Switzerland). By 1905, Nestlé's company had seventeen plants throughout Europe and one in the United States. See Pedrocco, "Food Industry," pp. 487–488.

57. Pedrocco, p. 489.

social groups, and we see this with regard to the field of gastronomic practices in France.

Toward the end of the nineteenth century, with the gastronomic field developing into a relatively distinctive and autonomous social universe, a thin fissure was exposed that would later expand into a fault line. On one side of the fissure stood entrepreneurs, managers, and industrialists seeking to maximize profit and expand their enterprises. On the other were the professional chefs, who, like other skilled artisans, tended to respond to the industrial imperative (toward large-scale enterprise, product standardization, and routinization of the labor process, etc.) like skilled workers everywhere, namely with a collective defense of their trade. Thus in the latter decades of the nineteenth century, small shopkeepers and artisans in the traditional *métiers d'alimentation* (including *chefs de cuisine, cuisiniers, pâtissiers, boulangers, traiteurs*) increasingly organized themselves into various *chambres syndicales* (union organizations) in response to the implantation of massive food-processing plants in the outskirts of Paris, several of which employed close to two thousand workers.[58]

The professional chef and the industrial manager represented social actors pursuing divergent career paths, who would tend to hold different aesthetic dispositions with regard to food and cuisine. Moreover, they gathered around institutions that tended to draw into their orbit those who were predisposed to one side or the other, with each represented by writers or spokespersons who articulated the logic and the value of their respective positions. Thus, on one side of the artisan/industrial divide stood Auguste Corthay, an industrialist who had once been a chef to the Italian royal family, who now extolled the modern virtues of preserved food ("Daily, the great factories will deliver tasty, freshly prepared and cooked food at very low prices. It will be the start of a new century!"); and whose book, *La Conserve alimentaire*, was published in four editions between 1891 and 1902.[59]

Corthay could well be regarded as the industrial counterpart of the gastronomes of the previous century. Whereas Brillat-Savarin had earlier

58. For example, once urban transportation made regional distribution possible, curing factories successfully turned pork butchering into a large-scale industrial process, and industrial dairies could achieve a monopoly over milk production. See Amy B. Trubeck, *Haute Cuisine: How the French Invented the Culinary Profession* (Philadelphia: University of Pennsylvania Press, 2000), pp. 80–81.

59. *La Conserve alimentaire* also became the title of the magazine that Corthay founded and that was published from 1903 to 1914. See Alberto Capatti, "The Taste for Canned and Preserved Food," in Flandrin and Montanari, *FOOD: A Culinary History*, p. 495.

presented a series of philosophical and aesthetic "meditations" on taste, the senses, the preparation of meals, the social character of dining, the table, and the body, Corthay offered up a practical disquisition on the methods of food processing and conservation and included recipes geared not to the senses so much as to industrial preparation and preservation. Only secondarily concerned with matters of taste, Corthay's recipes primarily focused on the proper amount of water, salt, sugar, oil, or baking soda added to the various steamed vegetables, fruit confits, or canned fish or meats that were laid out in his compendium of industrial foodways. It was a book that would have likely made connoisseurs of haute cuisine recoil in horror, for they would have viewed it as a cookbook of badly prepared food, as a collection of meditations on tastelessness, for it deliberately eschewed the skill of the chef/artisan in favor of the industrial machine.[60]

Subtitled *"Traité practique de fabrication*," it was essentially a book of industrial technique that eulogized the machinery of industrial production and that emphasized practical matters of quantity (weights, amount of produce), as one of the main objectives of industrial production is high volume. For example, one very brief description of a machine for pressing tomato sauce, a "passoire à tomate" indicated that two workers were required to operate the machine and that it could process one thousand kilos of tomatoes per hour (p. 57). Despite its stress on volume and labor investment, the book also presented a wide variety of processed foods, with recipes for six different kinds of canned peas and at least eight different preparations of canned sardines, for example. Corthay's book was essentially an industrial manual that placed both visual and narrative emphasis on the organization of the industrial kitchen and on the machinery of production deployed within it, presenting adoring images of the factory-kitchen and food-processing machines in celebration of the practical virtues of industrial technique.[61]

---

60. Auguste Corthay, *La Conserve alimentaire: Traité pratique de fabrication*, 4th ed. (Paris: Réty, 1902).

61. Machinery is a central theme throughout this 473-page book, one that pictures all manner of industrial-sized machines that clean, and steam, and cut, and chop, and puree, and separate vegetables, fruits, fish, meats, and fowl. Images that depict the spatial organization of production systems are presented in numerous drawings, such as one entitled "Vue d'un laboratoire à vapeur," which shows a workroom with six workers tending to eight large vats around the perimeter of the room, with five other workers sitting at a long table in the middle, busy processing (trimming, cutting) what look to be several large hams and piles of potatoes. Auguste Corthay, *La Conserve alimentaire: Traité pratique de fabrication*, 4th ed. (Paris: Réty, 1902), p. 29.

On the *other* side of this growing artisan/industrial divide stood the renowned chef Georges Auguste Escoffier whose classic *Le Guide culinaire* first appeared in 1902 and who came to virtually personify French haute cuisine through midcentury, presiding during a period when its symbolic imprint was perhaps most pronounced.[62] As we will see, he occupies a prominent place in the pantheon of haute cuisine, with a legacy marked as much by his contribution to the organization of the modern restaurant kitchen as by the considerable culinary artistry he displayed within it.

Corthay and Escoffier can be seen as having been emblematic of an emergent division in the gastronomic field between a culinary practice that valued the cultivation of finely honed artisan skills and aesthetic judgment, on the one hand, and, on the other, the industrial values of mechanization, standardization, time-thrift, and labor-saving techniques:

> Corthay regarded the factory as the natural heir to the kitchen and sent his products beyond the borders of Europe, while Escoffier insisted that food should be fresh: "Peas should be very green, picked and shelled at the last minute." . . . Corthay, however, claimed that "the harvest starts at the end of May and continues throughout the month of June. The sooner you use the vegetables, assuming the price allows it, the better the preserves will be." The taste and appearance of food was accompanied by other considerations: the right time to harvest, labor costs, constant availability, and the lack of seasonal barriers. In haute cuisine dishes are appreciated by the eyes, the nose, and the taste buds.[63]

In a reciprocally defining process not unlike that which occurred in other cultural fields, the emergence of an industrial cuisine in the latter decades of the nineteenth century helped to delimit (and elevate) the artisanship of the culinary arts. Thus did the professional chef rise to predominance at the very center of the gastronomic universe, as artist and artisan in relation to the industrial practitioners of industrial cuisine, but also as specifically male artisans in relation to the female purveyors of *domestic* cuisine. That is, the elevation of the professional chef was also accomplished through a social differentiation (a process that is always hierarchical) of the culinary

62. Escoffier's *Guide culinaire* remains a central text in the training of professional chefs. See Mennell, *All Manners of Food*, p. 157.
63. Capatti, "Taste for Canned," p. 496.

practices of the chef from "mere" everyday domestic cookery performed by housewives.[64] This required boring into powerful cultural bedrock that held women to be the "*gardiennes du feu*" and that considered culinary talent a matter of female nature rather than of human culture, with haute cuisine confronting such gender mythology by representing itself as a thing apart (and above).[65]

Over the course of the same period the increasing mechanization of the publishing process made possible the publication of numerous culinary journals, thereby aiding the process of social differentiation and reflecting it. A dozen culinary journals were founded in France between 1870 and 1900, intended either for men involved in professional cooking practice or for women engaged in food preparation or household management.[66] Among the most prominent of these journals, *L'Art culinaire* played a particularly significant historical role in placing the chef at the center of French gastronomy. Founded by chefs in 1883 as the journal of the Société des cuisiniers français, it was regarded as the leading professional journal of the day, and devoted itself to the everyday, practical concerns of the chef profession (including articles on the qualities of various foodstuffs, on the techniques of food preparation, and all questions related to the art and science of cooking; as well as occupational matters, such as the training of cooks and the system of apprenticeships). According to Trubeck, in contrast to other leading culinary journals, *L'Art culinaire* cultivated a distinctive readership: "*L'Art culinaire*'s editorial board knew exactly whom they wanted to captivate and influence: professional male chefs. And the editors of *Le Pot au feu*, *Le Gourmet*, and *Le Cordon bleu* knowingly concerned themselves with another community: urban bourgeois housewives and their female domestic servants."[67]

---

64. See Vicki A. Swinbank, "The Sexual Politics of Cooking: A Feminist Analysis of Culinary Hierarchy in Western Culture," *Journal of Historical Sociology*, vol. 15, no. 4, December 2002,, 464–494.

65. Represented by the expression "La femme naît cuisinière, l'homme le devient" [The woman is born a cook, the man becomes one] noted in Jean-Claude Ribaut, "Cuisine au féminin" in *Le Monde*, June 15–16, 2003, p. 18. According to Jack Goody, from as far back as ancient Egypt, male cooks had appropriated women's recipes for everyday cooking and transformed them into court cuisine, but French haute cuisine would have further reinforced this tendency because the rise of the chef profession in France was so closely bound up with nationalism, thereby raising the stakes involved and necessitating sharp social markers of differentiation. See Jack Goody, *Cooking, Cuisine and Class* (Cambridge: Cambridge University Press, 1982), p. 101; and see Swinbank, "Sexual Politics of Cooking," p. 469.

66. Trubeck, *Haute Cuisine*, p. 83.

67. Trubeck, p. 85.

It was the chef profession that supplied the journal with its editors and writers, and its goals were closely bound up with those of the Société des cuisiniers français pour le Progrès de l'art culinaire, the most important organization of elite chefs at the time (albeit one that shared a measure of high status with its rival, the Académie culinaire). Jointly, the Société and its journal, *L'Art culinaire*, sought to build a professional network of chefs, to create a cooking school, and to organize culinary expositions to promote haute cuisine (as well as to raise financial support for the school). The journal did more than simply enhance the organizational development of the profession, however, for it served an important symbolic role in advancing cuisine as transcendent, as an art, and as a cultural practice whose rightful place was at the very center of the national cultural patrimony. As its resident chef/poet wrote in 1888:[68]

Ô vous, qui de notre Art, embrassez la carrière,
Sachez sacrifier Presque la vie entière,
Afin de devenir cuisinier de talent:
Le début est aride, et le succès est lent . . .

Comme Art dont la valeur n'était pas contestée
Et toujours poursuivant la route du progrès
L'Art culinaire alors devint un Art français . . .

Although other prominent chefs made contributions as well, the recipes and menus of Auguste Escoffier were found in almost every issue of *L'Art culinaire*, and by 1890 he was well on the way to becoming the most influential chef of the Third Republic, the *capo di tutti capi* of French gastronomy at perhaps its grandest moment.[69] Escoffier's rise to prominence can be seen as having marked the unequivocal triumph of the professional chef in the struggle to achieve "jurisdiction" over the kitchen, or, more precisely, in the triumph of the chef of the restaurant (and hotel) kitchen over

---

68. Part of a poem that shared the title of the journal and was authored by its resident chef/poet, Achille Ozanne, in 1888 (and translated by Trubeck): "O you, who know our Art, embrace the career, Know that you must sacrifice almost your entire life; to become a talented cook: The start is barren, and success is slow"; and "As an art whose valor was not contested, And always in pursuit of the road to Progress. The Culinary art thus became a French art." See Trubeck, pp. 95–96.
69. Stephen Mennell, *All Manners of Food*, p. 174.

the managers of both industrial and domestic kitchens.[70] Thus the measure of autonomy achieved by the gastronomic field had its social expression in the dominance of the professional chef in the domain of the restaurant and hotel kitchen. Thenceforth, all the important marks of professional accomplishment, major awards of recognition, and the rites of institution that would truly matter, would be those framed in terms of the practices of professional chefs, their associates, and their institutions. That is, according to the evaluative criteria composed from within this sociocultural universe, it would be chefs, their restaurants, and their creations that would represent the principal objects of veneration, rather than the purveyors of industrial cuisine ("food service professionals" as they might be called today) for their products or processes, or indeed the family recipes and home-cooked meals prepared by the (mostly female) cooks of the domestic household.

The latter decades of the nineteenth century thus saw the consolidation of French gastronomy as a distinctive domain that was increasingly acquiring its own rules, regulations, and institutional forms and developing its own proper standards and methods of evaluation. In other words, it was increasingly a social world unto its own, having defined itself through a process of social conquest in which the professional chef had come to hold sway. It had established itself as a social world dominated by men and not women, and therefore as a cuisine that was distinguished apart from the cuisine of the private household. It was also a cuisine elevated above industrial process, a victory for professional chefs over their industrial counterparts. Thus the scale of valuation that became established in this world was one that was constructed not between craft and industry, as in the rest of the industrializing world where the skilled artisan was everywhere forced to defend his position and his traditional craft prerogatives against the encroachment of mechanized standardization and its insidious de-skilling effect. Rather the practice of the chef had come to occupy the space between art and craft, a scale of valuation that enhanced the position of professional chef.

"Society had little regard for the culinary profession" bemoaned Escoffier, before declaring that "this should not have been so, since cuisine is a science and an art and he who devotes his talent to its service deserves full

---

70. The concept of *jurisdiction* refers here to the link between a profession and its work and has been borrowed from the legal domain and applied to the sociology of the professions by Andrew Abbott in *The System of Professions: An Essay on the Division of Expert Labor* (Chicago: University of Chicago Press, 1988), p. 20.

respect and consideration."[71] In comparing the status of the chef to that of an artist Escoffier was, in effect, attempting an act of symbolic levitation by trying to raise the status of his profession through his assertion of it. For from a position atop the world of French gastronomy, a position secured by having codified haute cuisine with the publication of his *Le Guide culinaire* in 1902, Escoffier held the power to make such words count. Much like his predecessor, Carême, the philosopher-chef whose writings codified culinary practice in the nineteenth century, Escoffier's *Guide* set the terms for culinary practice in the twentieth century, quickly becoming the central text in the training of professional cooks, a position that it mostly still retains. Escoffier had advanced a more restrained cooking style than Carême, who's highly elaborated and expensively produced presentations marked haute cuisine as a spectacle of decadence, but both can be seen as having represented modernizing influences to the extent that they each contributed to the codification of gastronomic principles as well as to systematizing the process of culinary production.[72] Indeed, Escoffier was largely responsible for rationalizing (and institutionalizing) the modern organization of the professional kitchen. With the opening of the Savoy Hotel in London in 1889 under the direction César Ritz, Escoffier was provided with a stage upon which to work his symbolic magic, thereby permanently shifting the main venue of haute cuisine from the upper-class household to the gastronomic restaurant, in this case to the kitchens of the luxury hotels that were opening throughout Europe. In collaboration with Ritz, Escoffier opened restaurants in the grand hotels (the Savoy and the Carlton in London, and the Hotel Ritz in Paris) that demanded a higher volume of meal preparation in a relatively short time, and so Escoffier reorganized his kitchens along industrial lines, emphasizing the specialization of cooking functions, while strengthening the relations between cooking stations.[73] No longer were chefs mere glorified household servants. They could increasingly aspire to shape and command spaces of their own making that could attract inter-

---

71. Quoted in Andrew Dornenburg and Karen Page, *Becoming a Chef*, rev. ed. (Hoboken, NJ: John Wiley and Sons, 2003), p. 9.

72. As Ferguson convincingly argues, despite Carême's penchant for spectacular and exotic culinary display, his literary works established cuisine as a profession, with characteristic norms, regulations, and practices. See Priscilla Parkhurst Ferguson, *Accounting for Taste: The Triumph of French Cuisine* (Chicago: University of Chicago Press, 2004), pp. 50–53.

73. See M. Steinberger, *Au Revoir to All That* (New York: Bloomsbury, 2009), p. 20.

national visibility. In this way, Escoffier helped to secure for French haute cuisine a position of international culinary hegemony.[74]

But the elevation of the chef profession was not something achieved by Escoffier alone, nor was it simply a function of having secured, through the grand hotels, a prominent institutional platform (although that it did). While Escoffier played a critical historic role, and the luxury hotels provided a certain mise en scène by shining a spotlight on the work of the grand chef, the aura that would come to be produced around the star chef, the cult of virtuosity that became a virtual fetish in the world of haute cuisine, was equally generated by a relatively small group of culinary "big men" (plus one "big" woman). These four figures, all "larger than life" (larger, in literal terms, in their rotund figures, as well as figuratively, in their expansive personalities) had risen from within the ranks of the culinary craft in the early decades of the twentieth century to become charismatic personalities who seemed to be magnets for the press, for celebrities, and for men of power. Each of them, Ferdinand Le Point (called the "gentle giant of Vienne") at his Restaurant de la Pyramide; Eugénie "Mère" Brazier from her bistro on the rue Royale in Lyon; André Pic from Valence; and Alexandre Dumaine of la Côte d'Or in Saulieu, were distinctive "characters" as well as distinctive chefs. They drew to their restaurants the most prominent names from the worlds of art, literature, cinema, and politics, personalities who themselves were inevitably followed by the press, who, in turn, helped to construct these four chefs as celebrities.[75] Moreover, the glittering personalities they attracted had the effect of endowing French gastronomy with an air of glamour that further elevated culinary activity above the prosaic act of cooking. Through the prism of its socially constructed charisma, gastronomy appeared an alluring domain, a transcendent realm that came to reserve for itself a very special place in the French cultural imagination.

---

74. See Mennell, "Food and Wine," p. 179; Trubeck, p. 48; Dornenburg and Page, *Becoming a Chef,* p. 8.

75. The history of the *Michelin* star system is simultaneously a history of the consecration of the star chef, and, together, these four figures emerged, ironically, as the first real "personalities" of the culinary world, partially produced by the attention they attracted from celebrities previously certified in the worlds of art and politics. Pablo Picasso, Jean Cocteau, Salvador Dali, Sacha Guitry, Fernandel, Charlie Chaplin, the Aga Khan, King Edward VIII and Wallis Simpson, Léon Blum, and many others of the most prominent personalities of the mid-twentieth century frequented one or several of their restaurants. See the profiles of these four chefs in Jean-François Mesplède, *Trois étoiles au Michelin: Une histoire de la haute gastronomie française* (Paris: Grund, 1998).

To pursue an understanding of its social mechanics requires that we consider more than just those things that are normally associated with haute cuisine, for it is a domain that rests on more than just the material act of cooking. Just as importantly, social analysis requires attention to the production of symbolic practices. That means that we are concerned not only with the cultivation and the selection of foodstuffs or their circuits of distribution, or the social organization of the kitchen and the restaurant, or even the actual preparation and cooking of dishes, but equally with the social preparation of both the consumers and the producers of haute cuisine. In other words, the production of belief in haute cuisine as a particular sociocultural phenomenon is as important as the development of its culinary practices, which, otherwise left to their own devices, might have only limited cultural significance. For it is the collective system of belief that confers, acknowledges, and celebrates the significance of haute cuisine, thereby elevating it above mere cooking and, in France especially, rendering it virtually transcendent in sociocultural terms. The chapters that follow, therefore, are not exactly about food, or the ways we talk about food, or about cooking, or chefs, or diners, but about a domain of social practices in which these and other elements are brought to bear in relation to each other as a functioning social microcosm, as a distinctive field of social practices.

As we noted above, by the latter decades of the nineteenth century the field of gastronomic practices in France was becoming its own autonomous universe, having followed a path not unlike those of more advanced cultural fields like literature and art. At that moment it was in the process of constituting itself as a distinctive field with an array of institutional forms, including a structure of public eating establishments (increasingly hierarchically ordered) where its culinary creations were routinely displayed, consumed, and treated as objects of marvel; with an entire genre of books, manuals, and journals that codified its practices, venerated its practitioners, and formalized its methods of training, while maintaining its own system of gatekeepers and institutions of consecration to carefully manage entry into its ranks. An important, if not defining aspect of the French gastronomic field was the dominant position that had been assumed by chefs within it (specifically male chefs working in commercial, as opposed to household, kitchens), whose dominion was largely achieved through a process of collective self-promotion and jurisdictional conquest, not unlike that of other professions. The process was supported by the establishment of a network of grand hotels that served as prominent venues, where culinary artists displayed their works and where a gastronomic aesthetic was cultivated both for and by a clientele whose display of cultural refinement included the art of the table. Later, during the interwar period in the twentieth century, the status of the "maestro" chef would come to be elevated still further by association with those who had achieved notoriety in politics, art, theater, and film, and whose symbolic capital was increasingly converted by the print media into a common currency of "celebrity," transferable to the chefs who displayed it to enhance the luster of recognition that they had obtained in the gastronomic field.

Before proceeding we should recognize the problem we face in placing the chef at the center of an analysis of a domain that has been largely created by the chef himself. That is, the shape of the universe that we want to understand was largely sculpted by the hands of the victors in a social contest and has therefore been preconstructed by those who have successfully asserted their position and have been able to represent themselves as dominant. What this means is that we cannot necessarily assume that haute cuisine is itself the social object that needs to be understood to grasp the logic of French gastronomy. In other words, one might ask, what would it mean to maintain an exclusive analytical focus on haute cuisine (again, a domain largely created by those with particular sectoral interests) if it were merely the symbolic center, or just one part, of a broader field of gastronomic practices? This is not to suggest that chefs can be ignored in an analysis of French gastronomy, but it is to simply recommend that we proceed with caution, for there are at least four important analytical implications that flow from this recognition.[76] First, while our analysis must be concerned

---

76. The following chapters draw on a three-part database of professional French chefs that includes (1) dossiers of the thirty-six most highly consecrated French chefs during the decade of the 1990s (all were recipients of three stars in the *Michelin Guide* at some point during that decade), collected by the author and comprising biographical profiles of chefs culled from trade magazines within the chef profession and the restaurant industry in France, as well as articles from French popular magazines; (2) biographical data on 244 chefs who were profiled in the pages of *Le Chef* magazine between 1991 and 1998, a form of professional recognition that can be considered a secondary level of social consecration; and, (3) in order to help fill the gaps in nos. 1 and 2, I draw upon a compilation of professional résumés for over 1,400 members of the French culinary profession, which include 792 recognized chefs de cuisine and 640 culinary workers in secondary positions (including seconds de cuisine, sommeliers, pâtissiers, etc.) that have been assembled in a compendium published in 1998 by Les Éditions du Bottin Gourmand as *Les Étoiles de la gastronomie française 1998–1999*. Helpful too has been a study of French gastronomy that included interviews with sixty-six members of the world of French haute cuisine (including interviews with forty chefs/owners of restaurants with either one, two, or three stars in the *Michelin Guide*). The study was conducted by Isabelle Terence and published as *Le Monde de la grande restauration en France* (Paris: L'Harmattan, 1996).

with the central position of the chef in the world of haute cuisine, we should proceed in a way that remains focused on the social mechanisms by which chefs have been symbolically produced and reproduced as *central*. Thus, while haute cuisine may be but a small part of the gastronomic universe in material terms, it is crucial in symbolic terms, and so we must pay analytical attention to the processes and mechanisms by which such relatively marginal activity has been able to sustain its symbolic centrality.

Second, we should not assume that the boundaries around the gastronomic field are self-evident or that they can be determined a priori, because what we think of as the proper object of our analysis, at first glance, may very well be only that part of the social universe that the victors in a social contest meant for us to see; the process of delimiting the boundaries around a field may very well be an important part of what is at stake for the contestants in that field. In other words, the struggle over the definition of the legitimate boundary around a social field, as Pierre Bourdieu has shown in a wide range of other contexts, is often a crucial part of the stakes that animate the struggles that take place within that field (struggles over who and what legitimately belongs there, or does not). That is, in a social world shot through with struggles over recognition, the view that seems most self-evident to the observer at any given time may very well have been effectively prearranged, thereby ensuring systematic misrecognition. In analytical terms, therefore, we must be prepared to carefully construct and reconstruct what we understand as the very object of our analysis as we proceed, rather than relying on predetermined boundaries that appear to have been self-evidently "given" to us by the social world.

Third, our very way of viewing the position of the chef requires a certain break with the usual way that we look at cultural matters more generally. While we are accustomed to looking through an aesthetic lens to highlight the virtuosity of the individual cultural producer, we must instead look through a sociological lens to emphasize the process and development of the social context within which the cultural object is produced both symbolically and materially. In this case, it means that we must be prepared to lift the focus from the grand chef as the sole "creator" of the cultural object, haute cuisine, and view the social production and reproduction of the entire system of beliefs and practices that produce both the figure of the grand chef *and* the belief in his virtuosity.[77]

---

77. In my view this entails more than just an acknowledgment of cultural production as a cooperative process, as in Howard Becker's *Art Worlds* (Berkeley: University of California

Fourth, we should be prepared to distance ourselves from the effects that belief in the field may exert on us, in the sense of being aware that a stance that conveys reverence for haute cuisine provides the reader (and author) with endless opportunities to display the plumage of cultural connoisseurship by flaunting our own knowledge and appreciation of foods, wines, famous chefs, and notable restaurants. Moreover, because it radiates out from a symbolic French cultural center, which itself embodies a strong cultural marker as "French," we must be cognizant of the ways that Frenchness can render these things doubly exalted as objects of cultural veneration. The point is not to pretend to a contrived "reflexivity" that mainly advances the impression of our own thoughtfulness, but to take as part of the social reality that we are attempting to understand the social uses to which talk about and belief in haute cuisine may be put, and to find a place for that in our analytical model to help us make sense of it in relation to the entire field.[78]

Press, 1982), for example. Although grasping the collective dynamics of a cultural world is a crucial and necessary first step, a proper sociological analysis relies on a radically relational perspective that recognizes and seeks to grasp the logic of the internal differentiation of social actors, both individual and institutional, and that puts an analytical focus on both social life *and* its representations.

78. See P. Bourdieu, *The Field of Cultural Production* (New York: Columbia University Press, 1993), p. 35.

2

The Symbolic Economy
of French Gastronomy

To assist in our investigation of French gastronomy, it is useful to
follow a route taken by Pierre Bourdieu in his earliest investigations
of cultural production. With reference to haute couture, he noted
certain key characteristics of restricted markets for luxury cultural goods
that he would later employ in his analyses of other cultural fields: (a) the
rarity of the producer, rather than the rarity of the product, is where one
locates the source of value in restricted markets for luxury goods; (b) the
rarity of the producer is itself a function of the rarity of the position that the
producer occupies within a field of positions; and (c) faith in the magic of
the producer's signature (*griffe*) allows a certain transubstantiation to occur
through which the charisma of the producer is transferred to the cultural
object:

> It is in producing the rarity of the producer that the field of symbolic
> production produces the rarity of the product: the magical power
> of the "creator" is the capital of authority attached to a position,
> which can act only if it is mobilized by a person authorized, or bet-
> ter, if that capital is associated with a person, and with his charisma,
> and guaranteed by his signature. That which makes Dior is not the
> biological individual Dior, nor the House of Dior, but the capital of
> the Dior house, acting under the realm of a single individual who

is not only or necessarily Dior* . . . the imposition of the "signature" represents an exemplary case of social alchemy, an operation
of transubstantiation that, without anything changing the physical
nature of the product, radically modifies its social quality.[1] [author's
translation] [*Bourdieu here is referring to the case of the manager
who maintains the enterprise after the death or retirement of the
designer.]

How else to explain such brilliantly provocative and initially counterintuitive phenomena as Marcel Duchamp's "fountain," a ready-made replica
of a urinal that was successfully consecrated as fine art, other than with an
analysis that seeks to understand the position of the work and the artist in
the development and trajectory of an entire artistic field? Not only does the
analysis of the field afford an opportunity to comprehend the social and
institutional mechanisms capable of sanctifying, and thereby transforming,
mundane objects but also allows for an understanding of the acts of apparent
subversion of the field itself, like the forms of artistic sacrilege that Duchamp
originated and that has been commonplace in the arts since the 1960s.[2]

This is a perspective that views the artistic field as producing the value
of the work of art by producing and reproducing principles of difference
and separation (for example, between what is recognized as art and a simple
utensil, or between an artist and a plumber). It is thus the field that sets the
terms for the creation of the "creator," as well as the creation of the magical power invested in his "signature."[3] What else but a faith in such magic
could produce the enormous economic differences separating a work of art
that has been signed by a fully consecrated artist, and the value of that same
object (or image) when left unsigned, with an uncertain pedigree that could

1. Pierre Bourdieu (with Yvette Delsaut), "Le Couturier et sa griffe: Contribution à une
théorie de la magie," *ACTES de la recherche en sciences sociales*, no. 1, January 1975, pp. 21, 23.

2. As Bourdieu has written, "Paradoxically, nothing more clearly reveals the logic of the
functioning of the artistic field than the fate of these apparently radical attempts at subversion.
Because they expose the art of artistic creation to a mockery already annexed to the artistic
tradition by Duchamp, they are immediately converted into artistic 'acts,' recorded as such
and thus consecrated and celebrated by the makers of taste. Art cannot reveal the truth about
art without snatching it away again by turning the revelation into an artistic event." P. Bourdieu, "The Production of Belief," in *The Field of Cultural Production* (New York: Columbia
University Press, 1993), p. 82.

3. Bourdieu, "The Production of Belief," p. 28; and also see Pierre Bourdieu, "Historical
Genesis of a Pure Aesthetic" in *The Field of Cultural Production* (New York: Columbia University Press, 1993), p. 258.

be a mere copy or a fake?[4] This is faith that is not exactly accomplished through words or discourse but by the conditions (historical, institutional, structural) that grant a certain measure of power to words and by the reciprocally confirming relationship that prevails between social actors (individual and institutional) who occupy *positions* of close proximity in a field and so tend to have similar *dis-positions*. Such are the conditions in which words can be made to count and in which a strong sense of "belief" in the field can be produced. This always involves a certain collective misrecognition to the extent that it obscures the historical clash of social forces and competing interests that have shaped it to appear in a particular way, thereby excluding other possible ways of seeing.

The Production of Belief

Our analysis of the field of French gastronomy begins then, not so much with a focus on the chef, or even of haute cuisine as a cultural object, but with a focus on the production of belief in both the virtuosity of the chef and the value of haute cuisine. This entails attention to the set of individual and institutional agents who are collectively engaged in the production of this belief. This would encompass the various gastronomic "guides," trade journals and magazines, the journalists and the food critics, and the foundations and museums and the monuments; taking into account both established figures and rebels, the consecrators and the critics, from the more influential to the more marginal. While these social actors may seem completely peripheral to the cooking process under way in the kitchen and ancillary to the production of haute cuisine as a cultural object, they are central to the production of belief in the power of the chef and the power of the cultural object.

---

4. The art world is rife with struggles over attribution and authenticity of works of art, out of which has been produced an entire subindustry that adjudicates these struggles. Walter Benjamin sought to place this in a historical context in an analysis of the democratization of cultural forms that occurred in relation to the historical development of techniques of mechanical reproduction (photography, for example). See Walter Benjamin, "Art in the Age of Mechanical Reproduction," in *Marxism and Art: Writings in Aesthetics and Criticism*, eds. Berel Lang and Forrest Williams (New York: David McKay Company, Inc., 1972). While Benjamin's analysis contributed a great deal to understanding the social process of art, Bourdieu's conception of the artistic field reveals its limitations by demonstrating the value of analytically constituting a broader field of practices that include the art analysts themselves (including even the most critical of art historians) as actors contributing to a belief in the value of art, and thus as a crucial element of a sociology of art.

"A Master Class for the Masters"[5]

So what do you do when you're a Michelin three-star chef and the renowned travel guide decides that you should cook for a few of your colleagues? Well, not a few actually. How about 47 of the 49 Michelin three-star chefs in Europe? All the French men and women who share your stardom, along with those from England and Spain, Germany and Holland, Belgium and the Netherlands, Italy and Switzerland.

If you are Alain Ducasse you don't try to impress the chefs and the Michelin masters and a handful of journalists with sparks and somersaults, fireworks or cartwheels. Nor do you play it safe. Much to Ducasse's credit, he chose to create a seasonal menu that was at once classic and creative, ultra-modern and surprising, well-paced, and most of all satisfying. The setting was a lunch on Oct. 26 at his restaurant in the Hotel Plaza Athénée. It was a brilliant, blue-skied day, autumn leaves crunching beneath my feet as I walked along the Seine, trying to divine what might be on the menu.

For sure caviar, truffles, langoustines, sea bass, scallops and some sort of game. And so as not to play favorites, the wines would have to include a selection from some of France's best regions.

The purpose of the lunch was to say farewell to the Michelin Guide's director, Derek Brown of Britain, 60, and to usher in his successor, Jean-Luc Naret, 42, of France. It was a very nice reason for a party. You would have to be remarkably blasé not to be moved by all of this gastronomic talent gathered in one spot: There was the father of them all, Paul Bocuse of Lyon, seated next to the day's star: Ducasse.

The well-known were there—Alain Senderens of Lucas Carton and Jean-Claude Vrinat of Taillevent. So were some of the rising stars. . . .

At table, we began with a tiny turban of raw, glistening-pink langoustines topped with an exquisite dollop of the finest caviar, all set in a pool of pungent langoustine jelly. I am not a fan of raw langoustines—I prefer the pillowy fluff of the delicate shellfish lightly cooked—but I think that Ducasse may have made a convert. . . .

With such perfect starters, this would sure be a hard act to follow, but next came a refreshing rectangle of sea bass on a bed of citrus, served with a 2002 Chablis from Domaine William Fèvre, in a magnum, and a modern rendition of the classic, "lièvre a la royale," roborative in its traditional versions, here light and surprising in the Ducasse version.

. . . He's in a class apart," declared Vrinat, while Senderens pronounced the dish "a beautifully modern version of a true classic."

—Patricia Wells, former food writer for the *International Herald Tribune*

---

5. Patricia Wells, "A Master Class for the Masters," International Herald Tribune, November 5, 2004, p. 10.

The *Michelin Guide* is widely known as an institution that reigns supreme in the world of French gastronomy. Standing as sentinel at the gates of haute cuisine, the *Michelin Guide* and its system of consecration has served as an organizational foundation for the very *nomos* of the field of gastronomic practices, or the dominant principles of vision and division that establish its terms and its boundaries. Its supremacy largely resides in its power to consecrate and thus is an expression of one of the primary stakes in the gastronomic field, namely the monopoly of culinary legitimacy, or the monopoly over the power to assert (with authority) just who may legitimately call themselves and be legitimately called a "grand chef."[6]

First published in 1900, the dawn of the automobile age, by the Michelin Tire Manufacturing Company, and offered for free to drivers in an effort to promote automobile tourism, the thirty-five thousand copies of the first edition of the red-covered book contained maps of thirteen selected cities, listed the addresses of hotels, post offices, railroad stations, doctors and pharmacies, as well as service stations and the price of gasoline. Since then the *Michelin Guide* has been produced annually, apart from the periods of the two world wars and one other year (1921) that followed the change from being distributed freely to motorists to being an object of sale.[7] The *Michelin Guide* began classifying restaurants in 1923, which was a period in which the notoriety of French haute cuisine was on the rise. Escoffier was perched prominently at its summit and the rich and famous (increasingly tracked by the press) were beginning to flock to establishments run by a small but colorful handful of celebrated chef-proprietors. In 1933 a system of star designations that the *Michelin Guide* had previously introduced in selected locales was now expanded to cover restaurants across the country, thereby serving to further institutionalize the gastronomic cartography that Curnonsky had charted several decades earlier.

Even though the *Michelin Guide* was known for being a practical manual to the road and for maintaining a sizable readership among travelers, it was not until after World War II that it became widely recognized as *the* central reference of French gastronomy.[8] Annual print runs had fluctuated up and down in the 1920s, from sixty thousand to ninety thousand copies;

---

6. These points intentionally paraphrase Pierre Bourdieu's analysis of the operation of the literary field in *The Rules of Art: Genesis and Structure of the Literary Field* (Stanford, CA: Stanford University Press, 1992), p. 224.

7. Jean-François Mesplède, *Trois Étoiles au Michelin* (Paris: Éditions Grund, 1998), pp. 9–14.

8. Pascal Rémy, *L'Inspecteur se met à table* (France: Éditions des Équateurs, 2004), p. 110.

then they rose up and remained above one hundred thousand throughout the decade of the 1930s (publication ceased during the war years). They rose steadily after the war to six hundred thousand in the 1970s and leveled off to where they have (roughly) remained until today, oscillating between five hundred fifty thousand and seven hundred thousand copies annually.[9] This has meant that the *Michelin Guide* was likely to be found in the glove compartments of a sizable portion of French automobiles. At the same time its institutional status within the sphere of haute cuisine is only partially dependent on the size of its readership. Its impact and continuing importance is more the product of its restaurant rating system, whose cultural effects reverberate well beyond the gourmands and the travelers who rely on it for basic information about food and lodging on the road. In the domain of haute cuisine, and across the broad realm of French gastronomy, the *Michelin Guide* represents the supreme measure of culinary worth.

On its surface the star rating system is simple enough. The *Michelin Guide* retains a staff of anonymous inspectors charged with traveling the country, staying in hotels, eating in restaurants, and writing their evaluations. Their evaluations are then compiled and listed in an annual volume of some fourteen hundred pages that is organized alphabetically by city and town and that includes maps and various sorts of practical information on hotel and restaurant facilities across the country. According to the key at the beginning of every volume that explains the symbols employed (and that always includes an English version following the French text): "Certain establishments deserve to be brought to your attention for the particularly fine quality of their cooking. Michelin stars are awarded for the standard of meals served." Stars are awarded to very few restaurants in France, relatively speaking, and most of the thousands of restaurants listed in the guide receive no stars at all.[10]

---

9. Although precise sales figures are unavailable, after about 1970 the market for gastronomic guides expanded with the founding of *Gault-Millau*, *Bottin Gourmand*, and several others, so while *Michelin* continued to print about the same number of copies, its sales most likely remained fairly steady, but within an expanding market for such guides. Selected print run figures are provided in Mesplède, *Trois Étoiles*, p. 14.

10. The degree of luxury (and comfort) and the peacefulness of the setting of many of the other restaurants listed in the *Michelin Guide* are, however, designated by up to five *fourchettes* (forks), or "luxury in the traditional style" as well as color (with red representing a particularly "pleasant" establishment). In recent years, in addition to the star designations the *Michelin Guide* has begun to employ the symbol of the "Bibendum" tire cartoon figure to make special note of restaurants where one will find "Good food at moderate prices" ("less elaborate, moderately priced menus that offer good value for money and serve carefully prepared meals, often

There are three categories of *Michelin* stars, with one star representing (in the understated tone characteristic of the *Michelin Guide*) "A very good restaurant in its category," immediately followed by the notation that "the star indicates a good place to stop on your journey," offering a warning to the reader to "beware of comparing the star given to an expensive deluxe establishment to that of a simple restaurant where you can appreciate fine cuisine at a reasonable price." There are roughly between four hundred and five hundred restaurants in France awarded one *Michelin* star in a typical year (for example, there were 498 one-star restaurants listed in the 1990 edition and 405 in the 1998 edition). A two-star restaurant in the *Michelin Guide* is designated as one where you can expect to find "excellent cooking" that is "worth a detour" (there were ninety two-star restaurants listed in the 1990 edition, and seventy in the 1998 edition).

The highest rating for any restaurant in the *Michelin Guide* is a three-star designation, an award that has never been bestowed on more than twenty-seven restaurants in France in any given year (2004 was that year) and in recent decades the annual norm has hovered around twenty-one restaurants (from 1974 to 2001 there were never more than twenty-two three-star restaurants in any given year in France and no less than seventeen, although from 2002 to 2004 the numbers rose to twenty-three, twenty-five, and twenty-seven, respectively).[11] Three stars designate restaurants serving "exceptional cuisine" that are therefore "worth a special journey." As the *Michelin Guide* notes, "One always eats here extremely well, sometimes superbly. Fine wines, faultless service, elegant surroundings. One will pay accordingly!" Although the *Michelin Guide* exerts substantial influence on French gastronomy as a cultural field, it has not necessarily been used on an everyday basis by French people seeking a restaurant (or hotel). While many French families have been reputed to carry a copy of the *Michelin Guide* in the glove compartment of their car, a 1995 survey by *Le Chef* magazine and the marketing firm Sofres found that only 16 percent of those surveyed had consulted a gastronomic guide in the previous six months, although, of

---

of regional cooking"). While this "Bib Gourmand" designation is given visual prominence in the *Michelin Guide* that is nearly coequal to that of the stars, and while such recognition is undoubtedly extremely valuable for a restaurant's business, its purpose is information and not consecration, and holds none of the powerful symbolic effects that accompany the *Michelin* star.

11. Recent numbers of three-star restaurants culled from editions of the *Michelin Guide*; and for 1998, numbers are listed in Mesplède, *Trois Étoiles*, p. 204.

those who did, half had consulted the *Michelin Guide*.[12] Whether or not it is regularly used by the general public, however, it has played a crucial role in the structuring of the French gastronomic field.

A powerful mystique has enveloped the *Michelin Guide*'s restaurant rating system, a mystique that has been spun from a combination of elements, the most prominent being the cult of *secrecy* surrounding the restaurant inspection process. Not only is the precise number of inspectors who work for the *Michelin Guide* a secret but the individual inspectors remain scrupulously anonymous to the staff of the restaurants that they inspect, always paying their own bill when their meal is finished (unlike other restaurant critics in France, who typically would eat for free after identifying themselves to the restaurant management).[13] Moreover, the specific factors that distinguish, say, a one- from a two- and a two- from a three-star-rated restaurant remain largely a mystery, to the chagrin of those in and around the gastronomic field, as suggested in the following exchange:[14]

> *Néorestauration* **magazine**: How exactly your inspectors work is the question that burns on all lips. Is there a list of precise criteria?
>
> **Derek Brown (former director of the *Michelin Guide*)**: I cannot reveal our little secrets. It is part of Michelin's know-how. We work with a certain number of indicators but we don't follow a precise and detailed list of criteria. When we visit a restaurant we evidently meticulously pick up on everything that is of importance for the guide, but the judgment is a question of feeling, of experience.

---

12. The survey of 1,014 people in 1995 indicated that out of all the gastronomic guides available in France, of those who had consulted a guide 50 percent had consulted the *Michelin Guide* rather than any of the other sixteen listed (*Gault-Millau*, 23 percent; *Guide du Routard*, 9 percent; *Bottin Gourmand*, 3 percent; *Guide des Relais et Châteaux*, 3 percent; *Le Petit Futé*, 2 percent; *Champérard*, 1 percent; *Guide Lebey*, 1 percent; *Guide Pudlowski*, 1 percent; etc.). See "*Qui consulte les guides?*" in *Le Chef*, no. 75, January–February 1995, p. 52.

13. According to Echikson, the *Michelin Guide* was unique among gastronomic guides and food critics for paying their own way (William Echikson, *Burgundy Stars: A Year in the Life of a Great French Restaurant* [Boston: Little, Brown, 1995], p. 76).

14. *Néorestauration* magazine is an industry trade magazine, and Derek Brown was formerly the director of the *Michelin Guide*. Patrice Fleurent, "Derek Brown, Nouveau Directeur du Guide Rouge Michelin," *Néorestauration*, March 2001, p. 30n374 (author's translation). According to Echikson, when he was asked to distinguish between a two- and a three-star restaurant, the former Michelin director, Bernard Naegellen would only reply, "Three stars represent perfection, and two stars represent near perfection" (Echikson, *Burgundy Stars*, p. 76). Prior to Naegellen, who served as director from 1985 to 2000 (and who, reportedly, would speak with the press only on condition that his photo not be published), the identity of the *Michelin Guide* directors had always been kept a secret, too (p. 81).

Néorestauration **magazine:** That leaves a great part to subjectivity. . .
Derek Brown: That's true; it is not mathematical, but subjective. But we are trying hard to stay as objective as possible in our subjectivity. Recall that we are working to inform the reader as well as possible, and not to bring some professional opinion or another on this or that restaurateur. To know how to appreciate a hotel, a restaurant, is the essence of our know-how at Michelin.

Evidence that its almost cultish character tends to amplify its cultural resonance was made evident in the reaction to the publication of an "exposé" of the Michelin inspection process.[15] Although the contents of the book were relatively tepid as an exposé, the swirl of scandal surrounding its publication were as revealing as the book itself. The fact that it was penned by a former inspector, who had worked for Michelin for sixteen years and who claimed to have been fired for writing the book, and that Michelin had sought to prevent its publication was sufficient to generate considerable press attention. Months before the book even appeared *Le Monde* published a front-page article on the impending scandal that it promised, and the weekend edition of *Le Figaro* published a disguised photo of the book's author as part of a nine-page color spread on the *Michelin Guide*.[16]

Next to its legendary secrecy and anonymity, another key pillar of the Michelin mystique has been a cultivated *disinterestedness* in its display of disregard for commercial concerns, a widely recognized trait of the *Michelin Guide* that largely stems from the fact that for some eighty-five years it has accepted no advertising whatsoever on its pages (unlike other guides to gastronomy).[17] This appearance of disinterestedness has represented a sort of cultural "firewall" that seems to protect the evaluative process from any taint of a conflict of interest (in pecuniary terms at least), and whose effect

---

15. Rémy, *L'Inspecteur.*

16. It is surely a minor stroke of publicity genius to generate such a "looming scandal" several months prior to publication, but what is telling is that the threat of piercing the cult of secrecy surrounding the Michelin inspection process can generate such excitement in anticipation, not only in France but in the *New York Times* as well, albeit with the slightly sardonic inflection that might be expected. See Elaine Scolino, "Michelin Man Jolts French Food World," *New York Times*, February 25, 2004, p. D1, and "Michelin Man Rolls into Guide Critic" *New York Times*, April 28, 2004, p. D8. Moreover, the author's unsuccessful lawsuit against Michelin ensured steady publicity about the book for the rest of the year ("Fired Michelin Inspector Loses Appeal on Job Loss," *International Herald Tribune*, December 15, 2004, p. 3.)

17. Mesplède.

is to lend a strong measure of legitimacy and integrity. Of course, the ability of the guide to strike a disinterested pose is largely made possible by its comfortable position under the wing of the huge Michelin Tire Corporation, but by appearing to separate the judgment of culinary practice and artisanship from any risk of desecration by commercial interest, the element of disinterestedness can be seen as an important symbolic lynchpin for the entire edifice of French gastronomy.

The third ingredient of its mystique is the air of *timelessness* that the *Michelin Guide* appears to embody, the product of the combined effect of its age (over a century old), its serialized publication schedule (as an annual its publication has a ritualized quality), and its conservatism (in its essentially unvarying presentation, always dressed in the same red cover and organized according to the same format).[18] These elements operate in relation to one another to magnify a sense of timelessness, while also facilitating a ready transposition in the public imagination of the history of the *Michelin Guide* with the history of the gastronomic world that it has chronicled.[19] In addition, its ability to evoke a strong sense of trustworthiness is amplified by an association with a venerable family-owned and dominated industrial corporation that has been firmly implanted in the French economy for over a century.

The fourth component of the Michelin mystique is largely an effect of the previous three, and that is its mythical power of *consecration*, a power often recounted by the press and amplified by the simple fact that it occurs in a domain that has been at the center of the national cultural patrimony. A chef is realized as a significant cultural figure by receipt of a third-star in the *Michelin Guide*, with the publication of every new edition of the annual *Michelin Guide* widely anticipated and treated as a noteworthy media

---

18. It should be noted that the 2000 edition of the guide appeared with a new name, *Le Guide Rouge*, noting on the cover, "NEW with Text" although all that the editors added to the format were two brief lines of commentary, in characteristically flat style and without descriptive text. Thus, alongside the old symbols and pictograms were very brief characterizations of the restaurant's decoration or architectural style, along with equally brief and almost cryptic remarks on the cuisine (i.e., "refined cuisine," "current cuisine," "careful cuisine").

19. It therefore makes perfect marketing sense for the principal published history of the guide, *Trois Étoiles au Michelin* to be subtitled *Une Histoire de la haute gastronomie française* (Mesplède, *Trois Étoiles*). With regard to its conservatism, Echikson quotes one historian who described the Michelin family itself as a "citadel of 'catholic, paternalistic' values . . . a type of culinary Vatican' with 'secret, absolutist decision making.' . . . Almost alone among the world's great modern corporations, it is still directed by a family inner circle" (Echikson, *Burgundy Stars*, pp. 76–77).

event. Its air of cultural authority is thus both a cause and a consequence of its mystique, and this is made possible by a belief in its integrity as a gastronomic arbiter. The annual "scorecard" of winners and losers operates as a kind of serialized game that is the object of great interest to a substantial segment of the population (in a country where most three-star chefs are virtually household names).[20] But if the Michelin mystique helps maintain a belief in the cultural power of haute cuisine, it is a game in which both the losers and the winners alike tend to prevail, at least to the extent that it reinforces the place of the gastronomic field in French society.

But while its dominance as principal arbiter has been uncontested, Michelin is not the only guide that has wielded influence in world of French gastronomy.[21] The *Gault-Millau* guide, founded in 1969 as an alternative to *Michelin*, has also had an important role in the production of belief in haute cuisine, as much through its stylistic opposition to *Michelin* as through the direct influence that it exerts with its own system of restaurant ratings. Where *Michelin*'s reputation has hinged on its ability to represent itself as the venerable and eternal wellspring of gastronomic authority, an image cultivated by scrupulously concealing any effort at cultivation (i.e., through rhetorical understatement, stylistic conservatism, an absence of self-promotion), the *Gault-Millau* guide has sought to avoid such pretensions by advancing a very different stylistic persona. Founded in 1969 by journalists and food critics Henri Gault and Christian Millau, it emphasized gastronomic innovation and change, employing a more spirited language of descriptive embellishment to establish itself in relation to the *Michelin Guide*.

What it shared with *Michelin* was the national coverage of restaurants (roughly four thousand in every edition) and hotels across France, as well as a rating system of numerical scores (from ten to twenty out of a total of twenty) to designate "the quality of the cuisine and never the prices, the

20. In addition to more than half a million copies sold annually, the *Michelin Guide* receives some twenty-five thousand letters per year from readers who send in their judgments of restaurants, which are reportedly read by the inspection teams as part of the process of discovering new establishments and marking others for attention. It would seem to suggest the stakes that a substantial number of readers have in the process, for the letters are never printed in the guide itself (Mesplède, *Trois Étoiles*, p. 16).

21. As the author of one study of French restaurateurs put it, "For restaurateurs, the reputation of Michelin is already established. It is and remains the reference of the profession with regard to the standings." [author translation of: "La réputation du Michelin chez les restaurateurs n'est pas à faire. Il est et reste la référence de la profession en matière de classement." Isabelle Terence, *Le Monde de la Grande Restauration en France* (Paris: L'Harmattan, 1996), p. 118.

décor or the ambiance" (which were otherwise noted in the text itself).[22] Scores of more than thirteen in the *Gault-Millau* guide were visually overlaid upon one, two, or three *toques* (chef's hats) in the guide, with the highest-ranked restaurants receiving nineteen out of a possible twenty.[23] Scores were reached by an elaborate-sounding system explained as consisting of the information provided by "over a hundred correspondents" who cross the various countries where the guide is published, as well as "our investigators" in France of which there are "between twenty and thirty working in all zones," in addition to the information provided in questionnaires submitted by restaurateurs themselves and in letters from readers: "Their reports are transmitted to the editorial offices, the results are amended and validated by the editorial committee. . . . The investigator proposes a score to the directors of the Guide. The opinions of local correspondents are solicited on the score. The team investigates and the editors render their verdict. The score is then proposed to the editorial committee, which passes its judgment on to the senior management of the Guide."[24]

Unlike *Michelin*, the *Gault-Millau* guide made no attempt to maintain a cult of mystery around its restaurant ratings, fully disclosing its procedures and not keeping secret its "correspondents" and "inspectors." Not only did this limit its cultural authority, relative to *Michelin*, but *Gault-Millau* generally represented itself in a way that flaunted its lack of cultural affectation, a comportment that arrived at a point where it reportedly began to obtain a reputation for cronyism in its restaurant ratings, something that Gault himself conceded: "Since we were trying to get away from the Michelin style of gastronomic criticism—cold, impartial, and anonymous—our guide was personal and partial, and we became friends with many of the people we dealt with . . . Once you're the best friends with someone, how can you lower their rating or take away a toque?"[25]

---

22. From the page entitled "*Mode d'Emploi*" ("How to Use This Guide") at the beginning of every edition (translated into both English and German).

23. By the late 1980s the guide introduced a ranking of nineteen and a half, a score that was reserved for only one or two restaurants deemed to be almost transcendent in their quality. Generally, the numbers of numerically ranked restaurants tend to fluctuate in the *Gault-Millau* guide, but to give some idea of the number of restaurants ranked very highly, in the 2002 edition one counts twenty-one restaurants with a score of nineteen (the highest); twenty-six restaurants with a score of eighteen; and forty-two restaurants with a score of seventeen.

24. See the Gault-Millau website under the title "How Does It Work?": http://www.guides-gaultmillau.fr/telechargement/Comment_ca_marche.pdf.

25. Quoted in Echikson, *Burgundy Stars*, p. 101.

This determinedly "anti-Michelin," stance was also reflected in *Gault-Millau*'s promotional practices. So whereas *Michelin* has maintained the appearance of a strict separation between its commercial interest as an industrial corporation and the disinterestedness of its gastronomic guide, *Gault-Millau* has not been at all timid about mixing commerce and gastronomic judgment, routinely accepting commercial advertising in its guide. For example, one typical edition (2002) contained fourteen pages of full-page advertisements in the opening twenty-seven pages of text, and the last twenty-three pages of the volume consisted of nothing but ads of various sizes (mostly for wine and champagne producers).[26]

The Gault-Millau enterprise sells even more advertising space in its mass-market magazine, the *Gault&Millau* magazine. Formerly a monthly and in recent years published six times a year, the magazine, directed by Christian Millau for two decades is corporately managed. It displays advertising for a range of products, including automobiles, tourism, wineries, various regional specialties, and restaurant equipment, and contains articles about regions and their products, the recipes of specific chefs and their restaurants, and about the *Gault-Millau* guide itself. Both the magazine and the guide offer admiring profiles of both newly discovered and established chefs and of restaurants that have been recognized in the guide. The promotion of chefs or of restaurants that have been consecrated on its pages is a significant deviation from the form and the style of the *Michelin Guide*, which has forbidden those restaurants to which it has awarded stars from displaying the fact, both in the restaurant itself and in advertising promotions. By profiling (and thereby promoting) chefs in its magazine that its guide has recognized with a high restaurant rating the *Gault-Millau* guide is effectively able to enhance its own legitimacy in a process that simultaneously celebrates and ratifies its own star-making ability. For example, in the winter 1999–2000 millennial issue of *Gault&Millau* magazine where "The Eight Best Chefs of France" were announced, a thirty-page section profiled each of these grand chefs.[27] It began with a two-page photo spread of the eight "medal winners," all posed together in white chef's jackets, smiling, with each one holding out in front

---

26. While thirty-seven pages of advertising in a volume of just over one thousand pages would not normally be thought of as "substantial," the bulk of the middle material consists of the restaurant and hotel ratings, organized by locale, and printed blandly on rough paper in black, white, and red ink, whereas the front and back pages of advertising are multicolored, with visually arresting images, and are the most visually prominent section of the book.

27. "Palmarès 2000: Les huit meilleurs chefs de France," *Gault-Millau*, no. 337, Winter 1999–2000 (November, December, January), pp. 30–61.

of them a copy of the 2000 issue of the yellow *Gault-Millau* guide. Thus, in exchange for valuable publicity, the chefs were openly endorsing the very guide that had anointed them by offering them up as candidates for the *Gault&Millau* magazine's "Eight Best" in France. Such an obvious act of mutual promotion would have been inconceivable for *Michelin*, for it would have been regarded as a breach of the protective partition between commerce and gastronomy that it had always sought to scrupulously maintain.[28] At the same time, the *Michelin Guide* is able to return a certain profit from its stance, both in the sales figures and, just as importantly, in its standing as the supreme arbiter of gastronomic excellence, where faith in its "disinterested" judgment has been a vital ingredient.[29]

Of the two leading gastronomic guides in France, *Gault-Millau* has always represented itself as being the more dynamic, modern, less "stuffy" guide; open to discovering new trends that "tweaked the French food establishment" and that "debunked sacred culinary canons"; and set against the more stable, conservative, *Michelin Guide*, which is often seen as being preoccupied with the ratification of tradition. [30] It was *Gault-Millau* that first used the term "nouvelle cuisine" in the early 1970s to denote (and to enthusiastically advance in its guide and in its magazine) the trend toward lighter cooking and away from heavy, buttery sauces; the use of fresh, seasonal ingredients; and above all, to promote an ethos of culinary creativity among chefs. This essentially freed chefs to draw from a wider variety of ingredients, techniques, and styles, including foreign influences, and enjoyed a strong appeal to consumers who tended to be more urbane, adventuresome, and health-conscious; who were willing and able to pay higher prices (for smaller portions); and who appreciated the level of artistry that chefs

---

28. Accompanying each profile in this edition of *Gault-Millau* was a boxed insert, "Points of Reference" marking the key professional moments and accomplishments in the lives of each of the eight chefs, and it is telling that despite the fact that six of the eight have been recipients of almost certainly the highest accomplishment for a French chef, a third star in the *Michelin* guide, *Gault&Millau* magazine's mention of this award is conspicuously missing. At the same time, *Bottin Gourmand*'s profiles of each of these eight chefs notes their *Michelin* star rating along with their *Bottin Gourmand* rating (each received a four-star rating).

29. While its annual sales figures are not made public, according to Mesplède the *Michelin Guide* is published with an annual print run of five hundred fifty thousand to seven hundred thousand (Mesplède, *Trois Étoiles*, p. 14), while on its website *Gault-Millau* claims that the yearly sales of its guide are roughly seventy thousand, http://www.guides-gaultmillau.fr /telechargement/Comment_ca_marche.pdf.

30. William Echikson notes that *Gault-Millau* committed various forms of gastronomic heresy, including condoning the serving of red wine with fish, "touting the virtues of American wine," and promoting female restaurateurs. See Echikson, *Burgundy Stars*, pp. 88–89.

demonstrated in their restaurants. Yet we should not forget that while it was engaged in promoting nouvelle cuisine as the new culinary wave, *Gault-Millau* was simultaneously promoting itself as the new arbiter of modern gastronomy (contrasting itself to *Michelin*). Some have viewed nouvelle cuisine as an important social movement capable of redrawing the boundaries of culinary categories.[31] This seems exaggerated, for while the chefs promoted and endorsed by *Gault-Millau* engaged in new culinary practices the sharp boundary around nouvelle cuisine was short lived and had as much to do with the need for *Gault-Millau* to define itself, as it was to culinary practice. Plus, while a group of rising chefs were indeed creatively experimenting in their kitchens and promoting the use of fresh ingredients from local markets (and so moving away from traditional, heavier recipes) these were tendencies that had been under way for well over a generation. Several of the chefs who *Gault-Millau* identified with nouvelle cuisine had studied with Fernand Point (until he died in 1957), and he had long advocated using fresh ingredients from the market and simplifying the cooking process.[32] Paul Bocuse, the most prominent of the chefs whom *Gault-Millau* had stamped with a "nouvelle cuisine" label, had apprenticed with Fernand Point. His culinary practices indeed reflected the style of nouvelle cuisine, and Bocuse personified two other characteristics of the chef in the period of nouvelle cuisine: his ownership of his restaurant and his open pursuit of celebrity status. As Stephen Mennell noted, one key characteristic shared by most nouvelle cuisine chefs was that they were owners of their restaurants, a status that was relatively new.[33] Moreover, as the proprietor of the restaurant the chef has a material incentive to seek publicity (for the restaurant) and therefore celebrity status (for himself), a connection outlined by Ferguson and Zukin:[34]

> Chefs, especially those who own their own restaurants, appreciate and often actively cultivate publicity to gain a competitive advantage. For

---

31. I refer to two principal articles by H. Rao, P. Monin, and R. Durand: "Border Crossing: Bricolage and the Erosion of Categorical Boundaries in French Gastronomy," *American Sociological Review*, vol. 70, no. 6, December 2005, pp. 968–991; and "Institutional Change in Toque Ville: Nouvelle Cuisine as an Identity Movement in French Gastronomy," *American Journal of Sociology*, vol. 108, no. 4, January 2003, pp. 795–843.

32. Moreover, after returning from the Tokyo Olympics in 1964, Raymond Oliver and other grand chefs reported being very positively impressed by Japanese cuisine. See Stephen Mennell, "Food and Wine," in *French Culture Since 1945*, ed. Malcolm Cook (London: Longman, 1993), p. 180.

33. Mennell, "Food and Wine," p. 181.

34. Priscilla Parkhurst Ferguson and Sharon Zukin, "The Careers of Chefs," in *Eating Culture*, ed. R. Scapp and B. Seitz (Albany: State University of New York Press, 1998), p. 93.

their part, consumers more readily understand restaurants as social and cultural markers if they can associate them with "signature" styles of individual chefs. . . . Chefs' stardom also has clear connections with the self-conscious artistry of *nouvelle cuisine*, itself a beneficiary of a long-standing association of *haute cuisine* with art.

In contrast to the resolute facelessness of the *Michelin* guide, *Gault-Millau's* appearance was reflected in the public personas of its cofounders, each of whom were born and raised in relatively prosperous family circumstances and who seemed to personify the guide's image of dynamism, living their lives publicly, as Parisian celebrities: [35]

> They possessed flair and sophistication. Both dressed well, in the latest fashions, and once they became well known, the gossip pages recounted their comings and goings . . . Of the tandem, Gault had the sharper pen and wit, while Millau had a shrewder eye for business . . . In their heyday, the pair generated gross annual revenues of more than $6 million. Both lived the high life. Gault bought a giant apartment just opposite the Elysée Palace. He took vacations with his wife and children at a large country house near the old Huguenot city of La Rochelle, on the Atlantic coast. Millau furnished an elegant town house in the capital's sixteenth arrondissement and used his vacations for culinary explorations around the globe. He published the results in his magazine.

In an analysis by Isabelle Terence, a French sociologist, the respective outlooks of the two guides were systematically examined to see if their respective reputations (dynamism vs. stability) might be reflected in the practice of their restaurant ratings. A comparative analysis of the evolution of the standings of a sample of 119 restaurants listed in the two guides, between 1986 and 1990, found each of their respective symbolic postures reflected

---

35. Henry Gault (1929–2000), a doctor's son from a village in Normandy, graduated from a private lycée in Paris and studied science at the Sorbonne, before becoming a food journalist, working for an editor, Christian Millau, son of a prosperous family of *parfumeurs*, who had studied international relations at the prestigious "Sciences Po" and then law at the Sorbonne, before he too became a journalist. Quotation from Echikson, *Burgundy Stars*, pp. 86–87, and obituary entitled "Henri Gault, Writer on French Food, Dies," *International Herald Tribune*, July 11, 2000, p. 4.

and reproduced in the patterns of the guides' restaurant selections.[36] For example, she found that 66.4 percent of the restaurants maintained their standing in the *Michelin* guide over the course of the four years, while restaurant standings in *Gault-Millau* were much less stable, with 59 percent of restaurants changing their position, either up or down. She reported very little change in the *Michelin* standings over the short term, a pattern viewed as lending support to its reputation for stability; while *Gault-Millau* ratings were found to be more capricious: "the *Gaul-Millau* guide doesn't hesitate to downgrade restaurants that it had honored two years previously. Its fleeting promotions permit the guide to magnify each new edition in the number of promotions and to thus maintain a dynamic image."[37] Although the data was not strong enough to be able to determine the extent to which *Gault-Millau* actually "discovers" more new restaurants than Michelin, or whether Michelin tends to "confirm" already-consecrated restaurants, their distinctive symbolic representations (dynamism vs. stability) were expressed by their respective selection policies.

The two leading gastronomic guides appear to have straddled the line of stability in one other way as well, in terms of their respective financial positions. Whereas *Michelin*'s financial security has been assured as matter of birthright (as offspring of the venerable tire manufacturer), the financial position of *Gault-Millau* has been more unsteady in recent years.[38] The Gault-Millau business rose from rags to riches three decades ago, but has been in decline for some time. It thrived in the 1970s and early 1980s, with a circulation reaching as high as two hundred thousand, but has slipped steadily since, and its ownership has changed hands six times.[39] When the Gault and Millau partnership broke up in the late 1980s the enterprise was acquired by a large media conglomerate that reportedly edged Millau aside, leaving him as a figurehead. Although the overall business of the enterprise is down, the *Gault-Millau* guide is still published annually and continues to

---

36. Terence, *Le Monde*, pp. 114–124.

37. Terence, *Le Monde*, p. 123.

38. While the amount of subsidy that the Michelin Tire Company may divert to the publication of the *Michelin Guide*, if any, is unknown and unlikely to be divulged publicly by the notoriously secretive company, its tire business undoubtedly benefits from the gastronomic guide to the extent that it gains substantial benefits of recognition by its attachment to the virtually "sacred" status of gastronomy in the French cultural patrimony, and by extension to the rest of the world.

39. Bryan Miller, "Cooking Up a Storm," *New York Times*, March 15, 2003, p. A17. Current circulation figure for *Gault-Millau* magazine is noted as seventy thousand on the magazine's website.

matter in the world of French gastronomy with an influence that is still the envy of the various lesser gastronomic guides published in France.[40]

Though clearly a distant second in relation to *Michelin*'s supremacy, *Gault-Millau*'s significance lies primarily in its relational opposition to it. *Gault-Millau* and *Michelin* may serve as somewhat unequal gatekeepers to the gastronomic universe, but at the same time their differences represent an expression of the polarity that stretches across the French gastronomic field in two directions. Their stylistic differences can be seen as expressions of competing approaches to what constitutes laudable (and legitimate) culinary activity. It is the process of their interplay, including their putative competition, the discourse about their merits and their gastronomic values, and the various ways that they play out their proper roles of insider (*Michelin*) vs. outsider (*Gault-Millau*) that is what contributes to the production of a system of belief in haute cuisine. *Gault-Millau* may have always represented itself as the outsider, but both guides are products of the French gastronomic field and both are important agents of its reproduction.

But while the gastronomic guides have been very important, they are only a part of a system of production of belief that sustains haute cuisine in France. A cacophony of magazines and newspapers and their editors, journalists, and food critics can also be heard at any given time, a range of voices, some louder and more influential than others. Positioned differently in relation to one another as well as in relation to the practical and stylistic polarities that govern the field, some speak for more or less self-organized constituents (professional chefs, restaurateurs, industrial managers) while some are aimed at a varied audience of connoisseurs, occasional restaurant diners, or simple newspaper readers.

Journalists like François Simon, for sixteen years the critic for the newspaper *Le Figaro*, and Jean-Claude Ribaut, of *Le Monde* during the course of the same period, have been among the more prominent French food critics, but possibly even more influential was the American Patricia Wells,

40. While the promotional power of a high rating in a highly rated guide is significant, the importance of guides is actually quite minimal in a practical sense. A study commissioned by *Le Chef* magazine for the Sofres marketing firm in early 1995 found that "in the past six months" only 16 percent of restaurant customers had consulted a guide in making their restaurant choice. Of those 162 respondents, 50 percent had consulted the *Michelin Guide*, 23 percent had consulted *Gault-Millau*, while the various other guides included the *Bottin Gourmand* (3 percent), *Guide du Routard* (9 percent), *Guide Pudlowski* (1 percent), *Guide des Relais et Châteaux* (3 percent), *Champérard* (1 percent), and *Guide Lebey* (1 percent), a guide for Paris restaurants only. Study reported in Georges Golan, "Qui consulte les guides?" *Le Chef*, no. 75, January–February 1995, p. 52.

who served as food critic for the Paris-based *International Herald Tribune* (and prior to that for the French magazine, *L'Express*). For a quarter century Wells's writing was an enduring manifestation of the significance of French haute cuisine at an international level. It made her a sort of cultural envoy for French haute cuisine that was recognized and appreciated in France, while also placing her in a position to influence the restaurant choices of affluent American tourists and businessmen, who constituted an important part of the clientele for top French restaurants.[41] Like all food critics, Wells influence rested on her power to draw the public's attention to a chef or a restaurant; and working for the English-language mass media afforded her a considerable degree of (indirect) economic power. In his biography of the three-star chef, Bernard Loiseau, William Echikson recounted the particular anxiety with which Loiseau reacted to a visit from Wells:[42]

> Bernard was more nervous about Patricia Wells. The American critic had called to reserve a table for dinner and a room for a night at the end of February. Bernard thought Wells had the same demand for perfection as the judges from the Red Guide. His enthusiasm and food produced smiles of pleasure on almost all diners. Not with Wells. When she was eating, she almost never smiled. Bernard could not tell whether she liked what he was serving. And when he spoke to her, she never laughed at his jokes.

Whether or not Wells's aloofness was characteristic, she was not at all reticent about granting lavish praise on many chefs de cuisine over the course of her career (Bernard Loiseau included) and was well known for her particular appreciation of Joël Robuchon, who was one of a small handful of widely designated "superstars" of French cuisine, whom she designated "this century's finest chef" upon his retirement and with whom she collaborated on a cookbook (enjoying almost equal billing on its front cover).[43] Wells

---

41. Patricia Wells, *The French Kitchen Cookbook: Recipes and Lessons from Paris and Provence* (New York: William Morrow, 2013); and Patricia and Walter Wells, *We've Always Had Paris . . . and Provence: A Scrapbook of Our Life in France* (New York: Harper, 2009)

42. Echikson, *Burgundy Stars*, pp. 217–218.

43. Wells's offered this praise on the occasion of Robuchon's "first" retirement in 1996 (he has since come out of retirement to open another restaurant in Paris) in "Passing the Baton of French Gastronomy," in the *International Herald Tribune*, April 26, 1996, p. 13. In the Introduction to the book she indicated their mutual affinity: "I am not sure how and when the idea for this collaboration came about. It seemed to grow naturally, out of mutual professional respect and a vision of food that I shared with Robuchon, chef and owner of the Parisian restaurant Jamin," in Patricia Wells and Joël Robuchon, *Cuisine Actuelle* (London: Macmillan, 1991), p. 1.

Cuisine Actuelle

Patricia Wells

Presents the Cuisine of **Joël Robuchon**

"The strongest legacy a chef can bequeath is a core of chefs trained to reflect his style and manner. Joël Robuchon, who retired from the stove but not the food world in July, has done just that. This week and next, I turn my eye and palate to the current Robuchon endowment, beginning with Benoît Guichard. . . . In 16 years of visiting Paris kitchens I've probably spent more time in the presence of Guichard than any other chef. It's no surprise that this 35-year-old is not a household name, for he has spent the past 15 years in the shadow of his master. . . . Whether he spent his 16-hour work days in the 16th arrondissement kitchens of Jamin or Restaurant Joel Robuchon, or trained troops in the kitchens of a Tokyo chateau, his was not to reason why, but to flawlessly interpret culinary genius."

　—[from "Young Chef Dons Toque of a Master," *International Herald Tribune*, December 6, 1996, p. 13]

"One of the best new tastes in town comes from the kitchen of Dominique Bouchet, whose substantial track record includes stints in the 1970's as assistant to the chef Joël Robuchon and in the 1980's as chef at the then Michelin three-star Tour d'Argent and the then two-star Jamin."

　—[from "Updating the Grand Traditions," *International Herald Tribune*, April 4, 1997, p. 10].

"Mark my words: This may be the first, but not the last time you'll hear the name Frédéric Anton. One of a group of modest, hard-working, exceptionally well-trained chefs unleashed one year ago when Joël Robuchon closed his restaurant doors, Anton took over the helm of the illustrious Pré Catelan in the Bois de Boulogne several months ago. . . . As a Robuchon acolyte, Anton was responsible for ordering-then accepting or rejecting every leaf of lettuce, every grain of caviar, every squiggling langoustine that entered the kitchen. A perfect dish, as any cook knows, begins with absolutely fresh, flawless ingredients. In the kitchens of the Pré Catelan, Anton remarkably illustrates all he learned in the school of the master, then adds his own uncanny ability to nudge ingredients, create combinations that sing on the palate and, most of all, satisfy."

　—[from "Grand Old Restaurant Gets Great New Chef," *International Herald Tribune*, August 8, 1997, p. 10].

not only promoted the cuisine of Joël Robuchon, but looked after his legacy as well, nurturing the careers of many of his professional offspring, as the Cuisine Actuelle sidebar illustrates.

Among the many magazines and journals that have constituted the culinary press in France, several have been published for a mass-market readership of household cooks and gourmands, such as those of *Gault-Millau* and *Thuriès*. They have been magazines filled with recipes and practical tips from grand chefs that are directed at the household cook and magazine reader. *Thuriès*, a particularly lavish magazine in its presentation and production, with heavy, glossy pages filled with richly photographed dishes that highlight recipes, situates itself squarely within the world of haute cuisine.[44] While a magazine for the household cook and the magazine reader, it also presents itself as a magazine for the grand chefs. Upon opening an issue of the magazine the reader is greeted from the editorial page by a smiling image of Yves Thuriès in white toque. The editorials themselves tend to cultivate an in-house sensibility, so, for example, an editorial might be entitled "Homage to Our Masters," and every issue devotes a full four- to five-page spread to a single biographical profile of a noted grand chef or very high figure of the world of haute cuisine (complete with baby pictures and family portraits). The issues are organized thematically around particular seasons (spring or summer) or holidays (Easter or Mardi Gras) or specific foodstuffs (fish or venison) and this would seem to be more useful for household cooks and general readers than for chefs operating a restaurant kitchen.

As in virtually all media organs in the gastronomic domain, and well as in other cultural fields, the practice of mutual recognition is standard, since symbolic value can only be conferred by those people or institutions who already possess it (or whose specific function in the field is to dispense it). In the case of *Thuriès Magazine*, self-recognition by Yves Thuriès, the grand chef, is a way of maintaining the stature of the magazine as an authentic product of French haute cuisine, thus affirming its professional bona fides and thereby sharing a measure of its symbolic aura. For example, in an editorial to announce the end of his encyclopedic series and the begin-

---

44. The publisher Yves Thuriès, was a well-known pâtissier who won two prestigious titles for "Best Craftsman of France," and who published a cookbook of pastries, and who has owned both an expensive gastronomic restaurant and a bistro that is housed in the second hotel that he acquired. His glossy, *Thuriès Magazine,* first appeared in 1988 and by 1990 was publishing ten issues per year. It was a relatively expensive magazine (an annual subscription in France in the year 2005 was 79.60 euros or just over $100).

ning of a new publishing venture, Thuriès began by recounting his own accomplishments:[45]

> The love of my craft, all the knowledge acquired during the time of my [encyclopedia], and the obtaining of my two titles of Best Craftsman of France have been for me the great fortunes of my life. Add to this my wish to write and to transmit, and one understands why I have devoted twenty years of my life to the realization of this encyclopedia. It was in 1972, the works of pastry or of cuisine were not very numerous, or were dating from just after the war and were thus at times outdated. I therefore decided to write a first work on pastries. . . . In 1976, the obtaining of my two titles of "Best Craftsman in France" followed my designation of "Chef of the Year," creating the conditions that could not have been more favorable to the publication of my first book.

Further down on the same page, after presenting a résumé of the works that comprised his encyclopedic series on French gastronomy, the reader is presented with extracts of a sample of elegies and letters that he has received:[46]

> "In these collections, the entire culinary range is opened as one opens a Bible, emblazoned with the golden rules of the great culinary principles that are integrated harmoniously in the inventive personality of this exceptional chef." Michel Malapris: Président de l'Académie Culinaire de France.

> "But what touches me more in these works and which for all of us, Best Craftsmen of France, is our ideal, it is this obstinacy in always being better. Thank you, friend, Thuriès, for your beautiful example. I do not advance lightly in assuring you that the Best Craftsmen of France are proud of you and of your works." Louis-André Desquand: Président National des Meilleurs Ouvriers de France, Grand Prix National des Métiers d'Art.

> Diderot and D'Alembert in the 18th century depended on a monument, "La Grande Encyclopédie," known throughout the entire world.

---

45. Yves Thuriès editorial, "A Page Turns," in *Thuriès Magazine*, no. 54, November 1993, p. 1 [author's translation].

46. *Thuriès* "A Page Turns" [author's translation].

Pierre Larousse wrote and edited in the 19th century: *"Le Grand Dictionnaire du XIXème siècle."* Yves Thuriès has had his turn to make and to edit that which, for our days, is the greatest Encyclopédie Culinaire of all time. An incomparable memory of recipes covering the quasi-totality of the "Métiers de Bouche" S.-G. Sender: Fondateur de la première Bibliothèque Culinaire de France, Member of l'Académie Culinaire, Officier des Arts et Lettres.

Thuriès thus appended lavish elegies of his own accomplishments, issued by the representatives of significant organizations of consecration in the French gastronomic field. This included, in the case of Desquand, the head of an organization that had anointed Thuriès in the first place and that was thus making itself available a second time to reissue its stamp of approval, thereby demonstrating its own importance and, along with the others, exposing the reader to a carousel of mutual recognition and reciprocal self-promotion.

We observe similar processes with regard to *Le Chef* magazine, the principal internal voice of the chef profession in France. While those chefs de cuisine who owned their own restaurants would tend to also read other sources, such as the weekly *L'Hôtellerie* (a business newspaper for independent restaurant, hotel, and café owners), *Le Chef* served as the professional organ for chefs across various institutional locations. A monthly magazine that, in the 1990s, had a subscription rate of between five thousand and six thousand and a print run of roughly double that, *Le Chef* was primarily designed as a means of internal communication within the chef profession, functioning as an institution of peer recognition and occupational mobility.[47]

Its articles include reports on new culinary practices, notable names in the profession, new kinds of products on the market, changes in training techniques, results of contests and awards for chefs and its ancillary professions, reports on food and restaurant expositions, and so on.[48]

---

47. *Le Chef* reported a paid subscription rate in 1990 of 5,439 on a print run of 12,204 copies (and 6,503 paid subscriptions in 2015). In contrast, *L'Hôtellerie Restauration*, the weekly business magazine for hotels, restaurants, and cafes, had a paid circulation of 24,331 in 2015, according to "BOOK: Presse Professionnelle 2014–2015," published by ACPM (L'Alliance pour les chiffres de la presse et des médias) Paris, 2016.

48. While principally an organ of the profession, *Le Chef* is not devoid of commercial advertising. In a sample of issues published between October 1990 and April 1998 a count of between 20 percent and 50 percent of the magazine's pages were devoted to advertising copy, largely from companies in the food-processing industry and from companies selling restaurant equipment of various kinds.

The magazine serves as an important means of recognition and conse-cration of chefs in the field, but this role (as consecrator) must be renewed, upheld, and valorized by the central actors in the field, the chefs. So, for example, a year after awarding its 1996 "Chef of the Year" award to Alain Dutournier, chef de cuisine at Carré des Feuillants (a Parisian restaurant ac-corded two *Michelin* stars), *Le Chef* published an interview with Dutournier entitled *"Pourquoi Le Chef,"* by the magazine's president and managing dir-ector, that sought to elicit praise for the magazine from a chef whose power to sanctify had been partly furnished by the magazine itself:[49]

> *Le Chef*: You have been elected Chef of the Year 1996. You are a
> faithful reader of the review. How would you characterize it?
>
> **Alain Dutournier:** The magazine *Le Chef* is for us the hyphen that
> links all of the great family of cooks, those working in little
> restaurants, in the great restaurants, in the hotel chains, in in-
> stitutions, hospitals. This hyphen did not exist before *Le Chef.*
> Now, thanks to it, one sees all the many conjunctions between
> the people of our craft. One is better able to communicate, to
> participate in competitions. . . . *Le Chef* treats marketing, food
> hygiene, various subjects of innovation, and this craft, which
> remained somewhat insulated in its artisanship, has thus been
> made more open.
>
> *Le Chef*: You estimate that the magazine is nearly an indispensable
> tool of communication between chefs?
>
> **Alain Dutournier:** I am persuaded that it will largely overflow the
> borders because chefs abroad need to stay in contact with what
> is happening in France and in the regions. *Le Chef,* like Eur-
> ope, has to federate a large range of people. I think that *Le Chef*
> is somewhat perfect as a gathering place for this thick stew of
> cultures.
>
> *Le Chef*: Beyond the magazine, could you tell us, how are chefs of a
> certain level communicating between themselves?
>
> **Alain Dutournier:** Unhappily, we often don't have the time, nor
> perhaps do we take the steps to go and see what is happening
> with each other. One of course has friends and affinities in the
> profession, but the review, *Le Chef,* offers an entrée into the skills
> as well as the secrets. In the pages of *Le Chef* there are sometimes

49. *Le Chef,* no. 98, August–September 1997, p. 30.

pertinent pieces of advice that are best illustrated in visual terms. It thus permits passing along ideas to the young, whose spirit is open. Previously, they were getting information only from the chef who trained them. Now, with this media, they are seeing what is done in all the great restaurants. . . ."

Le Chef as an interviewer was thus seeking validation of its relevance to the profession; while the award-winning chef (made so by the magazine) appeared completely willing to provide recognition, and thus the Consecrated was consecrating the Consecrator. It is in this way that the "Chef of the Year" award has thus become "a gift that keeps on giving."[50]

Although the process illustrated above and in earlier examples may resemble the practice of product endorsement in commercial advertising, it is not money, which is only secondarily and indirectly present, that is the primary object of these transactions. The real gold standard is recognition, and while commercial success may very well come to those who have achieved a fair measure of recognition in the domain of haute cuisine, we would be mistaken to view the animating force as a simple pecuniary one. As we consider later on, there have increasingly been other avenues available to chefs for the pursuit of financial reward. Symbolic rewards are equally valuable via the professional sanctification that occurs in trade magazines, gastronomic guides, and award ceremonies.

What ought to be emphasized about the process of "mutual self-promotion" noted above (and demonstrated below) is that it is very much a collective social phenomenon. That is, the world of gastronomy is not exactly a world of individual actors rationally pursuing individual ends, so much as a configuration of social (and socialized) actors, institutional and individual, through which established reciprocal relationships are mobilized in pursuit of recognition and where advancement is more or less shared among those with whom one shares a common position within the field, as well as a common disposition toward it. In narrative form they may be presented as if they were examples of discrete interactions, thus accentuating the appear-

---

50. With reference to Mauss's expression from his analysis of *The Gift*: "We are together in society in order to expect, together, this or that result," Bourdieu has written: "For someone endowed with dispositions attuned to the logic of the economy of symbolic goods, generous conduct is not the product of a choice made by free will and virtue, a free decision made at the end of a deliberation that allows for the possibility of behaving differently; it presents itself as 'the only thing to do.'" from *Pascalian Meditations* (Stanford, CA: Stanford University Press, 2000), pp. 193, 193n21.

ance of discrete, individual acts in frozen frames. However, it would more accurately reflect the social reality of a field if they could be somehow set into motion, with the seemingly detached pieces hinged together to bring the various relational patterns into view. Accordingly, what we are essentially doing is taking a small portion of just one section of the gastronomic field and showing it as being linked, albeit unevenly, through reciprocal acts of promotion (as if we were viewing a moving samba line) whereby *Le Chef* magazine mobilizes the grand chefs to promote itself, while the grand chefs use *Gault&Millau* magazine to promote themselves; while in turn *Gault&Millau* magazine uses the grand chefs to promote the *Gault-Millau* guide, which promotes the grand chefs; and the grand chefs use *Le Chef* magazine to promote themselves. When viewing it in this way the collective and relational character of the gastronomic field reveals itself.

At the same time, the relations that constitute the field are not seamless, for they reflect various tensions or differences in orientation and disposition. For example, if the *Gault-Millau* guide has played the more innovative, less traditional "gatekeeper" to French gastronomy in relation to the *Michelin Guide* (in effect representing the "modern art" of the kitchen to the classicism and formalism of culinary art represented by *Michelin*); a voice that has been more receptive to commercial interests than Michelin, and others are even more strident in this regard. For example, *Néorestauration* magazine had been an unmediated voice for commercial and industrial cuisine since it was founded in 1972. In relation to what it regarded as the insularity of traditional French gastronomy, *Néorestauration* considered itself a "pioneer" and an "agitator of ideas" that would "carry a new image of a creative business of restaurants, whether it be institutional or commercial, ranging from fast food to the gastronomic table, and passing by theme restaurants, institutional canteens and all those supplying the profession, whether they be corporations of the food processing industry or those selling equipment to it."[51] As an unmistakable voice of industrial form within the gastronomic field, *Néorestauration*, along with the institutional forces it represents, have had a peculiar presence in the gastronomic field. While carrying enormous weight in material terms, they have a very limited symbolic presence.

The magazine *Néorestauration* has served as the primary trade magazine for the most industrialized sector of the gastronomic field, including chain restaurant companies, the fast-food industry, as well as *l'agro-alimentaire*,

51. Quoted in editorial marking the magazine's thirty-year anniversary entitled "L'Esprit des 'pionniers'" by Jean-Charles Schamberger, *Néorestauration*, no. 385, March 2002, p. 5.

the huge farm-to-table food-processing industry that is financed and owned by some of the world's largest multinational corporations. While seeming to operate a world apart from the domain and the practices of French haute cuisine, *Néorestauration* and the institutions it represents has functioned in a region of the field where economic logic holds sway, and unapologetically so. Recognition matters here, as in other regions of the field, but it tends to be granted for industrial innovation and economic success, rather than for aesthetic creation or the refinement of artisanal technique. For example, a 2002 *Néorestauration* article recounting the celebration that it had organized for 350 people on the occasion of its thirtieth anniversary, presented photographs of the trophy winners of its biannual "Innovation Awards." Of the forty-eight award recipients and presenters shown on the two-page spread of photographs, all were businessmen (except one) and were identified as top executives of large industrial, catering, or marketing firms within the industrial food sector.[52] Just one grand chef appeared in the group and, in general, chefs are not the central players on the pages of *Néorestauration*. So although the economic situation of independent commercial restaurants is not entirely ignored in the magazine, the magazine has not been an important medium for grand chefs and their careers, with an editorial focus instead on the business of corporate managers in food services, catering, chain restaurants, fast food, and industrial production.[53]

The nature of *Néorestauration*'s "Innovation Awards" certainly reflects this perspective. While the awards are accepted by individual executives from specific companies (with the figures for their annual business turnover prominently displayed), the awards themselves are granted for eight specific corporate products in various categories of prepared foods (i.e., "Vegetables, Cereals, and Starches" or "Culinary aids and fats") as well as in ten different categories of equipment (i.e., "Cooking," "Washing," "Distribution," etc.). The "Grand Trophy of the Jury" for the overall best food product was awarded to Bonduelle Food Service for its "Ready-to-use fresh sliced vegetables" and the "Grand Trophy of the Jury" for best overall piece of

52. All of the trophy recipients and those who presented the awards are identified by name and company under their photograph. In "30 Ans de souvenirs et d'émotions," *Néorestauration*, no. 387, May 2002, pp. 18–19.

53. It should be emphasized that while the relative significance of a medium may mean one thing with regard to strategic advantage or disadvantage from a certain position *within* the field, it means another thing from an analytical vantage point *outside* of it, where we would want to be able to understand the hierarchical relations (and the principles of hierarchy) that prevail across the entire field.

equipment went to the Nutri Pack Company for "Valvò Pack" (a device that facilitated both cooking and pasteurization in one package).[54] Here, too, it seemed that the promotional opportunities made available by the awards were as important as the awards themselves, as four finalists for each of the eighteen different award categories were prominently presented in a special supplement to the magazine in its February 2002 issue; while these winning companies and their products were profiled again in a sixteen-page section of the April 2002 issue. Then, as noted, the executives of these award-winning companies were presented to readers in the May 2002 issue, and so altogether there were three months of free promotional advertising made available for companies that normally purchase advertising space in *Néorestauration* to draw attention to their products. Two separate juries chose the winners, the one for "AgroAlimentaire" (prepared foods), which comprised twelve men and women, consisting of seven top executives for food-processing companies; one food service consultant; the chef de cuisine of the Ritz Hotel; and three journalists/writers for *Néorestauration* magazine. The jury that chose the award winners for "Kitchen Equipment" consisted of eleven men, including three high executives for kitchen equipment companies; three "technical directors" for large food-processing companies; an engineer for a food service company; three journalists from *Néorestauration*; and the chief veterinarian for the French Ministry of Defense.[55]

What is notable about awarding a "trophy" for equipment or for pre-prepared foods is that they are products of industrial practice where the measure of worth is the bottom line and where annual "turnover rate" and "market share" are the normal watchwords for denoting success and recognition. But here, the industrial sector had borrowed from the artisan culture of the chef profession in the form (and formula) of the culinary *concours*, the competitive contest of skill that is adjudicated by one's peers and that represents the characteristic method of recognition of the producers and the products of haute cuisine. Such concours are almost ubiquitous rituals in the domains of wine and of haute cuisine and the winners tend to carry them as important marks of pride throughout their careers.[56]

54. "Les Lauréats," *Néorestauration*, no. 386, April 2002, pp. 36–52.

55. Jury members and their affiliation identified in "Trophées 2002 de l'Innovation: Les Finalistes" special section of *Néorestauration*, no. 384, February 2002, pp. 2, 7.

56. In almost any single issue of *Le Chef* magazine one finds announcements of a broad range of awards, big and small, national and regional, such as the following from the January–February 1991 issue (no. 39): "le Prix Auguste Escoffier"; "the Jury of the Académie des Gla-

While there are hundreds of culinary concours or competitions across France, the one most coveted by chefs in France and that has been the virtual model for all of the others is the award of the Meilleur Ouvrier de France (MOF). Created in 1924 through competitions organized by the Société des meilleurs ouvriers de France, a nonprofit association that sponsors concours for some 220 different crafts across a broad spectrum of occupations, with the Métiers de Bouche (literally "crafts of the mouth") alone accounting for eleven different award competitions related to gastronomy.[57] The concours for "cuisine-restauration" will typically begin with several hundred candidates from whom are produced thirty to forty finalists, from which emerge just four or five award winners (between 1924 and 2000 just 131 of the bronze and enamel MOF medals had been awarded to chefs).[58] The most well-known winners of the MOF have tended to be those chefs-restaurateurs whose restaurants have held three *Michelin* stars, such as Jean Troisgros (1961), Paul Bocuse (1965), Alain Chapel (1972), Guy Legay (1972), Roger

---

ces"; the "Grand Prix de Cuisine Saumuroise"; "le Lauréat de l'Académie des arts et du vin"; "le Grand Prix du Terroir et le Grand Prix du Gibier" (for dishes made from the wines of Fitou, from the region Languedoc-Roussillon); "la Coupe d'Or de Marius Dutrey" (a national hotel award presented by Pierre Escoffier, grandson of the famous chef for the Société des cuisiniers de France); "le Trophée Coq Saint Honoré"; "Trophée Portzamparc" (ten award winners for the various wines from Macon in Burgundy). These sorts of awards are important markers in the careers of chefs de cuisine, sommeliers, pâtissiers, and all the other members of the culinary crafts, who prominently and routinely post such honorific forms of peer recognition in the profiles they give to the press and in directories where their names are listed. For example, see the profiles of chefs and other members of the culinary professions who are listed in *Les Étoiles de la gastronomie française, 1998–1999* (Paris: Les Éditions du Bottin Gourmand, 1998).

57. The "Society of the Best Craftsmen of France" was founded in 1929, five years after the award was first introduced, and the 220 crafts whose awards it sponsors are organized within nineteen different groups (i.e., "Crafts of the Mouth," including cuisine/restauration; pâtisserie; confiserie; boucherie; traiteur-charcuterie; boulangerie; maître du service de la table; glaces; chocolaterie; sommellerie; fromagerie); as well as "Crafts of Buildings, Public Works, and of the Architectural Patrimony"; "Audo-Visual Crafts"; "Crafts of Metallic Structures"; "Crafts of Hair Design and Aesthetics"; "Jewelry Craft"; and so on. Since 1952, the Meilleur Ouvrier de France has been recognized as a public utility, with the Ministry of National Education coordinating the competitions and with awards recognized as the equivalent of a diploma at the level of the baccalauréat plus deux. See Sylvie-Anne Mériot, *Le Cuisinier nostalgique* (Paris: CNRS Éditions, 2002), p. 178. The following website lists the métiers included in the MOF: http://www.aisne.cci.fr/pages/focus/metiers_mof.php?SSID=82ce4ff86ee84827b59ac52c5ab4f091.

58. See Michael Buller, *French Chefs Cooking* (Foster City, CA: IDG Books Worldwide, 1999), p. 17.

Vergé (1972), Joël Robuchon (1976), and Philippe Legendre (1996), but most of the three-star chefs have never won MOF medals.[59]

Competitions for the MOF in cuisine-restauration are held every four years. In a typical year, 1991 for example, the national finals were held at the high school of Hotels and Tourism at Saint-Quentin-en-Yvelines, where forty-three candidates (whittled down from three hundred and sixty-nine applicants in regional qualifying rounds) competed. The theme for the finals had been communicated to the finalists about two weeks prior and would be composed of three dishes that were to be prepared for ten people: one fish, one meat dish, and one dessert. The finalists were given five hours to produce their dishes in the school kitchens and to present them to a jury in a process described by one participant in the following way: [60]

> Completed dishes were brought into a tasting room. A jury of nine was set up at individual tables, twenty feet apart, with their backs to the windows to let in the natural light. Each category of dishes were awarded a score. The dishes were placed on a buffet table for presentation, with each member of the jury scoring the dish in terms of the theme and of the specific instructions for presentation. Each plate had to come out from the kitchen at the precise time that had been indicated to the candidate. Lateness was sanctioned. Latecoming dishes waited in a "hole" and would count against the candidate.

The MOF has been the most prestigious award that can be accorded a worker in any of the manual or service trades in France. The MOF is not the same as a journeyman's license to practice a particular craft or a right to work at a particular job site, which are rights based on the shifting and variable authority established in a history of union struggles with employers over the terms of employment. Rather, the MOF accords no explicit material rights, only the right of the medal winner to wear the French tricolor on their collar, a symbol that bestows considerable prestige among the members of the culinary trades, as well as beyond. Indirectly, material benefits surely flow to the medal winner, to the extent that any such mark of craft

---

59. According to the data developed for this study, at least twenty-three chefs whose restaurants have had three *Michelin* stars since 1990 are not included in the MOF brotherhood, including such well-known chefs as Alain Ducasse, George Blanc, Michel Guérard, Bernard Loiseau, Jacques Pic, Alain Senderens, Michel Troisgros, Marc Veyrat, or Antoine Westermann.

60. Author's translation of the description provided by Philippe Noël, "Vivement Bocuse! Le Parcours d'un candidat finaliste," *Le Chef*, no. 42, May 1991, pp. 38–39.

recognition is able to be successfully exchanged for jobs, salary, financing, and so on, but the process and the cult of the MOF seems carefully sheltered from any reference to the pecuniary. Even the practical skills that are demonstrated by the concours tend to be played down in favor of a more expressive, even sentimental discourse that emphasizes the traditional, time-honored qualities of artisanship. It is a discourse that is raised almost to the level of the sacred by a kind of transubstantiation, in which the award is made to signify the body and blood of the nation. Just such a discourse was evidenced in the official declaration by President Chirac to the MOF medal winners in 1997:[61]

> [*le meilleur ouvrier de France*]. . . is a title that is attached to our history and to its crafts and that have forever fashioned our life, our sensibility, and our culture and that have had an important place in the renown that France enjoys throughout the rest of the world. . . .
> It is a title that evokes talent, patience and, it is true, a love of work well done, the taste of perfection, and also the joy of creation . . .
> Guardians of ancestral traditions, the *meilleurs ouvriers de France* . . . in recalling their title with just cause, the indispensable conservatory of the know-how of the past. . . . Yes, the *meilleurs ouvriers de France*, who defend the high ideal of French quality, true to their roots in the traditions of yesteryear, but resolutely turned toward the future, are an essential element of the spirit of conquest that must be ours.

In recent years the jury for the final concours of the MOF has been headed by Paul Bocuse, arguably the most well-known chef in the world, and the juries themselves are normally composed of other notable French chefs.[62] Not only does winning the award mark one as highly prominent within the profession but simply being a finalist for the award carries high status and thus is often noted as being a significant accomplishment in its own right and often mentioned in articles in *Le Chef* and included in official biographical notices and publications.[63] But while winning the MOF medal

---

61. From "Allocution prononcée par M. Jacques Chirac," speech published on the Elysée Palace official website: www.elysee.fr/cgi-bin/auracom/aurweb/search/file?aur_file=discours/1997/BST. . . [translated by author].

62. See Buller, *French Chefs Cooking* p. 17.

63. The distinction of finaliste du Meilleur Ouvrier de France is among the career distinctions listed on the résumés for chefs (and affiliated culinary professions) that are included in the directory of the culinary profession published by Bottin Gourmand, *Étoiles de la gastronomie française*.

represents a major accomplishment among chefs, one that draws the attention of important institutions and social actors across the culinary world, and just reaching finalist status can boost the career of a young chef in the profession as well, by the time a chef reaches this portal, in many cases he has been preprepared for the role of grand chef. For example, of the nineteen MOF finalists for whom we have background data (out of a total of thirty-seven of the most highly consecrated French chefs) and who competed for the MOF in cuisine-restauration in 1991, twelve had either apprenticed or had otherwise previously worked in the kitchens of a three-star (*Michelin Guide*) restaurant, or had worked directly with a three-star (*Michelin Guide*) chef, or had won an important culinary award prior to achieving MOF finalist status.[64] This is not to suggest that previous recognition or association influenced the juries or entered into their deliberations, but by having inhabited an occupational milieu in the breast of haute cuisine, a young chef (and thirty-seven was the median age when they entered the finals) would have been daily exposed to the sorts of exacting standards and expectations, techniques, and overall demeanor of grand chefs and their aspirants. In other words, it is not a matter of simple, unadulterated "experience" or the specific culinary skills that win such contests but the social production of an outlook and comportment that reflects a measure of confidence in the experience that one has gained. In this sense, being stamped an MOF finalist might just as well represent the confirmation of one's place in a select group of chefs, as much as representing a sure point of entry into it.

Although profoundly important within the profession, the Société des Meilleurs Ouvriers de France is just one of the organizations that sponsor culinary concours in France and represents one of several associations of chefs with the ability to certify worthiness within the profession and to have its certification matter. Though somewhat less significant Les Maîtres Cuisiniers de France, the Chambre syndicale de haute cuisine française, and the Prix Taittinger perform similar functions, and there are various other organizations seeking to promote haute cuisine in France, such as

---

64. For example, six worked in three-star restaurants, three of the chefs had won the Prix Taittinger, a gastronomic concours for professional chefs (established by the family of Champagne producers); another had been an MOF finalist for the "Desserts" concours several years earlier, two had won a Prix Escoffier, and another the Prix Prosper Montaigne. The MOF finalist candidates were announced in *Le Chef* magazine no. 39, January–February 1991, p. 6. That we only have background data on half of the 1991 MOF finalists obviously limits what can be reasonably inferred here, but what is known suggests that a reasonably sizable number of the finalists had been well situated in the profession prior to reaching finalist status.

the Fondation Brillat-Savarin (private) and the Conseil National des arts culinaires (public) and the Académie culinaire de France (international). Operating in a more or less reciprocally confirming relationship to the principal magazines and journals of the chef profession, to the food critics, and to the gastronomic guides that we have noted, all the social actors, both institutional and individual, are bound to, established within, and living off the field of gastronomic practices. That is, among other things, they are all engaged with one another in struggles to impose a certain way of seeing the gastronomic world; and thus are collectively involved in the production of the value of the chef and of haute cuisine.[65]

The Social Organization of Haute Cuisine

While methods of training emphasize the centrality of craft-based knowledge and a master/apprenticeship relationship, the century-old brigade system that still prevails in most commercial kitchens was actually a product of the managerial cult of industrial efficiency prevalent in the late nineteenth century that had sought to break down craft-based knowledge and systems of production.[66] The brigade system was introduced by Auguste Escoffier to manage the large kitchens of luxury hotels, and included a more or less rigid and hierarchically organized division of labor between highly specialized tasks. Established as a method of bringing order to the inevitable chaos of a large, busy, and crowded kitchen, the brigade system was, and still is, based on a quasi-military structure in which authority is imparted from a central command over various workstations, each with their own distinctive responsibilities, with the goal of ensuring that all tasks are accomplished without duplication.

---

65. This sentence paraphrases a key point made by Bourdieu: "the subject of the production of the art-work—of its value but also of its meaning—is not the producer who actually creates the object in its materiality, but rather the entire set of agents engaged in the field. Among these are the producers of works classified as artistic (great or minor, famous or unknown), critics of all persuasions (who themselves are established within the field), collectors, middlemen, curators, and so on, in short, all who have ties with art, who live for art and, to varying degrees, from it, and who confront each other in struggles where the imposition of not only a worldview but also a vision of the art world is at stake, and who, through these struggles, participate in the production of the value of the artist and of art." P. Bourdieu, *The Field of Cultural Production* (New York: Columbia University Press, 1993), p. 261.

66. Auguste Escoffier set about to reorganize the restaurant kitchen to more efficiently serve the clientele of grand hotels, through a rigid subdivision of tasks, thereby conforming to one of Frederick W. Taylor's main *Principles of Scientific Management*. See Mennell, "Food and Wine," p. 179.

Generally speaking, the chef de cuisine (or chef) commands the entire operation of the kitchen, including supervision of all the work stations, ordering the food, and developing the menu. The *sous-chef*, or *second*, is the second in command, answering only to the chef, managing the weekly schedule, and helping supervise the specific station chefs (*chefs de partie*) who, depending on the size of the kitchen, would include some combination of the following posts[67]

- *Saucier* (sauté chef): responsible for all sauces.
- *Poissonnier* (fish chef): responsible for cutting and making sauces for fish.
- *Rôtisseur* (roasting chef): responsible for roasted foods and their sauces.
- *Grillardin* (grill chef): responsible for all grilled foods.
- *Friturier* (fry chef): responsible for all fried foods.
- *Entremetier* (vegetable chef): responsible for soups, hot vegetables, pastas, other starches, and egg dishes (traditionally the largest kitchens had a *potager* for soups and a *légumier* for vegetables).
- *Tournant* (swing cook): who works where needed throughout the kitchen.
- *Garde-manger* (pantry chef): responsible for preparation of all cold foods (salads, pâtés, cold appetizers).
- *Boucher* (butcher): responsible for butchering meats and poultry.
- *Pâtissier* (pastry chef): responsible for all baked goods, pastries, and desserts, although the pastry chef often supervises a separate kitchen made up of its own workstations in which,
    - a *confiseur* makes candies.
    - a *boulanger* makes breads and rolls.
    - a *glacier* makes frozen and cold desserts.
    - a *décorateur* prepares special cakes and displays.
- An *aboyeur* (expediter or announcer) takes orders from the dining room, relaying them to the appropriate station chef.

At the lowest rung of the kitchen staff are *commis*, or paid workers who help to prepare dishes at every station; and unpaid or nominally paid *appren-*

---

67. This outline of the brigade structure is drawn primarily from *The Professional Chef* by the Culinary Institute of America (New York: John Wiley and Sons, 2002), pp. 6–8; and from Terence, *Le Monde*, pp. 30–34.

tis, apprentices who do the most repetitive tasks (chopping, cutting, slicing) and are also assigned to specific stations, with both *commis* and *apprentis* working under the command and tutelage of the chef of the station; and the *plongeurs*, who are responsible for washing pots and pans and emptying garbage. If one were to show this graphically, on an organizational chart, flowing downward from the top would be authority and practical knowledge, while career aspirations would flow upward from the bottom.

A parallel structure of authority is maintained in the restaurant's dining room, where positions tend to be organized according to a comparable chain of command. At the top is the maître d'hôtel who manages the "front-of-the-house," trains the service staff, arranges seating, works with the chef to determine the menu, and generally serves as liaison to the kitchen. The maître d'hôtel exerts authority downward over the *sommelier* (or wine steward), the *chef de salle* (headwaiter in charge of service for the dining room), the *chef d'étage* (wait captain, who explains the menu to the guests and takes the order), the *chef de rang* (the front waiter assigned to ensure each table is properly set and supplied for each course and that food is delivered correctly), and the *commis de rang* (busboy, who sets tables, clears plates, fills water glasses, and assists the *chef de rang* and the *chef d'étage*).

The actual size of a restaurant's staff varies fairly widely according to the reputation of the establishment, but all restaurant kitchens in France tend to be organized according to the basic template of the brigade structure. The largest brigades can be supported in highly consecrated and recognized establishments, as well as in the largest hotels in the largest cities. One survey of restaurants awarded two and three stars in the *Michelin Guide* in 1988 found that of the seventeen three-star restaurants surveyed, 64 percent employed from fifty to ninety-nine employees (with the others employing from twenty to forty-nine employees); and the same survey indicated that among the seventy two-star restaurants, only seven employed more than fifty employees (and among these were several restaurants located in grand hotels that employed over 100 employees each).[68] Restaurants with a lower degree of notoriety would not be able to afford such large teams, unless located in a large hotel in a large city, where a consistently large clientele is assured. For example, while the Hotel Meurice in Paris was able to employ over 100

68. In some cases where a small inn was attached to the restaurant, the number of employees may have been inflated by the inclusion of staff working at the inn rather than the restaurant. See Terence, *Le Monde*, p. 30, whose survey sample was drawn from the 1988 *Michelin Guide*.

(72 in the kitchen and 30 in the *salle*) in its two-star restaurant; generally the size of the typical staff in an independent restaurant with a strong, but largely regional, reputation would tend to be much less. Thus, for example, the median number of employees in the thirty restaurants that were newly granted one star in the 2004 *Michelin Guide* was nine (this included both kitchen and *salle* staff combined).[69]

The structure of remuneration within the restaurant basically mirrors the brigade structure, with salaries in the kitchen generally higher than in the dining room. A 2003 industry survey conducted by *Néorestauration* magazine indicated that a typical chef de cuisine in a gastronomic restaurant (with no stars) had an annual salary in the previous year of 60,248 euros ($62,826 at the 2002 dollar exchange rate); which was one and a half times the rate of the *sous-chef* (45,281 euros per year); almost double the rate of a *chef de partie* (a pâtissier, for example, earned 33,295 euros per year); and four times the rate of a *commis* working alongside him (15,524 euros per year).[70] In 2002 the head manager of a gastronomic restaurant would have earned about 47,564 euros annually, a bit higher than the rate for a *sous-chef*; while a maître d'hôtel and a sommelier in a similar restaurant garnered salaries of 34,880 and 35,578, respectively.[71]

The various "role players" of haute cuisine (such as sommelier, pâtissier, fromager, maître d'hôtel) are also members of professional organizations that have their own structures of symbolic remuneration. That is, there are distinctive mechanisms of recognition that operate within each of the various métiers, often attached to institutions of professional association that serve as career escalators within the particular craft. The métier of sommelier, for example, has its own professional magazine and various concours are held throughout France and internationally. Through such

---

69. See profiles of new *Michelin* starred restaurants and chefs in *L'Hôtellerie*, supplement magazine, no. 2871, May 6, 2004, pp. 20–86.

70. Figures cited in "Emploi" a special supplement of *Néorestauration,* no. 404, December 2003, p. 20. Dishwashers typically receive the statutory minimum wage (SMIC) and in 2005 this would have been 11,790 euros per year, not including travel allowance, housing, and lodging benefits, which would have added 808 euros annually, according to "Nouveau SMIC Hôtelier" in *L'Hôtellerie/Restauration*, no. 2907, January 13, 2005, p. 12. A similar trade magazine survey conducted over a decade earlier (*Revue Technique des hôtels et restaurants*) showed a roughly similar kitchen salary structure, although somewhat less steep, with a chef de cuisine earning one and a half times the salary of a *chef de partie* and just under three times the salary of the *commis de cuisine* ("Les salariés dans la profession," *Revue Technique des hôtels et restaurants,* no. 500, June 1991, p. 80).

71. "Emploi" supplement in *Néorestauration,* no. 404, December 2003, p. 20.

institutions sommeliers are "made" by having been recognized by peers in associations that are recognized by their peers as being capable of judging. By passing through enough gates holding enough significance, for a long enough period of time, the sommelier can gain a level of recognition that is deep (within the métier) and broad (across the gastronomic field). In this way, and like a small handful of grand chefs, a sommelier, *chef de partie*, and various other "role players" are sometimes able to become veritable institutions in themselves.[72] The celebrated pastry chef, Gaston Lenôtre, achieved such a status. He was said to have revitalized pastry making in the 1960s via modern freezing techniques, the use of gelatin to stabilize mousse, and by lightening textures and lowering fat content of his pastries (in ways that prefigured the nouvelle cuisine cooking style). Similarly, master pastry chef Étienne Tholoniat (nicknamed "the king of sugar"), cheesemaker Pierre Adrouet, Parisian baker Lionel Poilane, and Lyon chocolatier Maurice Bernachon have all been legendary within their respective métiers, while becoming nearly as well known in French gastronomy as any of the most highly consecrated of the grand chefs.[73]

---

72. For example, Jean Frambourt twice won the concours for Premier Sommelier d'Île-de-France/Normandie, he was then elected president of the Association des Sommeliers de Paris; then president of "l'Union de la sommellerie française," and then president of l'Association de la sommellerie internationale and was termed "the world's ambassador for wine" in *Thuriès* magazine where he was profiled in a five-page spread, "L'Album du Chef" (no. 60, June 1994) (there are never page numbers included in the "L'Album du Chef"). A generation later, Olivier Poussier appeared headed along the same track, winning the Meilleur Sommelier du Monde in 2000, a decade after winning Meilleur Sommelier de France, and a career spent as *chef sommelier* at some of the most highly regarded restaurants (La Tour d'Argent, Ledoyen, Lenôtre); Patricia Cecconello, "Un sommelier au sommet," *Néorestauration*, no. 371, December 2000, p. 48. The gender distribution of consecrated sommeliers is less skewed than it is among the most consecrated chefs. For example, 37 of the 242 sommeliers recognized by Bottin Gourmand and listed in *Étoiles de la gastronomie française* were women, roughly 15 percent; while only 14 of the 933 chefs were women (1.5 percent). Similarly, among the 244 chefs profiled by *Le Chef* magazine between 1991 and 1998, only 7 were women (or just under 3 percent).

73. They are known among a wider public as well. For example, Lenôtre had a cooking school, a chain of sixty gourmet shops, has written six books of recipes, and (with chefs Bocuse and Vergé) opened the French Pavilion at Disney World in Florida, and bought the three-star Paris restaurant, Le Pré Catelan, profiled in Bernadette Gutel, "Gaston Lenôtre: La passion du beau et du bon," *L'Hôtellerie*, supplement magazine, no. 2668, June 1, 2000, pp. 6–14; and the fromager Pierre Androuet, ran a restaurant in Paris as well as five cheese shops, and wrote or coauthored six books on cheeses; while Étienne Tholoniat, the pâtissier, constructed an elaborately sculpted piece for the Saint-Etienne soccer club on the occasion of the quarter final of the Cup of Europe. Both men were profiled in "l'Album du Chef" for *Thuriès Gastronomique* magazine by Béatrice Balayé ("Pierre Androuet," no. 34, November 1991; and "Hommage à Étienne Tholoniat," no. 33, October 1991).

A key mechanism of consecration for such role players has been the concours held for the Meilleur Ouvrier for such specific crafts as pâtisserie-confiserie; chocolaterie-confiserie; glacier; sommellerie; fromagerie; boulangerie; boucherie; traiteur-charcuterie; and maître du service de la table (and that are separate from the concours for cuisine-restauration that we have considered previously). Such concours are not just established events through which time-honored craft methods are displayed, museum-like, to venerate traditional practices; they can also be a means of defining and advancing the collective interest by the members of a craft, in resistance to industrial methods, standardization, or international competition, all of which are potential threats to the livelihood of artisans. Thus, as Susan Terrio shows in her study of French chocolatiers, leaders of the primary national organization of artisan chocolate makers petitioned the Ministry of Education for some seven years to establish an MOF concours for the craft of chocolate before the first one was organized in 1990, and this was part of a broader effort to promote French chocolate in a market increasingly dominated by multinational firms.[74] In other words, the establishment of an MOF for chocolatiers was not simply a neutral act of veneration but was advanced as a mechanism of collective social closure in which one craft faction sought to buttress its position within the field relative to others.

The entry into the field of the individual producer, from virtually any position in social space, depends on the chef or the *cuisinier* having obtained the proper passkeys, both explicit and implicit. These include diplomas and other formal stamps of approval, officially acknowledged and codified in curricula and in state regulations as well as specific theoretical competencies that can be specified and tested in examinations. It also includes the acquisition of practical knowledge that is attained through a kind of osmosis, over time and through experience, in which the theoretical knowledge of the profession is absorbed and incorporated in the practice of practical activity in the kitchen (or the dining room). Becoming a chef means acquiring culinary knowledge "so perfectly mastered that it has become a natural automatism . . . a whole set of theoretical resources returned to the practical state, a state of practical sense," as Bourdieu put it with reference to a differ-

---

74. Among other things, she shows that small local chocolatiers were often opposed to the effort at national promotion and professionalization that the leaders of their Confederation sought to accomplish with the MOF concours, thus showing both that its establishment could be an act of struggle against larger social forces and that the "community" of French chocolatiers was not at all unified or homogeneous. See Susan J. Terrio, *Crafting the Culture and History of French Chocolate* (Berkeley: University of California Press, 2000).

ent social context.[75] The grand chef Joël Robuchon clearly articulated the notion of practical sense within the culinary realm:[76]

> No matter how proficient your staff is, there are certain cooking principles that cannot be explained, in words or in actions. And one of those is the fixing, or stabilizing, of flavors. For example, when I cook a ragout of truffles, there's a moment—you can tell by the aroma—when the full flavor of the truffle is being released, and it's at that point I have to intervene. And I have to know what to do: cover the pot; or add stock; or adjust the heat. If I don't jump in at precisely the right moment, the flavors disappear, lost into thin air. If I intervene at the perfect moment, the flavors are fixed forever. If you love cooking, the principle can be learned, but only by experience, by trial and error. . . . [T]he same goes for knowing when a dish is finished and when it's not. I like to give the example of a pot of tea. When you brew tea, there is an instant when it is underbrewed, an instant when it is perfectly brewed, an instant when it is overbrewed. It's not a principle that's easy to explain in simple words, but if you care about food, you'll make the effort to prepare that perfectly brewed pot of tea.

In addition to practical experience, I would suggest another element at work. What counts is not only the practical experience of the individual chef but experience that is organized in and through a wider system of formal and informal relationships. These are facilitated institutionally and elevated (symbolically) by what could be referred to as a "cult of lineage." By this I mean a source of symbolic power that runs through haute cuisine and that plays an important role in the acquisition of professional legitimacy, recognition, and influence. The phrase "it's not *what* you know, it's *who* you know" has usually referred to the concealed value of personal ties, usually with regard to entry into particular labor markets. In the gastronomic field, and perhaps other cultural fields as well, that phrase could well be restated as "it's not what you know, but who *you've known*."

Entry into the chef profession has largely operated via a relatively straightforward system of training and qualification that has allowed for

75. Pierre Bourdieu, *Science of Science and Reflexivity* (Chicago: University of Chicago Press), p. 51.

76. From an interview conducted by Patricia Wells in *Cuisine Actuelle: Patricia Wells Presents the Cuisine of Joël Robuchon* (London: Macmillan, 1991), p. 5.

several different routes into the kitchen. Traditionally, the apprenticeship system was the principal means of entry, a process through which both culinary techniques and professional comportment were learned through a combination of experience, absorption, and submission. Stories of apprenticeships served within the houses of legendary chefs (Paul Bocuse under the tutelage of Fernand Point and Mère Brazier; or Bernard Loiseau at chez Troisgros, etc.) still circulate in the lore of haute cuisine and most of the highly consecrated grand chefs began their careers as apprentices (thirty-two of thirty-seven served apprenticeships), but this system has changed in recent decades. While still a working arrangement, apprenticeship conditions have been transformed by state regulations that have limited the length of the working day and have mandated rest times for apprentices, in addition to other protections.[77] They have also been incorporated into the state education curriculum as programs that are more equivalent to "work-study" internship programs, pitched at a fairly high level of technical competence, than to the grueling stints of deference and degradation that characterize the lore of the traditional apprentice system.[78] Moreover, the training of apprentices has been increasingly integrated into the national education system through regional Centers of Apprenticeship Training in which fifteen- and sixteen-year-olds who are preparing for a basic diploma in a craft like cooking, spend six days of every month doing practical and theoretical work in a kitchen laboratory/workshop.[79] In this way traditional apprenticeship practices are integrated into the contemporary state diploma system, which, for most entering the culinary trades, is based on the CAP/BEP diploma (Certificat d'Aptitude Professionnelle/Brevet d'Études Professionnelles), the most basic qualifications of competency in a specific skilled trade. For most cooks and chefs these qualifications serve as the initial passkey to a paying job, and many of the most highly consecrated French chefs began

---

77. Echikson, in his biographical profile of the career of a three-star chef, notes that while Bernard Loiseau served a three-year apprenticeship working sixteen-hour days at the renowned chez Troisgros, his three-star restaurant offered six-month apprenticeships with eight-hour shifts, a workday that was then limited further by the state-mandated thirty-five-hour workweek. Echikson, *Burgundy Stars*, pp. 40–41.

78. Teachers in professional and technical high schools for the culinary arts, both public and private, are increasingly required to have high levels of technical expertise. After passing a qualifying exam, they must complete a two-year training program and a one-year internship in a technical high school and must master the economics and science of culinary production through a program heavy in both management and engineering. See Edmond Neirinck, "La Nouvelle formation des professeurs de cuisine," *Le Chef*, no. 36, October 1990, pp. 60–61.

79. Line de Miass, "L'Apprentissage, qu'est-ce?" *Le Chef*, no. 61, June–July 1993, p. 26.

their careers by training for a CAP diploma in cuisine. Of the thirty-seven most consecrated grand chefs, seventeen either worked toward or received a CAP diploma and seven went beyond the CAP to acquire more advanced skills in the form of a Baccaulauréat (BAC) or Baccaulauréat Technologique Hôtellerie (BTH). Twelve of the thirty-seven had no formal training at all.[80]

With whom one has served his or her apprenticeship not only marks a career but sets the arc of its trajectory as well. This is partly what's at stake with regard to the "cult of lineage" mentioned earlier, which refers to the heavy preoccupation in the profession with the hereditary career lines that chefs carry with them. When the heritage of one's career can be clearly and directly traced back to a highly consecrated chef one is permitted to essentially claim membership in a particular "kinship group," thereby gaining a measure of social capital on the basis of one's association with a particular master chef. Social capital, essentially a capital of association or of belonging, has held substantial value in the gastronomic field, particularly in its most rarified regions.[81] It is for this reason that in most writing about chefs it is almost obligatory to mention in whose kitchens a chef has worked, who has trained them, or whom they have trained—information that is important enough to be included in the curriculum vitae of a chef.[82] In part, this is simply a set of facts that serves the purpose of identification, locating a chef within a particular region of the gastronomic universe. However, identification can never be neutral where recognition is such an important part of what is at stake in the field, and the gastronomic field is structured hierarchically, like all fields. The conspicuous display of the amount and quality of the social capital one has accumulated (through magazine profiles, in interviews, in directories, etc.) amounts to an act of career advancement for the individual chef, of course, but all such claims of descent are also part of the process by which participants in a field determine where one justifiably "belongs." In other words, in setting such coordinates chefs are located in

---

80. Other research shows that fifty-nine out of sixty-three starred chefs entered the profession through either apprenticeships or specialized hotel/restaurant schools (Terence, *Le Monde*, p. 22); and 57 percent of cooks working in all forms of restaurant taken together (chain, institutional, and independent) held a CAP or BEP diploma (Sylvie-Anne Mériot, *Le Cuisinier Nostalgique entre restaurant et cantine* [Paris: CNRS Editions, 2002], p. 78).

81. This is essentially no different than the cult of lineage operating in various other cultural fields, most obviously perhaps the academic field, where the question posed to all doctoral students and recent Ph.D.'s: "with whom did you work?" is as important as the question, "from where did you receive your degree?" with both questions referring to the value of one's social capital.

82. Bottin Gourmand, *Étoiles de la gastronomie française*.

their "proper place" within the field, with the significance of social capital as a criterion of valuation thereby established, and circulated, and its value determined for the field.

Tracing the family lines among chefs (Roger Vergé begat Alain Ducasse, who begat Michel Sarran and Alain Solivérès, who begat Marc Mirretti, etc.) tends to benefit those at both sides of a relationship, across generations, and not only for the most recent or least established. For example, Alain Ducasse, arguably the most successful chef in the world, profits from his "family" ties to Roger Vergé (as well as to Michel Guérard and Alain Chapel, who he also claims as mentors) even though he may have come to surpass all three of them in professional recognition and notoriety.[83] Through an association with Vergé, Ducasse along with Solivérès and Sarran are able to display their roots in the patrimony of the profession; and, in turn, Roger Vergé displays his legacy to French cuisine by having it known that he trained both Ducasse and Solivérès.[84] While these lines may be invoked to establish legitimacy, they are neither strict nor exclusive, since multiple paternity claims do not seem to be a cause for controversy. It is thus not treated as a problem that Ducasse was trained by more than one notable chef, for example, or that both Michel Guérard and Roger Vergé each claim paternity in relation to Daniel Boulud, the chef/owner of the New York restaurant Daniel). These are relationships that are invoked, however fleeting or tenuous.

The preoccupation with legacy in French gastronomy reached perhaps its furthest expression with the formation of the Association of the Disciples of Paul Bocuse. Created in 1976 by close to 100 of Bocuse's former apprentices and commis who had come together from around the world to perpetuate the name and legacy of Paul Bocuse on the occasion of his fiftieth birthday. Two decades later, at a 1995 gathering of the group, one of his

---

83. Ducasse was the first chef to have two restaurants with three-star Michelin ratings ("Louis XV" in Monaco and the "Restaurant Alain Ducasse" in Paris) along with a portfolio that includes highly regarded restaurants in New York and Tokyo, a restaurant chain in France, several inns, a training school for chefs, and various chef-of-the-year awards and other honors.

84. Alain Solivérès is chef de cuisine at a Paris restaurant that holds two *Michelin* stars and three stars in *Bottin Gourmand*, "Les Élysées du Vernet." Michel Sarran's restaurant in Toulouse carries his own name and has two stars in the *Bottin Gourmand* guide. Vergé, Guérard, and Chapel are grand chefs with three *Michelin* stars and are mentioned prominently on Ducasse's website, and in various articles about him; while Ducasse is noted on the résumé of Vergé, and their connection is mentioned throughout the gastronomic press as well.

former apprentices recalled memories of the times passed with Bocuse and in the kitchen at Collonges au Mont d'Or:[85]

> At the breast of this little family affair, we considered ourselves the children of the father, Paul Bocuse, and we passed some unforgettable moments: hunting for blackbirds in the afternoon after a good snack, playing *boules* in the courtyard of the Inn, delicious evenings in front of the television. . . . At the same time, these three years of apprenticeship in the kitchen were very hard. We feared and respected Paul Bocuse, who was always at the ovens. The restaurant was open every day except for ten days in August and Paul Bocuse never missed a shift, except in 1950 for the finals of the MOF!

Bocuse, himself well known for his formidable culinary bloodlines descending from both Mère Brazier in Lyon and from the legendary Fernand Point of La Pyramide restaurant, where he served as an apprentice for two years, has spawned five winners of the Meilleur Ouvrier de France, who together constitute a sort of collective primogeniture.[86]

The formation of an association of "disciples" may be unique to Bocuse, but it really just represents a more organized and explicit expression of what has been an important means of professional valorization in the French gastronomic field. A collective consciousness of lineage binds the "family" of haute cuisine more tightly together, sharpening the professional endogamy that governs the most rarified regions of the field, but biological family ties also play a significant role. Among our thirty-seven highly consecrated chefs, twenty-one had parents or grandparents who had worked in the culinary trades as chefs, innkeepers, or café owners, while a previous study of gastronomic restaurants in France found that 75 percent of chefs hailed from families with industry ties, suggesting a high degree of social

---

85. The quote is from chef Jacky Marquin in Christel Reynaud, "Rendez-vous le 31 Décembre 1995: Disciples de Paul Bocuse," *Le Chef,* no. 39, January–February 1991, p. 16.

86. Roger Jaloux, termed his "spiritual son," and the brigade leader at Bocuse's restaurant at Collonges au Mont d'Or, and Christian Bouvarel, have both worked for Bocuse since the beginning, and together with the three other MOF winners, Jean Fleury, Francois Pipala, and Christian Tetedoie, are represented as the inner circle of the Association des disciples de Paul Bocuse. See Christel Reynaud, "Rendez-vous le 31 Décembre," p. 16; and Bocuse's published résumé in Bottin Gourmand's *Étoiles de la gastronomie française,* p. 76. For the history of Bocuse's relationship with Fernand Le Point and Mère Brazier, see Mesplède, *Trois Étoiles,* pp. 72–73, 144–145.

reproduction.[87] At the very least, such ties would have predisposed them from a very young age to consider cooking as a viable occupation, in addition to familiarizing them with basic culinary practices, internalizing the rhythms of restaurant life, and helping facilitate entrance into apprenticeships. In other words they would be coming of age with a kind of "feel" for the profession that others would have to acquire on the job, more gradually. Family ties have also served to tighten the enclosure of an already relatively closed universe of haute cuisine. Thus, among the grand chefs who have worked closely together in recent years, and who share three *Michelin* stars, are the twins Jacques and Laurent Pourcel (co–chefs de cuisine in Montpellier); the father-son teams of Michel and Jean-Michel Lorain in Joigny, and Marc and Paul Haeberlin in Strasbourg; while at least five current chefs are considered heirs of what have been considered culinary family "dynasties," three of whom (Blanc, Pic, and Troisgros) are considered virtual gastronomic institutions in themselves.[88] One analyst has suggested that the "dynasties" in French gastronomy have been rarer in Paris than in the provinces, where tradition and family ties tend to be more strongly valued and where their rupture represents a more significant event.[89]

The persistence of kinship ties would seem to represent a rough indicator of the (relative) autonomy of the French gastronomic field, for among the most highly consecrated (and thus most symbolically central) chefs, family ties in the profession would appear to facilitate a concurrence of socioprofessional with biological reproduction. That is, when we consider

87. Isabelle Terence (*Le Monde*) found that 50 percent of the two and three star chefs inherited their restaurants from their families (32 out of 66) and roughly 75 percent came from families where the parents worked in either hotels or restaurants (p. 22).

88. In addition to Gerard Boyer and Jacques Lameloise, who are descendants of well-known chefs, the chef Georges Blanc, born in 1943, is the fourth generation of the Blanc family to preside over a restaurant in Vonnas since 1872 (his sons reportedly work in the family business and his mother was once called "the best cook in the world" by Curnonsky); Michel Troisgros, born in 1958 is scion of the famous culinary family from Roanne who encompassed three generations of brothers and sons, including the grandfather Jean-Baptiste, the father Pierre and uncle Jean, and the brother Claude, now chef/owner of a Brazilian Troisgros restaurant; and Anne Sophie-Pic (born 1970) sister of Alain, daughter of Jacques, granddaughter of André Pic, and great granddaughter of Eugène, is the only woman among the ranks of the most highly consecrated grand chefs in France. Her expressed goal is to win back the third *Michelin* star that the family restaurant in Valence lost in 1995, shortly after the death of her father (Jean-François Mesplède, "Anne-Sophie Pic: Au nom du père," *L'Hôtellerie*, supplement magazine, no. 2590, December 3, 1998, pp. 4–7).

89. Guy Chemla, "L'Évolution récente des restaurants gastronomiques parisiens," in *Les Restaurants dans le monde et à travers les âges*, ed. A. Huetz de Lemps and J.-R. Pitte (Grenoble: Éditions Glénat, 1990), p. 45.

"family ties" in the very broadest sense to include the structures of professional lineage that are established through the apprentice system, the culinary backgrounds of chefs, and the number of familial dynasties capable of transmitting influence across generations, the gastronomic field can be seen as having retained a fair degree of autonomy from external judgment with respect to professional succession. It's not even that succession occurs primarily through such a relatively narrow funnel, although we have seen evidence suggesting that it does, but that the persistence of such patterns of professional endogamy suggest the degree to which succession remains protected from the logic of evaluation and judgment imposed from outside the gastronomic field (i.e., from the logic of the market, for example, or from the education system, both of which would necessitate other means of succession).

In practical terms, succession may operate through both familial and professional channels simultaneously, reinforcing both. For example, Pierre Orsi (chef de cuisine and president of the one *Michelin* star and three *Bottin Gourmand* stars restaurant Orsi in Lyon) did his apprenticeship with Paul Bocuse (and has been a member of the Association of the Disciples of Bocuse). Orsi subsequently went on to train the chefs Gérard Vignat, Jacques Rolancy, and Stéphane Gaborieau (who in turn has trained Pascal Cayeux, Sébastien Chambru, Sylvain Dereau, and Katsumi). Operating alongside this chain of professional lineage has been Orsi's family lineage, constituted by four sons who are all active in the restaurant industry in various countries (including his son Laurent, who apprenticed alongside Roger Jaloux at Chez Bocuse!).[90]

The effect of having passed through a highly consecrated restaurant as an apprentice or as a *commis* or as a *chef de partie*, would, essentially, be the equivalent of having worked alongside a highly consecrated chef. Being imprinted with an approved institutional stamp entitles one to display its aura, which carries with it a certain assumption that the experience of having worked in a duly recognized restaurant has prepared one for work in a restaurant worthy of comparable recognition, recommending one as "having what it takes" to operate at a similar level of skill, of comportment, and of overall professional standing. One is thus made a part of the "club" by

---

90. See the profile of Laurent Orsi by Georges Golan, "Un Lyonnais à Toulouse," *Le Chef*, no. 49, March 1992, p. 24. Lines of professional lineage were traced employing data presented in Bottin Gourmand, *Étoiles de la gastronomie française*. Paul Bocuse's son is not a chef but reportedly manages his father's Epcot center restaurant at Disney World in Florida.

having worked in a restaurant or with a grand chef recognized as being part of the club. The list of restaurants with the power to sanctify in this way would not be large and would not necessarily correspond to the list of chefs with great influence and recognition in the field. Just a few restaurants in France enjoy greater recognition than the grand chefs who have worked in them. Here one thinks of the Paris restaurants La Tour d'Argent, and Taillevent at the top of such a list, followed by Le Grand Véfour, and Ledoyen.[91] Similarly, and not surprisingly, the reputations of the most venerable Parisian bistros have usually hovered above that of the chefs who work there (i.e., Le Balzar, the Brasserie Lipp, La Coupole, etc.); but the most highly consecrated restaurants in France are normally unable to sustain a high level of attention and recognition without the active renewal provided by a highly consecrated and well-recognized chef/owner.[92] Emblematic was the case of Bernard Loiseau, hired to revive a venerable restaurant in Burgundy and whose own celebrity came to transcend it. The process of his accession is recounted in the following pages, with attention to the effects of the field in coauthoring his career.

The Social Production of Culinary Stardom

The grand chef, Bernard Loiseau, whom we met in the previous chapter, had a background not unlike other chefs of his generation. He was born in 1951 in the Puy-de-Dôme in the center of France and was raised in the industrial city of Clermont-Ferrand, a city dominated by the Michelin Tire Company. Although he attended Catholic school with the Michelin children, his social origins were much more modest than theirs, although not at all impoverished.[93] The eldest of three siblings, Bernard Loiseau was

---

91. The chefs de cuisine working at these restaurants are, respectively, Bernard Guilhardin, Philip Legendre, Guy Martin, and Ghislaine Arabian; all formidable by way of reputation and (particularly in the case of Legendre and Martin) are able to fully maintain the historic standing of the restaurants.

92. The case of La Tour d'Argent stands out for having outshone most of its chefs, but this was most likely a function of its longtime owner, Claude Terrail. Born and raised above the family restaurant on the banks of the Seine, Terrail personified the stylishness of a restaurant that was known as a magnet for celebrities, politicians, and diplomats. He thereby served as a cultural impresario at least as well as any of the grand chefs of the twentieth century. See Béatrice Balayé, "L'Album du Chef: Claude Terrail," *Thuriès Magazine*, no. 19, May 1990 (no pages).

93. Details of the life and career of Bernard Loiseau are drawn from a combination of William Echikson's *Burgundy Stars* and a dossier of published profiles drawn from professional trade journals, magazines, and gastronomic guides, including: *Le Chef*; *Thuriès*; *Gault-Millau* magazine; *Néorestauration*; and Bottin Gourmand, *Étoiles de la gastronomie française*.

an enthusiastic athlete, who was captain of the school soccer team, but an uninspired student and so, at the age of sixteen, he left school after failing to pass the qualifying examination for further study (BEPC). Loiseau would seem to have been predisposed to a life in the culinary trades, having descended from a long line of butchers on his mother's side and with a mother whose family owned an established charcuterie in the historic center of the city. Ironically, however, it may be that an equally important factor in the launching of his career trajectory as a chef was the fact that his father had departed from the family occupation, choosing instead to be a traveling hat salesman. As it happened, over the course of many years of travel his father had been stopping along his sales route to visit a little family restaurant in the small city of Roanne. The restaurant, long owned by the family Troisgros, is a name that came to acquire legendary status in the world of French gastronomy. When Loiseau decided to become a chef his father drew upon his Roanne connections to request an apprenticeship for his son, and one year later when an apprenticeship opened up he took it.[94]

From 1968 to 1971 Loiseau lived above the Troisgros restaurant, working in the way that apprentices in the culinary trade always did, namely very long hours, sometimes sixteen-hour days, six days per week, at the most menial tasks (hauling, peeling, preparing, polishing, etc.).[95] Only after many months was he permitted to use an oven, and although there are other ways to make one's way into the profession, and while it is more regulated now than it was in the past, the apprenticeship model has been and continues to be a common route for those with ambitions of becoming a grand chef.[96]

---

94. In the intervening year Bernard had gone to work in a pastry shop owned by a cousin where, Echikson notes, Loiseau reported having made a firm decision to become a chef: "I wanted to do more than just pastry . . . It was all show, no substance, painting with a small brush, instead of a large brush." Echikson, *Burgundy Stars*, p. 40.

95. Apprentices are now limited by law to eight-hour days, with at least twelve hours between shifts, a situation that, reportedly, has forced substantial modifications to the traditional system. As Pierre Troisgros told an interviewer, "How can you give somebody twelve hours off when you finish at midnight and have to begin at eight in the morning the next day? You can't, and that's the reason the old apprenticeship is breaking down" (Echikson, *Burgundy Stars*, p. 40). Apprentices tend to be paid at a rate of approximately one-third the rate of a cook and one-fifth the rate of a head chef in an independent restaurant (French government data cited in Sylvie-Anne Mériot, *Le Cuisinier nostalgique: Entre restaurant et cantine* (Paris: CNRS Editions, 2002), p. 81.

96. One study of highly consecrated restaurants (those with two or three *Michelin* stars) reported that of the sixty-three chefs interviewed, a full fifty-nine reported having apprenticed their way into the culinary profession. This same study cites a 1992 study of the hotel/restaurant industry conducted by the Rhône-Alpes regional authorities (the region that includes

Loiseau began his apprenticeship in the Troisgros kitchen at a fortuitous moment, for Pierre Troisgros, the most prominent member of this culinary family dynasty, was about to receive the highest form of sanctification, receipt of a third star in the *Michelin Guide*.[97] Just two weeks after Loiseau began his apprenticeship, Troisgros was granted his third star and, as legend has it, the seventeen-year-old apprentice expressly vowed that he too would one day receive three *Michelin* stars. It is perhaps revealing that this oft-recounted story has been featured not only in profiles celebrating a heroic Loiseau but in a hagiography of the *Michelin Guide* itself which, as we have seen, is the predominant institution of gastronomic consecration. For in a largely uncritical book of the history of the guide, one prominent food industry journalist and editor noted that "Bernard Loiseau had decided on that day back then that he would also have three stars"; while the editor of *Thuriès Magazine*, the stylish, glossy magazine wrote: "Fifteen days after he began, the 15th of March, 1968, the champagne flowed in this illustrious house in celebration of its third star. It left Bernard with a special feeling. He has been running after the stars ever since."[98]

The experience was undoubtedly a formative one for Loiseau, whose ambitiousness has been well-documented, but such quotes do more than enhance biographical detail; they offer analytical insight into the mechanics of the gastronomic field itself by providing a glimpse of the process of mutual constitution that prevails between and among the central actors in this social universe. For what was recounted, both in his lifetime and posthumous-

---

Lyon and Grenoble) indicating that only a 50 percent plurality of those in the profession acquired their jobs through apprenticeships (the others through professional hotel training programs or educational diplomas). See Terence, *Le Monde*, pp. 22, 35. As we'll see in the following chapter, this variation does not at all represent a contradiction. Apprenticeships have increasingly become less tightly linked to the grand restaurants, with apprenticeship training centers being established and becoming part of the system of state-authorized educational training. For instance, three-year apprenticeships now serve as preparation for the examination for a *Certificat d'Aptitude Professionnelle* (CAP). Line de Miass, "L'Apprentissage, qu'est-ce?" *Le Chef*, no. 61, June–July, 1993, p. 26.

97. Pierre and his brother Jean Troisgros, the second generation, are sons of restaurant/ hotel owners Jean-Baptiste and his wife, Marie, while Pierre is also the father of two sons, Michel (a well-known chef with whom he shares a third *Michelin* star at the family restaurant) and Claude (a highly regarded chef de cuisine and restaurant owner in Brazil), and a daughter Marie, who was a student at the École Hôtelière in Lausanne, Switzerland.

98. See Jean-Francois Mesplède, *Trois Étoiles au Michelin: Une histoire de la haute gastronomie française* (Paris: Éditions Grund, 1998), p. 152 (note that the book's title and subtitle place the *Michelin Guide* into the very heart of the history of French gastronomy). Also see Béatrice Balayé, "Bernard Loiseau," *Thuriès Magazine*, no. 28, April 1991, p. 7.

ly, was the near-mythic story of a future grand chef, who, while still a young apprentice, met his "maker" (the *Michelin Guide*) and gained inspiration by bearing witness to its transformative powers. Furthermore, it is a narrative tale that the maker *Michelin* (through its own storyteller) was able to use in a way that served to demonstrate and reinforce its power to make grand chefs! That is, social analysis can do more than just help us understand the social construction of the hero; it points us to the social construction of the hero-making apparatus. This would seem to then recommend a fuller examination of the mechanisms by which the reciprocally confirming circle of belief is sustained within the domain of French gastronomy, or any field of social activity. This includes an understanding of the social uses of myth and legend in the service of a system that symbolically elevates a chosen few of its inhabitants high above the mundane drudgery of restaurant work.[99]

Bernard Loiseau was still just a worker, after all; one who had left Troisgros in 1971 with CAP in hand (the basic diploma authorizing one to work in the culinary trade), having served an apprenticeship in a three-star restaurant owned by a very prominent grand chef. After an obligatory stint in the military where he oversaw a brigade of chefs in the kitchens of a French army base in Alsace, and several disappointing job-seeking efforts upon being discharged, Loiseau soon found a job in Paris cooking for a restaurateur named Claude Verger. An active businessman and entrepreneur, Verger eventually acquired six restaurants in Paris, for which he hired several Troisgros-trained chefs to work.[100] Loiseau was initially handed a job as chef at La Barrière de Clichy, a restaurant at the edge of the Paris city limits. Under the tutelage of Verger, reportedly an exacting boss, Loiseau developed a different cooking style, one that was light and that utilized fresh, seasonal ingredients. It was a style that he acquired at the moment that the food critics Henri Gault and Christian Millau were announcing their revolutionary "nouvelle cuisine," their designation for a putative culinary "movement" that, as it happened, gave their upstart *Gault-Millau* guide a very useful

99. Myth has been a crucial historical component of the gastronomic literary tradition, including the construction of the mythic figure of the gastronome, of great cooks, as well as of the genealogies of particular dishes, their techniques of preparation, as well as the sources of their names. See Stephen Mennell, *All Manners of Food*, 2nd ed. (Urbana: University of Illinois Press, 1996), pp. 270–271.

100. Echikson, *Burgundy Stars*, pp. 43–46. Claude Verger is not to be confused with the three-star chef, Roger Vergé, who was mentioned previously.

boost just as it was seeking to establish itself in a market for gastronomic guides long dominated by *Michelin*.[101]

A year later Loiseau became the chef at Verger's main Parisian restaurant, La Barrière Poquelin, located on the affluent Right Bank, where, according to Echikson, he quickly became comfortable with a Parisian clientele that included the very famous and the very rich, and where food critics began to notice his skills as a chef.[102] Soon after, Verger purchased a historic restaurant in the town of Saulieu, in Burgundy, two hours from Paris. Saulieu was a town that already enjoyed a certain standing in French gastronomy as the site of several highly regarded restaurants, largely due to its location on the traditional motor route between Paris and Lyon and points south. The most prominent of the Saulieu restaurants was la Côte d'Or, which, for over four decades, had been owned by Alexandre Dumaine, a very large figure in gastronomic circles.[103] Just as Verger began proceedings to purchase la Côte d'Or from Dumaine's successor, it lost two of its three stars, and Verger summoned Loiseau from Paris to be its chef de cuisine and to try to reverse the trend. Within just a few years, as Verger was preparing to retire, Loiseau purchased la Côte d'Or from him, but not before making two investments

---

101. Gault and Millau began publishing their guide in 1969 and denominated "nouvelle cuisine" in 1972, the same year that Loiseau was beginning his first real job as a chef. He was still an unknown and thus could not be counted among the chef "founders" of the trend (that title has been variously reserved for one or another combination of the following chefs: Paul Bocuse, Alain Chapel, Michel Guérard, Raymond Oliver, Roger Vergé, René Lasserre, and Jean Troisgros (and sometimes his brother Pierre)—see Jean-Francois Mesplède, "L'Union sacrée," *L'Hôtellerie*, no. 2570, July 16, 1998, footnote #1 and see Mennell, "Food and Wine," p. 180. The relative fluidity and variability of its genesis lends weight to the suspicion that the act of naming and representing it was as important for its establishment as anything that might have occurred in the kitchen. However, although various nouvelle cuisines have been announced at various points in French gastronomic history, this latest undoubtedly did identify some significant culinary innovations. The question is whether they deserve the scale of attention that they received, as a revolutionary shift in haute cuisine, and whether the heralding of a new cuisine may have partly been a marketing maneuver by Gault-Millau. Also questionable is whether nouvelle cuisine warranted the status of a social or "identity movement" (as some social scientists have designated it). See Hayagreeva Rao, Philippe Monin, and Rodolphe Durand, "Institutional Change in Toque Ville: Nouvelle Cuisine as an Identity Movement in French Gastronomy," *American Journal of Sociology*, vol. 8, no. 4, January 2003, pp. 795–843.

102. The restaurant received a rating of fifteen out of twenty in the *Gault-Millau* guide of 1974, according to Echikson a score that earned the young chef considerable attention, and indeed, the guide termed Loiseau "a remarkable chef" (*Burgundy Stars*, p. 47).

103. He was a large man in a physical sense, and in the sense that Dumaine was one of a handful of chefs who figured prominently in French haute cuisine during the interwar years and in its reestablishment after the war. His was a formidable heritage for Loiseau to attempt to match. Béatrice Balayé, "Bernard Loiseau" in *Thuriès*, no. 28, April 1991, pp. 7–13.

important to the business: he acquired a wife who was willing to work with him at the restaurant and he acquired a huge loan.[104] Loiseau became the chef de cuisine and proprietor of a restaurant that he would soon successfully return to a position of importance in the gastronomic world.

Loiseau's rise to the top of the culinary profession proceeded relatively quickly. In 1981, less than a year after purchasing la Côte d'Or, he won a second *Michelin* star for the restaurant; in 1984 the Hachette guide named him the "Best cook under 40"; which was followed, two years later, with the receipt of the highest four-star rating and the "Cook of the Year" honors in the *Bottin Gourmand* guide. Then in 1991 he won the "Chef of the Year" from *Le Chef*, the main trade journal in the profession, and achieved the goal of a lifetime for a French chef: receipt of a third star in the *Michelin Guide*. Nothing that followed was as important to Loiseau, even when, in 1999, he was named by *Gault&Millau* magazine as one of the "Eight Best Chefs of France" based on a poll of working chefs, while at the same time its Guide gave la Côte d'Or a score of nineteen on a twenty-point scale.[105]

In the decade prior to his death, Bernard Loiseau was widely considered a member of the unofficial "inner circle" of the leading grand chefs, a very tiny club that included Bocuse, Ducasse, Robuchon, and Troisgros, the grandest of the grand chefs, who were all on track toward legendary status in the domain of French gastronomy and whose names have often been invoked to personify French haute cuisine. Upon one's delegation as a member of this inner circle, one is basically authorized, unofficially, to represent haute cuisine to itself and to the rest of the world, while being decorated at the very highest levels of the state for one's work. Thus, Loiseau was

---

104. Besides purchasing the restaurant, he used the loan to refurbish the small hotel attached to it, with millions of dollars in renovations and additions. Having a wife to manage the front of the restaurant is thought to be essential to receiving a *Michelin* star, above all for the image of stability that it appears to convey. According to Echikson, Loiseau's first marriage only lasted a few years, reportedly because it had been consummated largely to satisfy this unspoken requirement (*Burgundy Stars*, p. 57).

105. It should be noted that only twenty-one chefs or restaurants receive four stars in the *Bottin Gourmand* guide, about the same number of annual three-star ratings given by the more prestigious *Michelin* guide, thus making it roughly equivalent in selectivity, if not in symbolic power. It also should be noted that "Chef of the Year" is awarded by *Le Chef* magazine on the basis of a poll of working chefs, rather than by a panel of external judges. Thus when Loiseau won his award it was reportedly based on ballot returns from between 750 and 950 chefs (who had been chosen on the basis of their citation in the *Michelin Guide*), each of whom were asked to vote for one chef on a list of ten finalists (see *Le Chef*, no. 46, November 1991, pp. 18–19.) The list of the "Eight Best Chefs of France" was published in the winter 1999–2000 issue of *Gault&Millau* magazine (no. 337, November, December, January).

awarded the Medal of National Merit in 1986, the second highest civilian award (after the Legion of Honor) and in 1995 was named a "Knight" of the Legion of Honor, the highest level of distinction for the highest of civilian awards.[106] Personally conferred by President François Mitterrand (who was known to have dined more than once at la Côte d'Or), it was only the second time that the award had been personally bestowed on a chef by the president himself (Paul Bocuse had been the first). What is most noteworthy, however, is NOT that a prominent cultural figure might receive such high recognition from the state, for cultural figures are routinely awarded state recognition in France, as they are most everywhere else (including the United States), but that a chef would be considered a practitioner of high culture, like a great novelist, or painter, or poet.

Through the decade of the 1990s Bernard Loiseau received the sort of popular adulation that accompanies a major celebrity. All of his professional honors and awards were able to be converted into more generalized recognition as the print and broadcast media popularized his swift rise within the profession, while at the same time the suddenness of his stardom and his smiling disposition augmented his media attractiveness. A regular on television, as author of some eight popular cookbooks and as a lively subject for interviews, Loiseau's name increasingly served as a trademark capable of selling products by endorsement (it graced various products, including a line of soups and prepackaged foods, and was featured in a marketing campaign for a well-known champagne company), in addition to various consultancy arrangements. His stock had risen so high in the gastronomic world that his company, Bernard Loiseau S.A. was listed on the Paris stock exchange, the first grand chef to have "gone public" in such a way. The public offering raised about $4.5 million, and according to Echikson, was used to pay off debt and to acquire two Paris bistros (Tante Marguerite and Tante Jeanne followed soon after his purchase of Tante Louise), as various other business ventures presented themselves.[107] In addition to la Côte d'Or, in which he reportedly invested some $10 million in renovations over two decades and

---

106. The Légion d'Honneur is an honorary distinction created by Napoléon Bonaparte in 1802. It is the highest civilian award and is granted for work deemed to enhance the reputation of France (in scholarship or the arts or science, etc.). It is awarded in one of five classes or levels of distinction, with "Chevalier" (Knight) being the highest.

107. For example, in 2001 Loiseau signed a consulting agreement to provide management services to a restaurant hotel project being built in Toulouse (Florence Jacquemond, "Projet de Bernard Loiseau en Haute-Garonne," *Néorestauration*, no. 378, July–August 2001, p. 14.) and see William Echikson, "Death of a Chef," *New Yorker*, May 12, 2003, p. 65.

which always comprised the largest part of his economic activity, he opened a boutique across from the restaurant that sold various souvenirs, including specialty foods, cookbooks, kitchen products, and so on, and opened a branch of his restaurant in a Sheraton Hotel in Japan (although an earthquake forced it to close after three years).

Loiseau was thus on an upward spiral at the time of his death, whereby the articles and interviews written about him were increasing his entrepreneurial chances and were helping to make him rich; which in turn augmented his attractiveness to the media as a celebrity, making him universally recognizable, thereby further enhancing his ability to make money. While we might recognize such dynamics as fairly common in Hollywood and the sports world in the United States, we would be right to ask how they came to be possible in the relatively closed world of haute cuisine, where the reigning ethos has always reflected the high value placed on skill and hard work in achieving culinary perfection. Neither fame nor wealth were traditionally central values associated with gastronomy, a domain where the goal of flawless creation through human artistry, and fidelity to the culinary knowledge of one's forebears have dominated the occupational culture. Unlike the artist or the craftsman, who might have once been expected to show disdain for the pursuit of commercial motivation or public recognition as being sacrilegious violations of the craft ethos favoring "the relentless pursuit of excellence as a badge of distinction," as sociologist Richard Sennett put it, Loiseau seemed to pursue both with unabashed enthusiasm.[108] Where was the restraint and moderation that had once seemed to reflect a self-confident bearing? It was not a matter of individual self-indulgence or greed, for Loiseau was not alone. Bocuse, Ducasse, Robuchon, and other grand chefs had been pursuing business interests as extensive as Loiseau's and seemed to cultivate a similar degree of celebrity recognition. If Loiseau was not simply a maverick in the world of haute cuisine, then, could it be that his extraculinary pursuit of wealth and fame was now becoming more acceptable for a French grand chef? If so, what had occurred in the gastronomic field, this relatively closed world of artisanship, to make the goal of profit making and fame both possible and acceptable? If culinary artistry and *artisanal* practice have been at the foundation of French gastronomy; and if, as we have noted, gastronomy is a central element of the French cultural patrimony, thereby placing it at the very heart of the French "cul-

---

108. Richard Sennett, *The Craftsman* (New Haven, CT: Yale University Press, 2008), p. 245.

tural exception," then such questions would seem to have implications that extend beyond the culinary sphere.[109]

French gastronomy seems enveloped in a struggle that has long been waged in other cultural fields and that has pitted mass markets against restricted markets and commercial value against aesthetic principle. As with other cultural practices, haute cuisine has been a practice in which time, craftsmanship, and the transfer of practical and theoretical knowledge from one's forebears have been highly valued, producing cultural goods not intended for a mass audience or clientele, but for a relatively limited circle of connoisseurs, aficionados, and cultivated judges. Distinctions made in haute cuisine over the routes of accession (whether via concours, guide ratings, reviews, etc.) are less for the elaboration of hierarchy in principle than they are for the endogamous (and thus relatively autonomous) character of gastronomic judgment. In other words, consecration and judgment are made on the basis of factors generated from *within* the field of gastronomy, rather than from standards that have been imported from without.

How is it then that grand chefs like Bernard Loiseau (or Bocuse, or Robuchon and the rest) who have spent their professional lives in single-minded pursuit of the long sought marks of gastronomic excellence (*Michelin* stars, a high score in *Gault-Millau*, winning or being named a "finalist" for the Meilleur Ouvrier de France, or a "chef of the year" award, or being recognized by a trade magazine or similar organ of the profession) were drawn by the siren-call of celebrity and financial gain? Why not be content with the prospect of gaining recognition for making a contribution to the cultural patrimony, or even entering the cultural pantheon? And, perhaps most importantly, what is it that transpired in the French gastronomic field that made it a site where ambition and greed could be readily and reasonably pursued?

---

109. See, for example, Alexandre Layareff, *L'Exception culinaire française: Un patrimoine gastronomique en péril?* (Paris: Éditions Albin Michel, 1998), p. 13; Serge Regourd, *L'Exception Culturelle* (Paris: Presses Universitaires de France, 2002); Sophie Meunier, "The French Exception," *Foreign Affairs*, vol. 79, no. 4, July–August 2000, pp. 104–116; and Phillip H. Gordon and Sophie Meunier, *The French Challenge: Adapting to Globalization* (Washington, DC: Brookings Institution Press, 2001).

3

Fast Food in France

A Market for the Impossible

A t the time it seemed that José Bové and his tractor could not have
chosen a more appropriate target for decapitation than that Mc-
Donald's outlet in southern France. It was 1999 in the small city
of Millau in the Aveyron region that Bové and his comrades from the Confédération Paysanne, a militant organization of French farmers, bulldozed
the construction site of a future McDonald's restaurant to protest a U.S.-
imposed tariff on Roquefort cheese.[1] Sporting a thick handlebar mus-
tache, and thus bearing a strong resemblance to Asterix, the popular French
cartoon hero, José Bové became an instant celebrity in France, propelling
him to the forefront of an emerging international movement against both
the World Trade Organization (WTO) and the introduction of genetically
modified organisms (GMOs) into French agriculture.[2] Everything, from
the company's global reach, its relentless standardization, and the garish
hyperbole of its promotional style to its hyperrationalized labor process—

---

1. Elaine Scolino, "Prison Looms for French Farmer, an Anti-Globalization Gadfly,"
New York Times, November 20, 2002, p. A9; José Bové and François Dufour, *The World Is Not
for Sale: Farmers against Junk Food* (London: Verso, 2001).

2. Wayne Northcutt, "José Bové vs. McDonalds: The Making of a National Hero in the
French Anti-Globalization Movement," *Proceedings of the Western Society for French History*,
vol. 31, 2003, pp. 326–345; Chaia Heller, *Food, Farms and Solidarity: French Farmers Challenge Industrial Agriculture and Genetically Modified Crops* (Durham, NC: Duke University
Press, 2013).

all overseen by a computerized accounting system capable of monitoring worker productivity at each of its cash registers, in each of its restaurants, anywhere on the planet—and its position in a system of industrial agriculture that seemed to threaten small farmers with extinction, recommends McDonald's as the embodiment of American-style neoliberal capitalism. But while the populist drama of a sheep farmer from the Confédération Paysanne fending off the American "Goliath" in a battle at the center of *la France profonde* was a brilliant piece of guerrilla theater, its compellingly simple narrative obscured important elements of the story of McDonald's in France. In this chapter this story is retold with a focus on the genesis of the market for American fast food in France in the 1970s and 1980s and in its relationship to traditional French culinary institutions and practices.

With an emphasis on speed, standardization, and the homogenization of taste, American-style fast food had always been viewed as the direct inverse of French gastronomy. Observers of both French society and of American popular culture had considered France thoroughly resistant to the spread of standardized eating practices generally, and fast food in particular.[3] Fast food, it was thought, would have only a limited appeal in France because "for many French people there is an association that good food is French and fast food is American and foreign and bad," as the sociologist Michel Crozier once told an American journalist.[4] One scholar of popular culture speculated that American fast food would only be successful in France as a comfortable "sanctuary" for American tourists visiting Paris and that the French could not "be expected to act in a culturally appropriate manner at McDonald's."[5] John Ardagh, British journalist and Francophile, expressly noted the poor prospects for the growth of fast food in France: "The French catering industry has never shown much skill at this very American style of packaged operation, so the quality is poor and the public are not interested. The danger, which seemed so real in the late 60's, of a mass invasion of France by this kind of cheap eatery has now mercifully receded. Fast food remains a marginal intruder, appealing mainly to tourists."[6]

3. For example, Anthony Sampson, *The New Europeans* (London: Hodder and Stoughton, 1968), p. 221; Mort Rosenblum, *Mission to Civilize: The French Way* (New York: Doubleday, 1988), pp. 418–419; and Conrad P. Kottak, "Rituals at McDonald's," Marshall Fishwick, *The World of Ronald McDonald* (Bowling Green, OH: Bowling Green University Popular Press, 1983).

4. Steven Greenhouse, "McDonald's Tries Paris, Again," *New York Times*, June 12, 1988, F1.

5. Kottak, "Rituals at McDonald's," pp. 53–54.

6. John Ardagh, *France in the 1980s* (New York: Penguin Books, 1982), p. 413.

When fast-food outlets first appeared in France they were treated as an exotic import; as an American cultural novelty that posed little threat to traditional French foodways. The stance of both guardians of haute cuisine in France and avid supporters of fast food was mostly one of indifference. For example, when asked whether he was concerned that American-style fast food might come to represent a threat to the future and viability of traditional French cuisine, the president of the venerable Académie culinaire de France responded with more indifference than urgency: "I don't know what they do, but I'm sure that their hamburgers are very good and are well prepared. Our cuisine is done differently. We eat different foods. I don't see it [fast-food] as a problem at all. It is a completely different thing."[7]

The president of the Chambre Nationale de la Restauration et de l'Hôtellerie, the main organization of employers in the restaurant and hotel industry, showed a similar lack of concern. When asked if traditional French forms of "fast" food, such as the bistro, would become threatened were American-style fast food to become popular, he conceded that while fast-food restaurants could shave off some business from traditional French bistros, particularly those unwilling to adapt to what he referred to as a more modern image of cleanliness and efficiency, he did not regard the situation as grave: "Fast food and bistros are complementary and the day that they would become the same, one of them would just have to disappear. But we need both the chains that people recognize throughout Europe and we also need the traditional patrimoine [heritage] and as the market evolves we will need to find a balance."[8]

This was similar to that taken by a key representative of the fast-food industry itself. The president of the fast-food employer's federation (and the CEO of a French-owned fast-food chain) noted the dynamism of fast-food outlets, relative to the traditional French bistros, but did not believe that the latter would be supplanted by the former: [9]

Bistros have not changed in a long time. They are typically male environments and with increasing numbers of women at work over

---

7. Author interview with Mon. Michel Malapris, president of the Académie culinaire de France, June 1989.

8. From author interview with M. Alain-Philippe Feutre, president of the Chambre Nationale de la restauration et de l'hôtellerie in June 1989. The word bistro(t) derives from the Russian word "bistroy," meaning fast.

9. Author interview with Laurent Caraux, former president of the Syndicat National de l'Alimentation et de la Restauration Rapide (SNARR), June 1989.

the last twenty years the bistros have not adapted to the new clientele. Women want to do other things during their lunch hour so they look to fast food, which is clean, where smoking is not permitted, where there are no surprises. The long term fate of the bistro? We don't know, and we in the fast food industry have been surprised that they haven't changed, that they're not copying a better image, quality of service, cleanliness. . . . [However] I don't think that 90% of people will be eating in McDonald's twenty years from now.

But two decades later fast-food restaurants were omnipresent in France. McDonald's was the largest private sector employer and the largest restaurant chain in the country, and France was the second most profitable market in the world for McDonald's.[10] While it never became a primary part of the everyday diet for most French people, over the next decades McDonald's would expand faster and more widely in France than anywhere else in Europe, opening more than twelve hundred French outlets, as the golden arches became universally recognized symbols and the fast-food way of eating became an important part of a rapidly changing French culinary landscape. The process by which this occurred is worth attention for what it indicates about the field of French gastronomy and its transformations.

Over the course of the early postwar decades, a broad and varied range of socioeconomic factors had been slowly altering French eating habits and, together, could be seen as providing a social backdrop for the rise of a market for fast food in France. Industry studies and social research identified such factors as the growing number of women in the paid labor force; the increase in spendable income of French adolescents; a weakening of family ties that placed less emphasis on family mealtimes; the expansion of the *journée continue*, or the working day without extended meal breaks; and increasing urban traffic congestion that discouraged workers from traveling home and back for their midday meals.[11] These were factors that permitted not only

---

10. Michael Steinberger, *Au Revoir to All That: Food, Wine, and the End of France* (New York: Bloomsbury, 2009), p. 9.

11. While 80 percent of women between the ages of twenty-five and forty-nine were in the French labor force by 2002, this had risen from 60 percent in 1975, according to *L'Économie française 2003* published by the Observatoire Français des Conjonctures Économiques (Paris: Éditions La Découverte, 2003), pp. 56–57. Other factors were cited in the following accounts: "Mangeurs fin de siècle" by Pascale Pynson and "Le Mangeur solitaire" by Michelle Rigalleau, both in *Nourritures*, ed. Fabrice Piault (Paris: Autrement, 1989); Claude Fischler, *L'Homnivore*

fast food but enabled a host of other changes in French eating practices, creating consumer markets for a range of institutional and industrial food systems. These included the industry of *agro-alimentaire*, a massive corporate agricultural and food-processing industry involved in the production, preparation, and distribution of frozen, processed, and otherwise preprepared foods, as well as the development of systems of institutional catering that located canteens and cafeterias along highways, in workplaces, in schools, and in hospitals.[12] But while such factors may have laid the groundwork for these various forms of "culinary modernization" overall, how was it possible for American-style fast food, and McDonald's in particular, to develop a market and embed itself in a society with such a rich culinary patrimony?

The Emergence of an Industry

Between 1969 and 1972 American chain companies in a variety of service industries (including hotels, commercial cleaning establishments, tax preparation and employment agencies, and fast-food companies) began expanding their operations abroad in response to what were perceived as rising labor costs, saturated domestic markets, and increased competition.[13] As part of this wave of overseas expansion, the McDonald's Corporation introduced its first restaurant outlets in Paris in 1972, which the industry reported as being the first such fast-food chain in the country.[14] But it was

---

(Paris: Editions Odile Jacob, 1990), pp. 175–217 ; as well as in industry sources, such as "Fast Food in France," Special Report No. 2, Economist Publications, 1987, and were traced in the annual reports of the Salon International de la Restauration Rapide, published by the Syndicat National de L'Alimentation et de la Restauration Rapide. For data on trends in working hours and the "journée continue," see Archibald A. Evans, *Hours of Work in Industrialized Countries* (Geneva: International Labour Office, 1975), pp. 83–86.

12. Jacques Bombal and Phillippe Calmin, *L'Agro-alimentaire* (Paris: Presses Universitaires de France, 1980); Fischler, *L'Homnivore*; and for an international survey of the industry, see Alessandro Bonanno, Lawrence Busch, William H. Friedland, Lourdes Gouveia, and Enzo Mingione, eds. *From Columbus to ConAgra: The Globalization of Agriculture and Food* (Lawrence: University Press of Kansas, 1994).

13. Max Boas and Steve Chain, *Big Mac: The Unauthorized Story of McDonald's* (New York: New American Library, 1976), p. 153.

14. The historical record from within the industry has been somewhat fluid, with varying accounts offered up by different players. The chief employer organization, SNARR (Syndicat National de l'Alimentation et de la Restauration Rapide) initially located the first fast food in France as a McDonald's restaurant in Paris in 1972, while the trade magazines *Néo Restauration* and *Revue Technique* indicated that American-style fast food had been introduced a year earlier, by companies that are no longer in business (with names such as Crip-Crop, Dino-Croc, and Chicken Shop). More recent accounts in the McDonald's Annual Reports identified the first McDonald's outlet as being opened in Strasbourg, France, in 1979.

not a particularly smooth landing in France. McDonald's had signed a contract with Raymond Dayan, a local franchisee, for a license to open twelve restaurants under the McDonald's name, with the option of opening many more throughout the Paris region. The license was reportedly offered to Dayan in exchange for royalty payments that were well below the normal McDonald's rate, and it was suggested that Dayan was only offered such favorable terms for his franchises because the company had never expected that its fast-food restaurants would have much success in France.[15] Several years later the company initiated a legal challenge to the French franchisee, contending that Dayan had mismanaged his outlets by allowing the level of cleanliness to drop below the McDonald's standard.[16] The lawsuit was ultimately successful and eventually brought the French franchises back under corporate control. However, during the period that the lawsuit was under way, a stretch of nearly eight years, McDonald's was unable to expand its operations in France. This temporal gap was important because it permitted French companies to open fast-food chains in a completely undeveloped market and to establish the "fast-food formula" in France. Once established it set the stage for a rapid expansion of the fast-food market in the 1980s.

In the initial surge the French fast-food companies tended to exhibit the characteristics of what sociologists call "organizational isomorphism," for between 1972 and 1976 French entrepreneurs opened fast-food hamburger outlets closely modeled on the McDonald's formula.[17] With American-sounding names like Chicken Shop, Dino-Croc, France Quick, FreeTime, Magic Burger, B'Burger, Manhattan Burger, Katy's Burger, Love Burger, and Kiss Burger, these were restaurant businesses that not only sold hamburgers and other American foods produced in assembly line fashion but intentionally packaged, displayed, and marketed them as "American" foods in restaurants whose designs and internal spatial symbolism borrowed heav-

---

15. This was the assessment of industry representatives interviewed by the author in June 1989 (see notes 4 and 5 above), but it was also a view expressed June 30, 2000, by the journalist Bertrand Le Gendre, "McDo Made in France: La restauration rapide à la conquête de l'Hexagone," an article reissued in a compilation published in the magazine, *Le Monde 2*, September 11, 2004, p. 78.

16. Several of the journalists and industry managers interviewed for my earlier study indicated that they thought the McDonald's lawsuit against its French franchisee was very likely a pretext to reclaim franchises that were more successful than the company had anticipated.

17. See Howard Aldrich, *Organizations and Environments* (Englewood Cliffs, NJ: Prentice-Hall, 1979) and Paul DiMaggio and Walter Powell, "The Iron Cage Revisited: Institutional Isomorphism and Collective Rationality in Organizational Fields," *American Sociological Review*, vol. 48, April 1983, pp. 147–160.

ily from the American fast-food model. One industry trade magazine attributed this "strange mimicry" to the "exoticism of the hamburger": "The evolution of fast food in France gives rise to a flowering of signs based on the American model. If this strange mimicry—which only [the fast food] pastries have resisted—is manifested in the burger sector, it is because the product is still for us eminently exotic."[18] Indeed, in the early 1970s pretty much everything about American fast food was exotic for the French, from its products, to its methods of fabrication, to the restaurant spaces where it was sold, to the ways of eating that it entailed. It thus had to be presented to both French producers and French consumers as worth their investments.

Potential French entrepreneurs and investors were introduced to the concept and methodology of fast food in the business press, particularly in the branch of the press specializing in mass food preparation and distribution. The most significant of the trade magazines devoted to introducing, explaining, and promoting the fast-food industry was *Néo Restauration*, its first edition appearing in April 1972, just as the first McDonald's was being constructed in the suburbs southwest of Paris.[19] Thus, in its inaugural edition, *Néo Restauration* described fast food to its readers in the most basic terms:[20]

1. "It is a formula based mainly on the mass phenomenon";
2. "In the United States, fast food is a restaurant";
3. "Where one can eat in, either standing or sitting";
4. "Where one can take a dish away and eat it in the car or at home, or on the grass";
5. "It is sold at a very cheap price (hamburger=1.10 french franc). In fast food, the price is half the cost of a traditional snack-type meal, so there is no discount policy in fast food."[21]

---

18. Quoted from "Ces noms étranges venus d'ailleurs" [These strange names from elsewhere] in *Néorestauration* magazine (no article author), no. 136, March 1984, p. 38. [author translation].

19. While the first fast-food restaurant in France was identified by the chief employer association, SNARR, as the McDonald's outlet that opened in Creteil in June 1972, there had actually been earlier attempts to introduce fast food by French fast-food companies, including Crip Crop (July 1971); Chicken Shop (March 1972); Croq' Minute (May 1972) as documented by *Néo Restauration*, no. 6, October 1972, pp. 102–103. As a student in Paris I recall eating in a Wimpy's, a British fast-food chain on the boulevard Saint Michel in 1970. While the date is not of great concern, it is interesting to note that the industry's version of its history advances an image of "success" by ignoring previous fast-food "failures."

20. *Néo Restauration*, no. 6, p. 27.

21. "Verra-t-on le fast food en France avant 1980?" [Will there be fast food in France by 1980?], *Néo Restauration*, no. 1, April 1972, p. 27. No author listed. The early issues of the magazine (1972–1973) were written as "*Néo Restauration*" with two words in the title.

The article focused on the profit potential of the industry, outlining approximate costs (and expected returns) in owning a fast-food restaurant and offering estimates of infrastructural and investment requirements (for land, building construction, labor costs, merchandise costs, etc.), while underscoring the spectacular growth and profitability of the fast-food market in the United States. Significantly, the magazine made clear to its French readers that fast food was not primarily a gastronomic undertaking but a commercial/industrial one. "Paradoxically, it is not the French restaurateurs who have taken the initiative, but the largest vending [distribution] groups, for whom diversification seems to hold more promise. The distributors are inspired by the Americans: first cautiously, then with application, finally with passion. Indeed, they have been fortunate to be able to read their own future in the pages of a major economic history book, that of the United States."[22]

In a subsequent edition of the same trade magazine, two industry consultants wrote of the labor cost savings to French employers of the American model of fast food, especially in relation to traditional cuisine: "Due to its operational methods a fast food restaurant does not require the presence of a highly qualified chef, whose salary is very high, nor that of other specialized cooks. This is of course an advantage, necessitating a part-time, non-specialized workforce mainly composed of students and housewives."[23]

The organization of the fast-food restaurant took particular forms and required specific food production technologies, most of which were still very unfamiliar to French businessmen. The new technologies were often described and evaluated in articles published in the trade magazines, while the companies supplying technologies for industrial kitchens were prominent advertisers on the pages of those very trade magazines. The magazine *Néo Restauration* published a report in its second edition documenting the "Basic Equipment of a Fast Food Kitchen" that described the five basic machines necessary for a fully automated fast-food restaurant (in 1972). The machinery consisted of a pressure fryer, a breading machine, a special cupboard for preserving foods at correct temperatures, a refrigerator, and

22. "Verra-t-on le fast food," p. 26. And the director of a French fast-food management company was explicit about this, writing: "Fast food is above all an industry and the champion of all categories in this industry is the hamburger, which represents 70 percent of the turnover of fast food, because it is certainly the product that has had the most success and that better corresponds to the industrial norms of operation of this type of restaurant." See William Moore, "Management pour une industrie," *Néorestauration* magazine, no. 112, March 1982, p. 52.

23. R. Halstead and E. von Mayrhofen, "Le Fast Food, oui . . . mais comment réussir?" [Fast food, yes . . . but how to succeed?] in *Néo Restauration*, no. 16, September 1973, p. 14.

a machine for cooking hamburgers.[24] The article included a sketch of the system for dispensing soft drinks and mixing carbonation with flavored syrups, as well as a map of a fast-food kitchen area, indicating where the various machines and furniture would normally be situated. A section "Techniques et Méthodes" subsequently became a regular feature of the magazine.

Marketing practices were still very undeveloped in French industry in the 1970s, and particularly so in the restaurant business, and so in the early stages of the fast-food market the business literature continually stressed the importance of marketing and advertising for establishing and maintaining the market for fast food:[25]

> Fast food is an extremely competitive and therefore very lively activity. Publicity that is well-organized, well-coordinated and original, with an aggressive "marketing image," are not only essential for a particular type of operation, but must be integrated into its life.
>
> It is a form of extremely sophisticated communications and is, in fact, an art. If it is used skillfully, it can motivate people, create needs, influence behavior, change habits, and ultimately determine the characteristics of our society. . . . At the current stage of its development, fast food in Europe faces a double challenge, to introduce into the European market the new concept of the fast food restaurant; as well as its unfamiliar merchandise such as the hamburger, cheeseburger, milkshake, etc.

The model for successful marketing strategies, along with every other element of this emergent industry, was to be found in the United States, where fast-food companies maintained considerable advertising budgets, and where television advertising was a key marketing platform.[26]

In the formative years of the industry in France, *Néorestauration* [as it was called after 1973] and other trade magazines acted in the role of cultural interlocutors, explaining the business concept of fast food to readers and providing a forum to its practitioners.[27] For example, Raymond Dayan, the

---

24. H. Bourcier, "Équipement de base d'une cuisine fast food," *Néo Restauration*, no. 2, May 1972, pp. 41–44.

25. Halstead and von Mayrhofen, "Le Fast Food, oui" p. 14.

26. The annual advertising budgets of the major U.S. fast-food chains were highlighted in "Publicité des chaînes de fast food," *Néo Restauratione*, no. 3, June 1972, pp. 50–51.

27. Other trade magazines promoting the fast-food sector were *Revue technique des hôtels et des restaurants*, which went out of circulation in 1990, and *Resto Flash*, a supplement to the trade magazine, *Hôtellerie* (now *Hôtellerie Restauration*).

first owner of McDonald's franchises in France, was asked in a *Néo Restau-ration* symposium in 1972 about the slow sales of takeaway food:[28]

> Fast food is not known in Europe. The public does not know what it is. We face this problem every time we open a restaurant. Fast service means nothing, it is not easily translated. In our profession the first thing to do is to have an education campaign addressed to the public! For them fast food is not a restaurant, you have to convince them. Second, we must show that fast food is especially designed to sell for take away rather than for consumption on site. If you remember, the USA, when McDonald's began, there were no seats! People came, took, ate in the car, and that was all! Gradually seats were added!

A later edition of the magazine would feature a promotional illustration that had been displayed by the French fast-food company, Chicken Shop, in which its customers were offered a visual demonstration of the process of ordering food to take away from the restaurant (showing cartoon characters taking their food from the restaurant "to eat at home," or "at the office," and "without losing time").[29]

With its $5 million annual advertising budget for television ads and posters, and with the financial clout to obtain the most valuable real estate locations in the largest cities for its restaurant sites, McDonald's was always the most visible fast-food company in France, and this even when 80 percent of the fast-food hamburger restaurants in France were still largely owned by French firms.[30] Real estate was a key marketing strategy because streets with a steady stream of pedestrian traffic would ensure large num-

28. "Le Fast Food: réalité ou encore incertitude?" [Fast food: reality or uncertainty?] *Néo Restauration*, no. 6, October 1972, p. 105.

29. Under the heading "Techniques and Mèthodes," the article, by D. Majonchi was entitled "Chicken Shop: Le fast food français à l'américaine," *Néorestauration*, no. 86, January 1980, p. 23

30. McDonald's advertising figure from *Marketing in Europe* no. 296, Economist Publications, July 1987, p. 48. As late as 1989, French firms owned 618 of the 777 hamburger fast-food restaurants in France, according to "La Restauration Rapide en France" in *Revue technique des hôtels et restaurants*, no. 473, March 1989, pp. 98–107.

bers of customers and also associate the company brand with central sites of cultural and historical significance.[31]

By 1976, several French companies had begun to apply the fast-food model to traditional French food products, mostly baked goods like brioche, croissants, sandwiches on baguettes, and pastries. Called *"viennoiseries,"* they were modeled after the hamburger restaurants to the extent that they were chain establishments (two or more businesses at separate locations with a common ownership) that sold at a counter low-cost, packaged food items that were meant to be consumed in place or taken away. But as with all chain establishments it meant a more or less rigid degree of standardization in their production systems, marketing strategies, and restaurant designs.[32] The viennoiseries sold traditional French foods under brand names designed to retain a French identity, the most prominent being La Brioche Dorée, Aubépain, La Croissanterie, and Pomme de Pain. France was one of the very few European countries that responded to the expansion of American fast food by adapting traditional national foods to the fast-food formula.

Once McDonald's was free of its legal entanglements and it regained control of its French franchises, it began a program of rapid growth on the French market, expanding from its 15 restaurants in 1983 to 150 in 1990 to 353 in 1994 and beyond (see Figure 3.1). This rate of expansion required considerable investment in real estate and advertising, and this posed a problem for the newer and smaller French firms to enter, grow, and retain a place in the market. The situation prompted a process of concentration within the French fast-food industry, with the acquisition, merger, or parceling of many independent companies with one of the larger corporate "groups" in the food industry.[33] Over the course of the 1980s these large groups, relying on the financial resources provided by their basic or historical position in either food processing, commercial catering, or hotel chains, moved to diversify by entering (from a horizontal or vertical position, and

---

31. When McDonald's expanded its operations in France, after 1982, it located its restaurants in the most important sites in Paris and in the downtown centers of the largest cities (Lyon, Marseille, Bordeaux, Toulouse, etc.).

32. See D. D. Wyckoff and W. E. Sasser, *The Chain Restaurant Industry* (Lexington, MA: Lexington Books, 1978).

33. An editorial in the trade weekly *L'Hôtellerie* pointed out that the requirements of competition, heavy investment, labor intensivity, shrinking profit margins, and the pressures of international expansion were factors that increasingly reserved the fast-food sector exclusively for the largest industrial groups. See *"Rapidité oblige"* in *L'Hôtellerie*, no. 2214, July 4, 1991, p. 32.

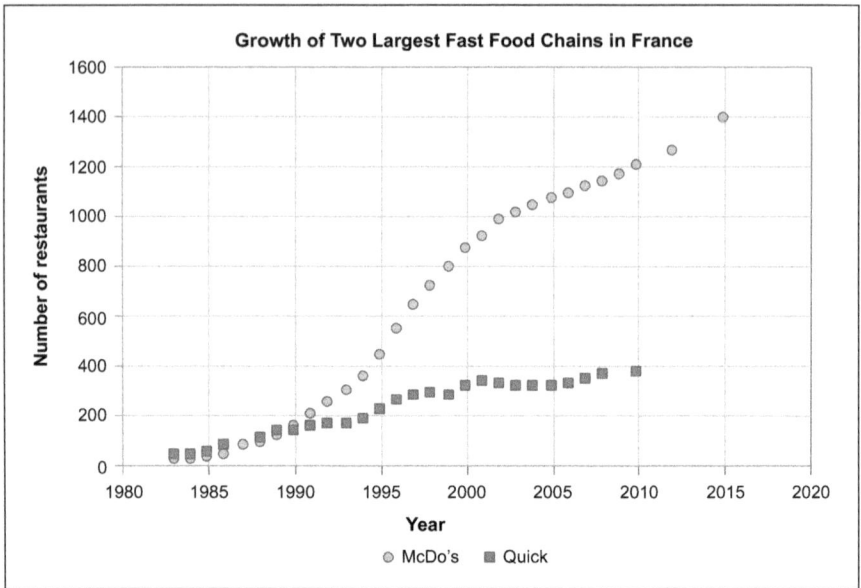

Figure 3.1 Growth of Two Largest Fast Food Chains in France

largely through mergers, acquisitions, and joint ventures) various catering markets.[34] So the development of the fast-food industry in France occurred as part of a more general "oligopolization" of the food-processing and catering industries.

Within just a few years, most of the French fast-food chains were absorbed into one or another of the larger commercial restaurant groups, providing them with a stronger financial structure in which to operate and compete with the much larger and more heavily capitalized American fast-food firms, particularly McDonald's. Ironically, when the fast-food industry developed in the United States, the ideology of the small entrepreneur and "democratic capitalism" were central features of the industries' self-definition. Ray Kroc, the founder of McDonald's, was a heroic figure in the business press

---

34. For example, 132 Quick Burger and Freetime hamburger restaurants were absorbed into the Casino Group, a food conglomerate whose restaurant division had a turnover rate (*chiffre d'affaires*) in 1990 of $700 million. Similarly, ACCOR, an industry group with over 250 various catering establishments, absorbed a great variety of fast-food restaurants; and Group Le Duff acquired 109 fast-food restaurants. See D. Goodman and R. Rama, "Socio-Economic and Technological Developments in the European Catering Industry: Evidence from the United Kingdom, Spain, and France," published by the Directorate for Science, Research and Development, Commission of the European Communities, no. 143, February 1987, Brussels.

where he was portrayed (and portrayed himself) as the personification of the "self-made millionaire."[35] Figuring prominently in American business folklore, Kroc started out as a traveling salesman—selling Florida real estate, paper cups, and the six-pronged Multimixer milkshake beater—and consequently spent two decades traveling the country and observing the growth of convenience foods and their production systems. In 1954, Kroc bought the McDonald's name from two brothers who had run a successful group of roadside hamburger stands in Southern California, with a plan to develop an assembly line system of inexpensive hamburger restaurants and to sell franchise rights to those willing to buy the use of the name, the methods, and the marketing process. Within four years, Kroc was opening his one hundredth restaurant.

The franchise system of distribution and ownership provided a strong impetus to the growth of the industry in the United States. The "franchise" (whose root is the Old French word *francher*, meaning "to free" from servitude) was a method of dispensing merchandise only to licensed distributors that afforded rapid growth and penetration into a market by relying "on the capital or borrowing capacity of the franchisee, as well as the franchisee's knowledge of local markets and real estate situations"[36] It expanded rapidly in the 1950s as a reaction to corporate growth, for the franchise seemed to be "the last frontier of the independent businessman," and Ray Kroc, with his legendary promotional zeal, sold the franchised drive-in restaurant as "the answer to an American dream . . . we're teaching people how to become successful small businessmen"[37] In the Cold War context, franchising thus created the appearance of an opening for newly "enfranchised" small entrepreneurs and furnished a timely ideological message of individualism, free enterprise, and entrepreneurial capitalism.

However, franchising was *not* the predominant method of distribution for fast-food chains in France. Of the nine largest fast-food chains operating in 1990 only one company, Manhattan Burger, had a higher percentage of

35. The image of Ray Kroc and of his business were cultivated in industry sources like the following: "Mirror, mirror on the wall," *Forbes*, no. 106, November 1970, p. 21; "For Ray Kroc, Life Began at 50, Or Was It 60?" *Forbes*, no. 111, January 15, 1973, pp. 24–30; "I'm the Hamburger Man" (interview) in *Institutions/Volume Feeding Magazine*, no. 71, September 15, 1972, pp. 73–88; "Appealing to a Mass Market" (interview), *Nation's Business*, no. 56, July 1968, pp. 70–74; and see the autobiography of Ray Kroc, written with R. Anderson, *Grinding It Out* (Chicago: Henry Regnery, 1977).

36. Wyckoff and Sasser, *Chain Restaurant Industry*, p. lviii.

37. Boas and Chain, *Big Mac*, pp. 130–133.

TABLE 3.1 FRANCHISED FAST-FOOD RESTAURANTS
IN FRANCE (1990)

Company	No. Franchised Units	No. Total Units	% Franchised Units
McDonald's	105	150	70.0
Quick	19	132	14.4
La Brioche Doree	18	109	16.5
Manhattan Burger	10	13	76.9
Pomme de Pain	5	36	13.9
Aubepain	4	17	23.5
Burger King France	4	22	18.2
La Croissanterie*	0	89	0
La Viennoiserie*	0	47	0

*Drawn from 1988 data published in *Revue Technique des Hôtels et Restaurants*, no. 473, March 1989.
Source: Figures extracted from 1990 franchising figures for commercial restaurants, published in *Revue Technique des hôtels et restaurants*, "Dossier restauration commerciale," no. 496, March 1991.

franchised outlets than McDonald's, and this was on a much smaller base of operations (see Table 3.1). Generally, as McDonald's expanded in the French market, it sold franchises to its restaurants in the provinces, while retaining as company-owned enterprises its less risky outlets in the Paris region, and so the percentage of franchised restaurants increased.[38]

Early on in its development then, the French fast-food industry was drawn into the vortex of established (and developing) industrial conglomerates. It was thus not accompanied by, nor was there much of a structural basis for, the kind of ideological representations that had been advanced in the United States. But while an ideology of "rags to riches" mobility may not have been as firmly attached to the industry in France, it provided opportunities for labor exploitation that were extremely attractive to French entrepreneurs.

The Promise of Labor Control

The development of the fast-food market brought a variety of innovations to the French service sector, not least of which was a proven method of controlling labor and cheapening its cost as the basis of a mass market for restaurants. Unsurprisingly, proindustry accounts of the fast-food phenom-

---

38. Data on McDonald's franchise restaurants in 1999 indicated that 85 percent of its 720 restaurants were franchises, a figure up from 70 percent in 1990. See T. Royle, *Working for McDonald's in Europe: The Unequal Struggle?* (London: Routledge, 2000), p. 31.

enon rarely referred to the hyperrationalization of labor in considering the "pioneering service innovations" of the industry, focusing instead on the consumer experience of "service" and thus enacting the radical dislocation between consumption and production that has been a key symbolic attribute of societies subjected to neoliberal transformation.[39] So, for example, the main industry account of McDonald's noted that as the company expanded abroad, it was "exporting America's well-developed systems for conveniently serving consumer needs," and that in Europe it was creating a mass market for restaurants where "there were virtually no family restaurants, and thus for the middle class eating out was always a special occasion."[40] But what such accounts fail to mention is the production process upon which "mass markets" are based.

Just as the market for fast food was being created in France, one analyst explained that the technological rationality of a McDonald's outlet was so well-developed that it required just fifteen minutes for McDonald's to train a new worker, who could then achieve maximum efficiency in one half-hour, making it "economically feasible to use a kid for one day and replace him with another kid the next day."[41] Such a degree of routinization was the result of a range of innovations designed to minimize human judgment in the preparation of the product. Fast food was prepared with the use of timing mechanisms, beeping signals, premeasured quantities, and computers submerged in the cooking oil to enable frying foods to uniform specifications. In place of the numbers of a cash register, keys were labeled with the abbreviated names of items ("lge. fries," "big mac," "med coke," etc.), making it unnecessary for the cashier to know the actual price of any item, while the machines were programmed to automatically remind workers to suggest dessert or other items to the customer who has not ordered it.[42] The overall accounting system of a McDonald's restaurant was so computerized that it allowed managers "to determine immediately not only the dollar volume for the store, but the amount of each item that was sold at each register for any given period."[43] The fast-food labor process combined the application of contemporary computer technology to "Taylorism," the systematic separation of the mental from the

---

39. See R. Fantasia, "Dictature *sur* le prolétariat: Stratégies de répression et travail aux États-Unis," *Actes de la recherche en sciences sociales*, vol. 138, June 2001, pp. 3–18.

40. J. Love, *McDonald's: Behind the Arches* (New York: Bantam Books, 1986), pp. 417–419.

41. B. Garson, *The Electronic Sweatshop* (New York: Simon and Schuster, 1988), p. 21.

42. See R. Leidner, *Fast Food, Fast Talk: Service Work and Routinization of Everyday Life* (Berkeley: University of California Press, 1993).

43. B. Garson, *Electronic Sweatshop*, p. 28.

manual components of the labor process. For French entrepreneurs it offered service sector managers the ability to deploy labor as flexibly and as cheaply as possible, while providing the means to effectively monitor its productivity. A 1982 management guide to opening a fast-food outlet in France strongly recommended a level of computerization comparable to that employed by McDonald's, and a systematic study of the labor process at France Quick, which was (and continues to be) the second largest hamburger fast-food company in France, reported a comparable level of computer rationalization, indicating that all of the leading French-owned companies had aspired to replicate the McDonald's system.[44]

In addition to technological innovations, American fast-food companies brought a virulent antiunionism to the French service sector. It was a position cultivated in the United States by the McDonald's Corporation's deep and explicit antipathy toward unions, a stance expressed openly by the chief of labor relations at McDonald's three decades ago when he asserted "unions are inimical to what we stand for and how we operate," and who acknowledged that McDonald's maintained "a powerful union resistance movement. . . . As a result, McDonald's stores today are strictly nonunion shops."[45] In France, which has been organized with a different system of labor relations, McDonald's had entered a society where unions were still largely accepted, where they had fairly deep institutional roots, and where their institutional impact was broader than in the United States, and particularly so in the service sector.[46] Consequently, even though few fast-food workers were union members in France during the first two decades of the industry, they enjoyed more protection than did fast-food workers in the United States. In France, most fast-food companies, and thus most fast-food workers, including workers at McDonald's, were automatically included in a national collective agreement under the name of the employer association, SNARR (Syndicat National de l'Alimentation et de la Restauration Rapide) with three main French trade union groups. The agreement concerned wages

---

44. See Y. Van De Calseyde, *Ouvrir un Fast Food* (Paris: Editions B.P.I., 1982), pp. 90–92; and H. Bovais, "Analyse stratégique d'un fast food," unpublished Mémoire de Maîtrise, Paris 1987.

45. Quoted in J. Love, *McDonald's: Behind the Arches*, p. 397. It is a statement as true today as it was in 1986.

46. The different ways in which unions are embedded in the United States and in France are outlined in R. Fantasia and K. Voss, *Hard Work: Remaking the American Labor Movement* (Berkeley: University of California Press, 2004), esp. chap. 1. [This is an enlarged edition of R. Fantasia and K. Voss, *Des syndicats domestiques* (Paris: Raisons d'Agir Éditions, 2003).]

and working conditions and included much of what might be contained in the collective bargaining agreement between an individual company and a union in the United States. During its first fifteen years in France, McDonald's policy in the employer's organization was to refuse to recognize the trade unions.[47] Only after a series of well-publicized labor struggles in France in the 1990s did McDonald's join the employer's association, soon becoming president, and the company eventually agreed with the unions to establish several joint works councils (*comité d'entreprise*), moves viewed by critics as mostly cosmetic and resulting in few concrete gains for most fast-food workers.[48] At the same time, with a higher statutory minimum wage than in the United States, the wage rates of French McDonald's workers were roughly 63 percent of the average French wage in the 1990s, as against 36.7 percent in the United States.[49]

With the rise of the industry in France, companies relied on a workforce that was heavily part-time and contingent, following in the assessment of one analyst that "part time and temporary working is central to the way in which fast-food companies operate."[50] A 1987 European Union study of the European catering industry predicted that the increasing penetration of the fast-food industry was on track to "accelerate the substitution of labour intensive craft-based food preparation by industrialised mass production methods," and that "occupational structures will become increasingly characterized by unskilled, low paid, part-time jobs with high rates of turnover."[51] Although it is difficult to discern the independent effects of the fast-food industry on these rates, between 1971 and 1988 the part-time labor force in France nearly doubled, reaching almost a quarter of the female

47. As one official of the French union CFDT asserted, "The company has a resistance to unions that is incredible." See Royle, *Working for McDonald's in Europe*, p. 103.

48. McDonald's went on to sign company agreements with the unions (in addition to the industry's sectoral agreement), and out of this have developed the establishment of several works councils (although some union representatives viewed this as more of a public relations exercise rather than a change in the company's employment or labor relations policies). See Royle, *Working for McDonald's in Europe*, pp. 104, 134–138.

49. See table comparing McDonald's gross wages and average gross wages in fourteen European countries for 1998 in Royle, *Working for McDonald's in Europe*, p. 157.

50. Royle, *Working for McDonald's in Europe*, p. 72. In a published guide to opening a fast-food restaurant in France, the author obliquely advised potential investors, "Of course there are a number of people working part-time, a situation that can affect 40% or 60% of staff." See Van De Calseyde, *Ouvrir un Fast Food*, p. 74.

51. Goodman and Rama, "Socio-Economic and Technological Developments," p. 49.

labor force.[52] It tended to be French-owned hamburger chains that hired part-time labor to a much greater degree than viennoiseries, pizza places, or other types of fast-food chains operated by French firms. This suggests that the "organizational isomorphism," which was being applied to production systems and marketing strategies, was also being extended to labor allocation.[53] A recruitment hand flyer obtained at the opening of a new McDonald's restaurant in eastern France in 1991 noted explicitly some of the characteristics of the labor force that was being recruited. It read: "If you are between 16 to 25 years old," "We are proposing: Part-time employment with hours adaptable to your availability" and listing among the potential benefits "the possibility of continuing your studies while working." The hamburger chains that dominated the French fast-food industry from the beginning seemed to serve as the vehicles for fashioning an "American-style" labor force of young, flexible workers, to go along with the "American" system of labor control in the restaurants.[54]

The Social Space of Fast Food

Before the fast-food industry took off in the 1980s, the hamburger was largely considered a novelty in France, sold at such fashionable places as

52. In 1988, 23.8 percent of women workers and 3.4 percent of male workers were working part time, both figures that had nearly doubled since 1971, according to data reported in M. Forse et al. *Recent Social Trends in France, 1966–1990* (Montréal: McGill-Queen's University Press, 1993), p. 111.

53. A 1982 industry survey found that 49 percent of the employees of the hamburger chains were part-time, but only 20 percent of workers in viennoiseries, 14 percent in pizzerias, and 10 percent in fast-food sandwich shops. From: "La Carte 82 de la Restauration Rapide," in *Néorestauration*, no. 118, October 1982, pp. 25–36 (no author listed). Although the proportions may have risen throughout the industry in subsequent years, in 1982 McDonald's was not yet dominant in the French market, suggesting that the "flexibility" made possible by part-time labor may have been partly modeled on the success of the American fast-food industry.

54. In the nineteen fast-food restaurants visited for this study in 1991, about 90 percent of the workers on duty were under twenty-five years old, with an average age of about twenty. The managerial staff generally seemed older, roughly thirty to thirty-five years. These estimates are fairly close to the data offered on the workforce at France Quick in a study conducted several years earlier. There, the average age of the workforce was twenty-one years old, and the managerial staff between twenty-six and twenty-eight years old. Students were favored by management because they were seen as "more available" to work varied hours and to take part-time hours, while the unemployed were less favored because of the view that "they demand too many hours and then when they find something better they go." Still, the average length of employment was reported to be just three months at that restaurant. See Bovais, "Analyse stratégique d'un fast food," p. 4.

Le Drugstore on the Champs-Élysées, an object of "snob appeal and well-filled pocketbooks . . . the favorite of the smart set, from Vatican ambassadors to movie stars."[55] And as late as 1979 a restaurant-industry trade magazine could still write that "fast food remains a purely American product, something new, somewhat snobby and very Parisian, so much so that the last fashion show by Daniel Hechter included a buffet catered by McDonald's."[56] Although hamburgers and high fashion might seem incongruous to Americans and to the French today, in France of the 1970s it represented a "taste of the other" as a prominent French journalist put it, somewhat exotic and mildly transgressive, an attempt at a reverse snobbery in response to what Jean Baudrillard characterized as the "sickly cultural pathos," and the "fetishism of the cultural heritage" of the old France.[57] The perceived American culinary taste for simplicity and informality were regarded as trendy and fashionable in France because for several decades "American" styles and methods of modernization had been promoted as innovative and cutting edge. For those whose ambitions or actual social position were grounded in certain spheres of social and economic life, things associated with the most "modern" trends tended to hold great appeal.[58] It was a cultural orientation personified by the postwar formation of a "new bourgeoisie" of professional managers, not bound by the traditional values of the old families, whose manners were "a mixture of the asceticism of the partisan fighter and easy-going 'American-style' simplicity."[59] These "young wolves" as Boltanski termed them, were less bound to tradition and the classical bourgeois manners of the "old lions" of heavy industry, and were increasingly schooled in the techniques of marketing, advertising, and the needs of a globalizing market, distinguishing themselves through a "rhetoric of technocracy and the 'new-bourgeois' lifestyle, associated at work with internationalism—the executive with the briefcase at the airport and at home with 'light' food, 'modern' furniture and a passion for films

55. Quoted in Boas and Chain, *Big Mac*, pp. 154–155.

56. "Fast food, l'an de la réussite," in *Néorestauration*, March 1979.

57. The journalist Pau Moreira, quoted in "Les aventuriers du goût méconnu," in *Nourritures*, ed. F. Piault (Paris: Autrement, 1989); and J. Baudrillard, *America* (London: Verso, 1988), p. 100.

58. See, for example, I. M. Wall, *The United States and the Making of Postwar France 1945–1954* (Cambridge: Cambridge University Press, 1991); and L. Boltanski, *The Making of a Class: Cadres in French Society* (Cambridge: Cambridge University Press, 1987); and see P. Bourdieu, *Distinction: A Social Critique of the Judgement of Taste* (Cambridge, MA: Harvard University Press, 1984).

59. Boltanski, *Making of a Class*, p. 106.

rather than opera."[60] This is not to assert that French managers were necessarily the primary consumers of fast food but merely to suggest that the "break" with traditional cultural practices that was under way was bound up with American forms of modernization generally, offering a cultural and aesthetic "script" (from a "universe of stylistic possibilities") through which traditional bourgeois lifestyles were being reframed.[61] A degree of social legitimacy was thus conferred on those lifestyle practices (including eating) that could be regarded as "new" and as "American." Ironically, just as the new bourgeoisie were symbolically turning away from traditional haute cuisine in France, the middle and upper classes in the United States were increasingly turning toward "continental cuisine" as a mark of distinction. As one analyst noted of the United States, "By the late 1960s, and early 1970s, from Bangor to San Diego, cities whose finer restaurants had been endless variations of the steak, lobster, and roast beef theme began to sprout restaurants called L'Auberge"; or restaurants generically labeled "continental" or "European" and which were dubbed "Maison de la Casa House" by the humorist Calvin Trillin.[62]

As the market for fast food took form in France, who actually were the "*fastfoudeurs*," (as industry trade magazines sometimes referred to consumers of fast food)? Although the categories employed were rough ones, figures drawn from marketing studies and reports produced at two points in the 1980s indicate that there were some fairly clear social differences in the consumption of fast food (see Table 3.2). Marketing studies commissioned by the fast-food employers association, SNARR in 1986 and 1989 grouped senior managers, industrialists, and professionals into a single category.[63]

60. Boltanski, *Making of a Class*, p. 106. Also see J. Marceau, "France," in *The Capitalist Class: An International Study*, ed. T. Bottomore and R. J. Brym (New York: New York University Press, 1989), p. 64; and P. Bourdieu, L. Boltanski, and M. de St. Martin "Les stratégies de reconversion," *Information sur les Sciences Sociales*, no. 12, 1973, pp. 61–113.

61. In Bourdieu's terms, the stylistic possibilities available across the field of gastronomic practices will tend to cohere with the dispositions of the habitus of the class fraction under analysis. In this case, the French "new bourgeoisie" of executives in the more dynamic commercial industries were predisposed to the new and less encumbered forms of eating. See Bourdieu, *Distinction*, p. 208.

62. H. Levenstein, *Revolution at the Table* (New York: Oxford University Press, 1988); C. Trillin, *American Fried* (New York: Vintage Books, 1979).

63. The marketing studies drawn upon were a 1983 study produced by a private marketing firm that was based on an exit survey of one thousand consumers in eight French cities, as well as an opinion poll, reportedly of a random, representative national sample of two thousand persons, *"La Restauration Rapide"* (Paris: Marketing Office, 1984). Two later surveys (1986 and 1989) were commissioned for the fast-food trade association, SNARR (Syndicat National

This grouping of occupational elites made up only 8 percent and 7 percent of fast-food customers in 1986 and 1989, respectively, while manual workers constituted only 5 percent and 2 percent, respectively, though manual workers (*ouvriers*) were at least 40 percent of the French labor force at the time. So in general terms fast-food restaurants were inhabited by neither proletarians nor the bourgeoisie in the first years of their operation in France. Like the boundary between manual workers and clerical and commercial employees that Bourdieu discovered with regard to general food consumption practices in France, there became an evident boundary between white-collar employees and manual workers in relation to the consumption of fast food as well.[64] White-collar workers ("*employés*") made up the largest percentage of fast-food customers in 1989, at 32 percent while constituting just 21 percent of the labor force. While the traditionalist tastes of manual workers certainly might have been a factor in these differences, fast food may not have been a clear point of departure for the expression of class differences in any event, for in the early stages of the fast-food market the restaurants were neither near factories nor working-class neighborhoods. Initially, fast-food restaurants were spatially concentrated in the downtown centers of the larger French cities, where those who worked in offices, banks, and retail stores had easy access during lunch periods, while those manual workers employed in factories and large industrial sites would have been more likely to eat in (subsidized) company cafeterias. So space relations and social space were likely overlaid in ways that are not easily disentangled, and when middle managers and self-employed artisans (who together represented 19 percent of fast-food consumers) were added to the category of white-collar employees, the result was a large urban workforce that accounted for half of all fast-food consumers.

During the period that fast food was being introduced into France, there were clear differences between men and women consumers, but the data available suggest that it was in flux. Between 1986 and 1989, 5 percent more men and 5 percent fewer women were reported as having eaten in fast-food restaurants overall, while the gendered character of the market for the two broad kinds of fast-food establishments became somewhat less pronounced (see Table 3.2). The viennoiseries, selling traditional French items, such as sweet pastries and croissants in chain restaurants embodying

---

de l'Alimentation et de la Restauration Rapide) and were based on surveys of one thousand consumers in fast-food restaurants in Paris and Lyon.

64. Bourdieu, *Distinction*, p. 180.

TABLE 3.2 PROFILE OF FRENCH FAST-FOOD CONSUMERS
(1986/1989)

	Overall Fast Food (%)[†]	Hamburger Fast Food (%)	Viennoiseries (%)
A. Occupational category (% of work-force):			
Senior managers, industrialists, professionals (8.7%)	8/7	9/6	6/9
Middle managers, artisans (16.4%)	18/19	20/20	16/17
White collar employees (21.2%)	30/32	18/26	35/39
Manual workers (42.4%)	5/2	7/3	3/2
Retired, unemployed*	–/8	–/6	–/12
Students*	–/32	–/40	–/19
Farmers/farm laborers	1/0	1/0	0/0
B. Gender:			
Men	44/49	60/56	29/41
Women	56/51	40/44	71/59

*Categories employed in 1989 study only.
[†]Slash is between values for 1986 on left and 1989 on right.
Source: Marketing data derived from studies commissioned by SNARR for the 1986 and 1989 fast-food exhibitions, "Salon de la restauration rapide," Paris; labor force data is from "L'Évolution des effectifs salariés en France depuis 1954," *Problèmes Économiques*, no. 2088, August 31, 1988, pp. 2–7 (no author listed). Percentages of occupational categories are incomplete because portions of labor force data are compatible only with the categories used in these marketing studies.

many elements of the fast-food formula (food sold at a counter, to be taken out or eaten on the premises, employing standardized baking processes, high lighting levels, large and brightly colored menu displays, etc.) had a very high female to male clientele ratio of 71:29 in 1986, which dropped to 59:41 in the 1989 study. It was suggested that a key reason that viennoiseries were initially "gendered" in this way had to do with the fact that traditional cafés, particularly those in local residential neighborhoods (rather than on large boulevards of the major cities) were largely male preserves and not particularly welcoming to women, while the new viennoiseries were regarded as cleaner, brighter, and safer environment for women.[65]

Equally or perhaps even more significant than gender and occupational/class divisions was age as a social factor characterizing the consumer base of

---

65. This was the view put forward by two representatives of the Fédération Nationale de L'Industrie Hôtelière, a trade association representing café owners, restaurateurs, and hoteliers. Interviews in June 1989 in Paris.

fast food during its formative period. A marketing study conducted for the fast-food employers association in 1986 found that 59 percent of all the paying fast-food customers were under the age of twenty-four, while 81 percent of customers were under thirty-four years of age.[66] As a growing market, it was in some flux, and by the 1989 study the percentages had slipped somewhat, to 50 percent of consumers under twenty-four years old and 78 percent under thirty-four years (see Table 3.3). Still, the fast-food market was a youth market in France. This was particularly evident for hamburger restaurants, where 83 percent of customers were under thirty-four years of age and 57 percent were under twenty-four years (in contrast to the viennoiseries, where the percentage were somewhat less pronounced (at 72 percent and 42 percent, respectively). These differences were probably due to the fact that when the fast-food formula was adapted to traditional French foods they were considered less authentic to adolescents who were seeking an authentic American food experience. Focus group interviews with French lycée students in 1991 indicated that while "McDonald's" and "fast food hamburger restaurants" were viewed as distinctly American cultural products, viennoiseries did not have nearly the same degree of cultural appeal.[67] So when queried about their experiences of eating at fast-food outlets, none of the forty-eight students (in nine focus groups) offered the example of or even mentioned viennoiseries as a form of fast food or as a fast-food restaurant. This was similar to the invisibility that marketing studies found with regard to the "image of fast food." As part of a larger study of the fast-food market, industry sources found that in the mind of French consumers, "the viennoiserie occupies a place apart" and that "in sum, the viennoiserie is not considered the same as the concept of fast food."[68]

---

66. "Fastfoudeurs, qui êtes-vous en 1986?" a study commissioned for the Fifth Salon de la Restauration Rapide, by SNARR (Syndicat National de l'Alimentation et de la Restauration Rapide) in 1986.

67. The author conducted focus groups with students between the ages of sixteen and eighteen in May 1991 at the Lycée des Glières in Annemasse and Lycée de la Versoie in Thonon-les-Bains, two small cities in eastern France. Nine groups of four or five students each were asked to say which commodities (or categories of commodities) they considered to be distinctly "American" things, and only those commodities that all the members of each group could agree upon were listed. All the members of eight of the nine groups agreed that "McDonald's" or "fast food hamburger places" (both terms were employed interchangeably) were specifically "American things or commodities." No other commodity or category received as clear an identification as "American."

68. "Fastfoudeurs, qui êtes-vous en 1986?" commissioned for the Fifth Salon de la Restauration Rapide by SNARR.

TABLE 3.3 PROFILE OF FRENCH FAST-FOOD CONSUMERS BY AGE (1989)

Age	Overall Fast Food (%)	Hamburger Fast Food (%)	Viennoiseries (%)
Under 18	5	7	3
18–20	18	21	13
21–24	27	29	26
25–34	28	26	30
35–44	12	11	13
45–54	4	2	7
Over 55	6	4	9

Source: Data from marketing survey commissioned by SNARR for the 1989 "Salon International de la Restauration Rapide," Paris.

Certainly, a part of the reason that both young adults and white-collar workers frequented fast-food restaurants was that they were inexpensive relative to traditional restaurants. In the mid-1980s the average price of a meal in a fast-food hamburger restaurant was about half the price of a plat du jour in a café or brasserie, while the cost of a meal in a pizzeria was about a quarter or less the price of a meal in a "good restaurant" (a one "toque" restaurant, not a four "toque" luxury restaurant).[69] In other words, that those *under* eighteen frequented fast-food restaurants less than those *over* eighteen was largely a function of their spendable income, which for those between fifteen and eighteen years amounted to an average of just $30 per month (in 1991), while students between eighteen and twenty-four years old had between $200 and $400 per month and young workers of the same age had from $400 to $1600 per month of spendable income.[70] At first glance this might seem to simply reflect a "taste for the necessary," which is never a simple matter in any case, but to understand the "impossible" rise of a market for fast food in France requires analytical attention to the symbolic representations embodied in fast-food consumption, where the taste for fast food was a retranslation of the "taste" for a certain lifestyle.

---

69. One "toque" was the lowest ranking by *Gault&Millau* magazine, designating restaurants that were not particularly expensive but that served what the magazine considered to be good meals, worthy of mention. Prices of fast-food meals were surveyed in the trade magazine, *Revue Technique des hôtels et restaurants*, no. 473, March 1989, p. 100, and in "Les fastfoudeurs se mettent à table," a marketing study produced for the Eighth Salon International de la Restauration Rapide by SNARR in 1989.

70. V. Lecasble, "Ils pèsent 400 milliards de francs," in *L'Évènement du Jeudi*, June 6–12, 1991, p. 100.

The Taste of Americanism

In their marketing strategies, fast-food companies sought to figure out which sectors of the population would be most inclined to eat in their establishments, and that largely meant those who were predisposed to breaking with tradition and trying new things. The category "*décalé*" (meaning "offbeat" or "shifting") was used to refer to forward-looking "cultural rebels" whose tastes in cultural goods would tend to diverge from dominant cultural patterns.[71] A concept derived without analytical rigor as a sort of ersatz sociology, an industry source nevertheless estimated "*décalage*" to encompass 20 percent of the population, a group denoting young, affluent, urban dwellers who were "studying beyond the bac" or who had recently completed their studies. Described as being "level-headed and prudent in appearance" while "their conformity masks a deep psychological marginality. . . . With their rejection of tradition, and their search for novelty at any price, most of the new products target the *décalé* through a media that strongly resembles them in style."[72] For an industry whose future depended, to a considerable degree, on a population willing to break with traditional habits and conceptions about restaurants, a marketing strategy oriented toward "youth as decalage" necessitated that fast food be marketed in a way that encouraged the transgression of traditional cultural forms. The president of the fast-food employer's association emphasized that when fast food was first introduced in Paris it was especially "popular among the young as an expression of rebelliousness" and that "those Parisians who were drawn to it on that basis then are now having children and are not bound to traditional ways . . . in the 1980s fast food has made inroads in the provinces, and here [again] it is the young people who are the main customers."[73]

In the realm of fashion and lifestyle, "décalage" was often closely bound up with images of the United States, a society viewed in France and everywhere, both positively and negatively, as the embodiment of the future. In the 1980s those who consumed fast food were the younger sisters and brothers (and increasingly the children) of the 1968 generation who had been in

---

71. The term derived from *décaler*, meaning "to bring forward," and was posed against "*recentré*" (meaning "refocused"), which the marketing literature employed to refer to those with conservative cultural tastes, "*valeurs stables*" ("stable values").

72. Quotation from "La restauration rapide en France: 725 units en 1983," *Revue Technique des Hôtels et Restaurants*, March 1984, p. 98.

73. Quote from an interview in Paris in June 1989 with Laurent Carraux, who was president of SNARR.

active revolt against French Algeria, U.S. imperialism, police repression, and bureaucratization of work and school. This was a generation of post-1968 cultural "rebels" who, in the 1970s and 1980s were increasingly drawn to American cultural iconography in the form of dress, music, slang, film, and television. They often eschewed traditional French cultural codes in favor of James Dean posters, T-shirts, sneakers, and American television and rock and roll, thereby offering a sardonic reply to the revolutionary graffiti of May 1968: *"Êtes-vous des consommateurs ou bien des participants?"*[74] In 1991 French lycée students were asked, in focus groups, why they thought many young people in France had seemed to adopt American styles of dress (blue jeans, sneakers, sweatshirts, baseball caps, etc.), and they responded in terms of the cultural texturing, saying: "it is loose-fitting, casual clothing"; "it isn't serious clothing"; "the clothing is more fun, it is very colorful and relaxed"; "the clothing is a fantasy."[75] Their characterizations centered on the playfulness, informality, and relaxed (*"décontracté"*) style, in contrast to traditional French styles, which they viewed as "too expensive and not for young people" and asserting that "we prefer something different, something new, modern, and different." In general, their stylistic outlook on clothing closely approximated their relationship to eating in fast-food restaurants.

All restaurants are sites of ritualized behavior where one finds, as in all rituals, "highly stylized, repetitive, stereotyped events, occurring in special places, including costumes and set sequences of words and actions."[76] As the market was being established the rituals of a fast-food outlet were completely new to the French, and represented a significant departure from the more formalized rituals governing traditional restaurants. For example, observations made at the opening of a new McDonald's outlet in the Haute-Savoie region in 1991 showed customers utterly failing to grasp or respect the rules for queuing along the counter, showing no regard to the cash registers as signifying the front of the queue.[77] Of course, there is no obvious reason why anyone would automatically form lines perpendicular to

---

74. Trans.: "Are you consumers or participants?"

75. See note 66 above.

76. See S. Strasser, *Never Done: A History of American Housework* (New York: Pantheon Books, 1982), p. 297.

77. In July 1991, I spent several hours at two different times of the day observing customer behavior at the grand opening of a McDonald's restaurant in a city of seventy-five thousand in the *Haute-Savoie* region of eastern France. Because it was the very first fast-food chain restaurant in that region, I reasoned that for at least some of the customers it would be their first experience in a fast-food restaurant.

the counter at each of the cash registers, and the employees at the counter of this restaurant, for whom it was presumably their first active day on the job, spent a good deal of effort trying to coax customers to their particular cash register.[78] During the busier of the two periods that I observed, an assistant manager placed herself in front of the counter to serve as a "guide," answering occasional questions from customers and directing them to available places at the counter. The fact that someone was assigned this task suggests that the company anticipated some initial difficulties for those unfamiliar with the ritual process, and there were indeed some moments of chaos at the counter on that first day of business.

The nature of "service" was a key element differentiating fast food from traditional restaurants. Going out to a restaurant had meant being served by others, whereas one went to a fast-food outlet to engage in "self-service," something which was still a relatively new practice for the French in the 1970s and 1980s.[79] Today, self-service seems a reflexive and trivial set of activities for Americans and French people alike, but to those who were unaccustomed to being "participants" in the restaurant service process, and for whom employees and customers consisted of distinct roles, interactions that blurred the customary role expectations of customers and employees would have "marked" the interactions and the setting as new and as different.[80] When focus groups of French adolescents were asked what aspects of fast-food restaurants most appealed to them, they indicated "self-service" as being an important part of the experience (i.e., "you can choose your own place to sit"; "you don't have to wait to be served"; "each person orders directly from the cook"; and "you simply pay individually, so you don't have

---

78. My observations of the disorderly lines at this fast-food outlet in France mirror quite closely the observations of queuing behavior at a Dutch fast-food restaurant as well. A social anthropologist observed that "there is a kind of instant emigration that occurs the moment one walks through the doors, where Dutch rules rather obviously don't apply and where there are few adults around to enforce any that might." P. H. Stephenson, "Going to McDonald's in Leiden: Reflections on the Concept of Self and Society in the Netherlands," *ETHOS: Journal of the Society for Psychological Anthropology*, vol. 17, no. 2, June 1989, pp. 226–247.

79. Supermarkets, a widely used form of self-service, only become widespread outside of Paris in the late 1960s and early 1970s (see Chapter 4), while it was not until the 1980s that large numbers of the French began eating regularly in self-service cafeterias. See J. Maho and P. Pynson, "Cantines, comment s'en débarraser?" in *Nourritures*, ed. F. Piault (Paris: Autrement, 1989), p. 200.

80. One can imagine that a venerable Parisian café would go out of business if it suddenly posted a new policy of self-service, requiring customers to serve themselves, bus their own cups and glasses, and so on. Because fast food was perceived as different, meaning as new, as *American*, as modern, it tended to be treated differently, as a place apart.

to bother dividing up the check among everyone"). They enjoyed going to fast-food restaurants (as against traditional restaurants) because, as a number of the young people noted, it was "easy," and this was largely because it was a place with few adult interlocutors. There was no maître d'hôtel to pass, no waiters to engage when ordering food, or being served, or having to pay at the end of the meal.[81] They enjoyed eating in restaurants where, in their eyes, "there are no rules." Although there certainly were "rules" for eating fast food, they were based on fewer formalities than in traditional restaurants and (for many) in their own homes. Observations participants made in focus group interviews included these: "the tables are not set, they are clear"; "there are no utensils and you can eat by hand"; and "you can take the food in your hands and eat it just like that" (mimicking eating with two hands). Eating by hand was considered "fun" and "different," as was the practice of having "each thing wrapped individually" and the way that one "can just choose to eat one thing, one doesn't have to order several courses," and "at any time of the day" rather than at specified meal times. Young people viewed the fast-food restaurant as "an informal place, a place for young people" as one commented. This respite from the adult world, with its rules and proper manners, was also expressed in their comments on the visual and aural atmosphere: "You really feel the American atmosphere—the noise, the bright colors, the dress of the staff"; and "you can talk loudly and nobody minds"; and, "it is loud and colorful, it isn't ordered"; "there is more agitation, more noise."[82] This was essentially a playful world that permitted young people to engage in eating practices in a manner that was untroubled by the rules governing the adult world of the traditional restaurant. If we add to this the young workers behind the counter of fast-food restaurants, along with marketing initiatives by the industry to create "family friendly" restaurants, with child seats, play areas, toys, and birthday parties for children, all within a bright, colorful atmosphere decorated with cartoonish promotional displays, we can see the fast-food universe as an infantilizing world. Although certain elements of these chains were eventually changed as the market became more deeply rooted and more differentiated in France, during the first fifteen years, as the market was becoming established, a

---

81. Although several agreed with one student who missed the "human contact" with the waiter and with other customers in the restaurant, most of the students seemed to find the minimal contact with adults as being one of the more positive features of eating in fast-food restaurants.

82. Comments were made by the participants in at least one of the nine focus group interviews conducted in May 1991 at two lycées in eastern France. All five participants in the group where they were expressed agreed with them.

childlike atmosphere and appeal was what the fast-food companies intentionally sought to create, and youthful consumers were drawn to it in large numbers. The president of McDonald's France was clear about this when he stated in 1988 that "traditionally, children hated stuffy French restaurants as much as the restaurants hated having the children."[83]

Ironically, but unsurprisingly, fast-food companies represented themselves as a revolt against tradition. That is, despite the fact that McDonald's, Burger King, Quick, and the other French fast-food chains were massive capitalist corporations (or were owned by them), to establish themselves in a society where gastronomy was deeply embedded, institutionally and culturally, they promoted themselves as vehicles of cultural transgression and rebellion. McDonald's was quite explicit about this. For example, one television ad that ran in 1994 consisted of a child's voice reciting proper table manners ("Don't put your elbows on the table"; "Don't play with your food"; "Don't eat with your fingers"; "Don't act like a clown"; "Don't make noise at the table"; etc.), while different images of people eating in a McDonald's in ways that corresponded to each edict (people eating with their elbows on the table; playing with their french fries; eating with their hands; joking and having fun). A child's voice concluded the ad by announcing, "It's how it goes at McDonald's." Another ad, in 1993 showed a torpid-looking wedding procession making its way through a small French village, out of which a young boy (looking particularly bored) suddenly bolted down a side street followed by his concerned father, and into a McDonald's restaurant where all was bright, lively, and colorful, in what amounted to a reversal of the Pied Piper fairy tale, with the adult being lured away by the child. While such reactions against convention were representations that French young people would have been inclined to appreciate, the adolescents interviewed for this study in 1991 expressed no intention of abandoning traditional cafés in favor of fast-food outlets.[84] That is, they made clear distinctions between

---

83. When McDonald's opened in Paris, it explicitly sought to market its outlets as "family restaurants" because, as the president of McDonald's France stated, "when we started positioning ourselves there was no other restaurants in France that went after families." Greenhouse, "McDonald's Tries Paris, Again," p. F1.

84. Some sixteen thousand cafés were lost in France, between 1978 and 1984, a period when the number of fast-food outlets was growing rapidly, but it seems that fast food was only a small part of the reason for the decline. More significant, according to some industry marketing analyses, had been the exodus of population from rural villages, combined with housing improvements that were increasing consumption and entertainment opportunities in the home, including television. See D. Legoupil, *Débits de Boissons* (Paris: Centre d'Étude du Commerce et de la Distribution, 1985); and Greenhouse, "McDonald's Tries Paris, Again."

cafés and fast-food restaurants, viewing them as completely different kinds of places, to be used for different activities. For example, others agreed with the student who explained: "We go to the cafe to drink, not to eat, and in a cafe we can sit and talk for a long time or a short time, and this isn't possible in fast food places"; and another noted that "you just wouldn't linger for a long time in a fast food restaurant like you would in a cafe," and "a cafe has another atmosphere, for after meals; you stay there for a long time, but you don't in fast food restaurants." In contrast to fast-food restaurants characterized by their *informality*, traditional cafés were appreciated for their *spontaneity*, places of convivial social interaction. In cafés, more chairs could be added to a table to accommodate a continuous stream of new arrivals; and was a place where you might very well know the bartender, the waiters, and other customers personally: "the café is more human—you can feel the presence of people; there's a warmer atmosphere there, people are not in a hurry" as one student noted (and the others in her focus group agreed).[85]

Of course, company policies in many fast-food chains had expressly sought to remove the "warmth" of human interaction in the service process through the enforcement of scripted and timed communication by employees in their interactions with customers, along with technologies like those that automatically prompted employees to "suggest" food items to customers.[86] These, plus the uniform-dress required of fast-food workers, represented policies that reduced the expression of individuality of restaurant employees. The bright, bold colors of the employee uniforms were viewed by the adolescents interviewed as a central and characteristic feature of American fast-food restaurants. When asked about the features of fast-food outlets that recommended them as "American," employee costumes was a frequent reply. As one student noted, "It is very different from what we're used to, with the workers dressed in ridiculous costumes, with a little cap and a name plate on their chest." Research on workers at a France Quick fast food restaurant in Paris in 1986 indicated that wearing a uniform was a

---

85. When McDonald's first entered France the seats in their restaurants were bolted to the floor, as they were in the United States. When announcing the opening of their first company-owned Paris outlet, the press release explicitly mentioned "movable free-standing chairs" as one of the few "deviations to the traditional formula" that the company was making in the French market, in press release entitled, "16th French McDonald's Opens in Paris" (distributed by McDonald's System of France, Inc., Paris, January 26, 1984); and later recounted in "Experience McDonald's of France, Where Food Is an Experience," *McDonald's Management News*, February 1988, p. 5.

86. See R. Leidner, *Fast Food, Fast Talk: Service Work and Routinization of Everyday Life* (Berkeley: University of California Press); and B. Garson, *Electronic Sweatshop*, p. 28.

regular source of complaint.[87] According to an industry guide for prospective fast-food employers, employee uniforms were important for the image of the brand by furnishing "an indispensable strand of fantasy to display the appearance of young and active personnel," and additionally to "differentiate the personnel according to their capabilities."[88]

Mostly, it was the "atmosphere" of the fast-food restaurant that was the major attraction to young people, and this distinguished it from all other kinds of eating establishments in France. There were particular symbolic characteristics of the internal space that immediately marked it off as a "different," as an "authentic," and as an "American" place. A key element was its lighting intensity, which was extremely bright in relation to traditional French eating spaces. Whereas traditional French cafés, restaurants, and brasseries normally had an internal average lighting level ranging from 121 to 320 lumens; in fast-food outlets the average lighting range was between 440 to 1000 lumens.[89] In contrast to the relatively understated and indirect lighting patterns, color schemes, and surface textures in traditional French eating places, in fast-food restaurants the lighting intensity of the internal space created unusually luminous conditions that were magnified by the broad, multicolored menu board displayed above the counter, illuminated from behind by fluorescent lights that reflected off the shiny, stainless steel surfaces of the countertops. The radiance of the atmosphere created a sense of spaciousness and a level of visual incandescence that marked the fast-food outlet as a decidedly un-French space.

In its atmosphere and its rituals, a key element of the appeal of fast food has been its "spectacular" quality. Just as it seemed to Americans when it arrived as a culinary innovation in the 1950s, when fast food appeared in France it embodied all the elements of what the architect Robert Venturi

---

87. Bovais, "Analyse stratégique d'un fast food," pp. 47–49. To consider the extent to which employee uniforms added to the particular imagery of the fast-food restaurant, one might imagine the response by French waiters and by their customers in a traditional café or restaurant were they to suddenly be required to wear brightly colored and somewhat absurd costumes. It would likely provoke militant action by the waiters and open ridicule by customers.

88. Van De Calseyde, *Ouvrir un Fast Food*, pp. 19–20.

89. Median lighting levels ranged from 110 to 260 lumens in traditional cafés and restaurants to 480 to 850 lumens in fast-food outlets. In March 1991, each of seventeen establishments (seven fast-food hamburger and viennoiserie outlets and ten traditional establishments, including restaurants, brasseries, and cafés) were measured with a photometer during daytime hours. Lighting levels were measured in what appeared to be the dimmest and the brightest sections of each establishment, thereby producing a low and a high range, indicated by the two figures for each type of establishment.

and his colleagues in their book *Learning from Las Vegas*, termed "a pleasure zone"; or a place where lightness, the quality of being in an oasis separated from the surrounding environment, a heightened symbolism of the internal space, and an ability to engage the visitor in new forms of role-playing, made for a distinct, and special experience.[90] It was something that was understood perfectly by Ray Kroc when he declared that "when you are in this business you are in show business!"[91] As it entered the French market the fast-food restaurant must have indeed seemed like a "pleasure zone" for many French youths, with its playful, phantasmagoric atmosphere representing it as a place of cultural transgression, and thus a rejection of the aesthetic of Frenchness: of the old, the venerable, the traditional (and the parental). But if its stylistic features were decidedly "un-French," its cultural associations were unmistakably "American."

For many adolescents, their first experiences with fast food were tantamount to tourist experiences: "The first time I went it was like I was visiting the United States, but after that it became more normal, but it is still interesting." In focus group interviews, participants reported not just that they were "fed up with formal things and fast food places are youthful, a change in one's way of life," and that fast-food restaurants were "relaxing and easy" but that McDonald's and other fast-food hamburger restaurants represented "an American way of life"; "hamburgers and coke is a way to live like an American"; they "allow you to feel the American atmosphere," "an American experience of friendliness." The basic characteristics of a "genuine" fast-food restaurant (the lighting, the colors, the noise, the sense of space, the informality, the participation) taken together were viewed as "American" and this was something that held great importance for many young people.

It was a cultural aesthetic cultivated within reciprocally confirming peer groups of adolescents for whom American cultural goods were perceived as being new, advanced, inventive, cutting edge, and therefore "cool." In the realm of cultural consumption, "coolness" could be considered a form of "subcultural capital" that young people are seeking to accrue by making substantial investments in music, clothing, celebrity, lifestyle, as well as in the cultivation of knowledge about all of these things. Their liminal status in society has often accorded youth a special situation in Western societies, including France. With their family ties loosening, and without settled

90. R. Venturi, D. S. Brown, and S. Izenour, *Learning from Las Vegas* (Cambridge, MA: MIT Press, 1989).

91. Boas and Chain, *Big Mac*, p. 140.

families of their own, nor established in occupations or careers, adolescents can be viewed as postponing the process of "social aging," or the process of being socially fixed to a position in the class structure, through a heavy investment in cultural forms allowing them to maintain what Sarah Thornton called a "fantasy of classlessness."[92] In a survey of the cultural practices of the French commissioned by the Ministry of Culture and Communication between 1973 and 1989, it was found that the increasing length of time that French young people under the age of twenty-five were spending either in schools or living with their parents had had a significant effect on the homogenization of cultural tastes among adolescents, regardless of social background.[93] This finding was indicative (or suggestive) of the existence in France of a generalized "youth culture" that was relatively independent of class background and occupational position. The survey also found, however, that after the age of twenty-five (after leaving school, entering careers, starting families, etc.) the cultural tastes and practices of French youth tended to become more closely linked to their relative position in the social and occupational hierarchy. While the diffusion of cultural forms like rap and hip-hop in the years that followed may have introduced a degree of politicization and attentiveness to social questions in cultural expression, until then youth culture had essentially been an analogous system of social valuation, largely floating above the material realities and struggles of class inequality and driven by the ideas, practices, and an aesthetic that favored differences over style rather than struggles over class.[94]

92. In a useful adaptation of Bourdieu's analysis of how bourgeois adolescents "express their distance from the bourgeois world, which they cannot really appropriate, by a refusal of complicity whose most refined expression is a propensity towards aesthetics and aestheticism" (Bourdieu, *Distinction*, p. 55), Sarah Thornton has shown how "coolness" operates among British youths as a form of subcultural capital, based on fantasies of classlessness in a highly stratified society. See S. Thornton, "The 'hip' versus the Mainstream," in *The Subcultures Reader*, 2nd ed., ed. K. Gelder (London: Routledge, 2005), pp. 188–190; and see her study of British "rave" culture in *Club Cultures: Music, Media, and Subcultural Capital* (Hanover, NH: University Press of New England, 1996). Also, many years ago Talcott Parsons made the point that youth enjoy a temporary and relative freedom from necessity, in T. Parsons, "Age and Sex in the Social Structure of the United States," *American Sociological Review*, vol. 7, no. 5, October 1942, pp. 604–616.

93. O. Donnat and D. Cogneau, *Les Pratiques culturelles des Français 1973–1989* (Paris: La Découverte/La Documentation Française, 1990), pp. 254, 276.

94. See A.J.M. Prévos, "The Evolution of French Rap Music and Hip Hop Culture in the 1980s and 1990s," *French Review*, vol. 69, no. 5, April 1996; and A. Williams-Gascon, "Voices for the Voiceless: Graffiti and Social Issues in Contemporary France," in *France at the Dawn of the Twenty-First Century Trends and Transformations*, ed. M.-C. Weidmann Koop (Birmingham, AL: Summa Publications, 2000), pp. 115–133; and B. James, "French Rap and the Art of Vandalism," *International Herald Tribune*, July 4, 1991, p. 20.

It was more than a little ironic that American cultural goods should be considered "cool" in France, where opposition to American cultural, political, and economic practices had been so persistent and so sharp for so long.[95] Indeed, it is likely that this very French reflex toward anti-Americanism was what made its reverse seem to be an appealing stance to take. One observer of French cultural politics called it *Americanophilia*, "a widespread enthusiasm for American mass culture that is shared by French people at large (and particularly young people) and that is far from being the preserve of a trendy Parisian in-group."[96] For trendy Americans, paradoxically, it was French (and European) cultural goods that held a special status in the 1970s and 1980s. Educated elites could earn marks of distinction from their peers by displaying their knowledge of and appreciation for all things "foreign, "European", and "French" from cinema, to cars, to clothing, to electronic goods, to food, at the same time as typical American mass cultural goods would be considered inferior, if not repulsive.

The improbable success of fast food in France stimulated a reaction from the French government, with the creation in 1989 of a National Council of Culinary Arts by the Ministry of Culture. Headed by the president of the Chambre Syndicale de la haute cuisine française, the council was charged with "protecting the culinary patrimony" through a wide-ranging program that included an inventory of the major sites of French culinary heritage, the establishment of a national Day of *Gourmandise*, and the creation of a museum and a conservatory of culinary heritage to promote research, mount expositions and organize educational activities in primary schools.[97] Although not explicitly framed as a response to American fast food, Jack Lang, a former Minister of Culture and a celebrated figure in the French Socialist Party, was outspoken against American "cheap commercialism" and

95. See R. Debray, "Confessions d'un antiaméricain," in *L'Amérique des Français*, ed. C. Faure and T. Bishop (Paris: Editions François Bourin, 1992), pp. 199–220; D. Lacorne, J. Rupnik, and M.-F. Toinet, eds. *The Rise and Fall of Anti-Americanism* (New York: St. Martin's Press, 1990); D. Strauss, *Menace in the West: The Rise of French Anti-Americanism in Modern Times* (Westport, CT: Greenwood Press, 1978).

96. Quote by B. Rigby, *Popular Culture in Modern France: A Study of Cultural Discourse* (London: Routledge, 1991), p. 163.

97. The design of the project included the drafting of senior chefs to teach three-week courses to eleven-year-old primary school pupils on taste, culinary history, and regional cuisine, a practice that became firmly institutionalized. See the outline for the project in the trade weekly, *L'Hôtellerie*, no. 2138, January 4–11, 1990.

the "ravages wrought by its popular culture throughout the world."[98] When pressed by a journalist to acknowledge a relation between the formation of the new council and the growth of American fast food, Lang acknowledged, "I'm no fan of hamburgers," before going on to explain more diplomatically that the pedagogic efforts of the council were simply to defend the culinary heritage: "Our children will be better armed to savor the wonders of life, especially in this beautiful country. France has developed the art of living which we all need to rediscover and safeguard."[99] That the rapid growth of the fast-food market was occurring during a period in which the language of "productivism," the market, and the entrepreneur-as-hero were being openly promoted by the governing Socialist Party, with Jack Lang as a very visible representative, was quite a paradox.[100] For the attempt to defend the cultural patrimony against "cheap commercialism," while simultaneously encouraging "market forces" as the most reasonable arbiter of human affairs was a contradiction, since "cheap commercialism" is the very definition of mass consumer markets.

Moreover, with its focus on the preservation and defense of the culinary patrimony the protectionist response to fast food overlooked the wider consequences of "Americanism" for French society. For in addition to contributing to the standardization and homogenization of taste, the fast-food industry also brought with it a model for the computerization, rationalization, and de-skilling of the service sector labor process, along with an increase in part-time and student labor and a dogged antiunionism. These had been key features of McDonald's success in the United States, thereby making it a model for French businessmen hoping to enter the game. After having carefully followed the growth and profitability of the industry in the United States, they looked to fast food as an innovative and adaptable system that could provide companies that had the capital to compete with the large American firms with a potentially lucrative expansion of the chain restaurant market in France. For the industrial producers of this new cultural form, the fast-food phenomenon was part of a larger process

98. D. Pinto, "The Left, the Intellectuals and Culture," in *The Mitterrand Experiment*, ed. G. Ross, S. Hoffman, and S. Malzacher (New York: Oxford University Press, 1987), p. 222.

99. Quoted in A. Riding, "Paris Schools Add a Course a la Carte," in *New York Times*, February 6, 1991, p. C1.

100. See S. Berger, "French Business from Transition to Transition," in *The Mitterrand Experiment*, ed. G. Ross, S. Hoffman, and S. Malzacher (New York: Oxford University Press, 1987), pp. 187–198.

of restructuring and diversification within a French commercial restaurant industry that was increasingly dominated by large industrial food groups.[101] The changing ownership structures of these industrial groups did not seem to indicate strong cleavages between the ownership of fast-food outlets and traditional restaurants. For example, Eliance, the restaurant branch of the Elitair industrial group, owned two Maxim's gastronomic restaurants at the same time as it owned two Aubépain fast-food viennoiseries and was in the process of entering into a joint venture with Burger King to open several hamburger outlets; Groupe Fabien SAAL owned two Magic Burger outlets and, reportedly, twelve various "higher scale restaurants"; while in addition to its ownership of fifty-three fast-food viennoiseries, Groupe Holder owned several traditional bistros and restaurants.[102] In other words, although fast food represented a cultural transgression, or a break with tradition for its mainly young clientele, as well as for the gatekeepers of the cultural patrimony and the institutions of haute cuisine, for French investors and entrepreneurs "business was business" and a matter of economics not culture. While it certainly must have appeared silly and crass and formulaic to those captivated by haute cuisine and traditional cultural forms, McDonald's, Burger King, and their various French kin did not exactly enter "France," but they entered the most industrialized (and industrializing) region of the French gastronomic field. This was not the part of the field where artisanal culinary practices were executed by grand chefs, or where restaurants competed for *Michelin* stars; but where a place for American fast food had already been set and prepared.

---

101. See Chapter 4 for more on this process.

102. The ownership patterns of the large industry food groups were profiled in "Les 50 premiers groupes," in the trade magazine, *Revue Technique des Hôtels et Restaurants*, no. 496, March 1991, pp. 59–74.

4

Industrial Cuisine and the "Magic" of Americanism

S tandardization is the foundation of all industrial practices and has been the basic operating principle of the fast-food method. In the realm of foodways, standardization violates the strong bond between food and region that is evoked by the French concept of "*le terroir*." "Terroir" is a term for which there is no real English equivalent, but above all it refers to "distinctiveness": the distinctive products of the land, the distinctive qualities of a specific region or place, and the distinctive or characteristic human practices (knowledge and techniques) of cultivation that are applied to this region or land. Thus an object of le terroir is the product of both the natural qualities of a specific region and the specific human practices that render it sublime. Standardization is a suppression of the distinctive, and the overarching imperative governing McDonald's and other fast-food chains is that each unit be more or less the same everywhere, regardless of where they may actually be located. So no matter where a fast-food outlet may be located, its products, its design, and its methods of production are detached from the immediacy, distinctiveness, and particularity of that place. So, whereas the French idea of le terroir draws our cultural imagination to the specificity of region and place, the American idea of fast food essentially seeks to dissolve it.[1] This is not to say that the fast-food market had no "proper place" on the French landscape, for its restaurants were eventually located in what could be considered its "natural habitat," the suburban commercial strip.

The Commercial "Strip" in France

When the McDonald's Corporation won its lawsuit against its original French franchisee it began an extremely aggressive and extended expansion in the French market, opening nearly one new outlet per week in France from 1989 all the way to the present.[2] In the first decade of its expansion, McDonald's sheer size gave it the capital base to permit it to occupy sites for its restaurants in the most expensive downtown centers of the largest French cities. So as the company began to expand in the French market, McDonald's (at the time, reportedly, the world's largest owner of retail real estate) bought some of the most expensive real estate in Paris for its outlets on the Champs-Élysées, the rue de Rivoli, the boulevards St. Germain and St. Michel, and so on, and as it expanded in the provinces, it located restaurants in the historic centers of the largest cities.[3] From this economically and culturally prominent position, often in close proximity to important tourist destinations, McDonald's was able to locate itself on the French landscape in places that were both spatially and symbolically central.[4]

---

1. In recent years McDonald's France has been adapting part of its menu to include French food tastes, offering various traditional French *casse-croûte* (snack) foods, like ham and cheese on a baguette, and serving goat cheese in salads and reportedly using grass-fed beef in its hamburgers. See, for example, "France as a Fast Food Nation," February 2013, in *The Connexion*, an English-language newspaper published in France, available at http://connexionfrance.com /McDonalds-casse-croute-menu-France.

2. From 150 restaurants in 1989, McDonald's currently has 1,384 restaurants in France; having averaged one new restaurant opening per week for twenty-five years. See Figure 3.1.

3. So, for example, in 1989, the Rhône-Alpes region (which includes Lyon) had 131 fast-food outlets and Provence-Alpes-Côte d'Azur (which includes Nice and Cannes) had 122 outlets, while the more rural regions of Franche-Comté and Limousin had 15 and 8 outlets, respectively. These numbers were drawn from a report prepared for the 1989 "Salon International de la Restauration Rapide" and provided to the author by the president of SNARR.

4. This was a purposive corporate strategy designed to "market" and introduce the brand in France, while attracting pedestrian traffic into its restaurants located near crowded tourist sites. French fast-food companies made comparable real estate investments to compete with McDonald's and other American companies, well aware of the symbolic value of having a restaurant on what is regarded as a prestigious site. See F. Jacquemond, "Lieux de vie, lieux de culture," in *Revue Technique des hôtels et restaurants*, no. 497, April 1991, pp. 67–72; and "La Carte 82 de la restauration rapide," in *Néorestauration*, October 1982, pp. 25–35.

However, in the early 1990s, McDonald's began to expand outward, opening restaurants across the country in smaller cities with populations as low as twenty thousand (including towns like Millau in the Aveyron region, where it became a target for José Bové and his compatriots), as well as in the suburbs of all large French cities. It was in these suburban (or *"périurbain"*) spaces that many of the newer fast-food outlets were opened in the 1990s, with some 50 percent of new outlets including a "drive-in window," thus permitting customers to order food and drive it away without leaving their automobiles. Although the drive-in window had been a relatively widespread method of retail food sales in the United States for decades, it represented a completely new practice of retail "convenience" in France. Ironically, the placement of McDonald's in these new French developments replicated the suburban commercial strip where fast food had been born four decades earlier in the U.S. market. Indeed, what had once been a distinctly American commercial ecosystem, French "commercial zones" had been developed along the outskirts and on the peripheral routes into French cities since the early 1970s, bearing more than a passing resemblance to what Americans have known as the "commercial strip" or as "sprawl." These commercial zones were formed along the heavily traveled access roads into French cities, superimposing the aesthetic of a Las Vegas on the pattern of the ancient *faubourg.*[5]

Often established along the same routes as *grandes surfaces*, or "big box" supermarkets (and hypermarkets), French *zones commerciales* are relatively unregulated commercial strips, visually punctuated by billboards, automobile dealerships, garden supply stores, furniture outlets, motel chains, bowling alleys, and fast-food restaurants. The brightly colored structures and extravagant architectural styles of retail chain businesses like Conforama, Castorama, Monsieur Meuble, Monsieur Bricolage, BUT, and McDonald's, together can be seen to emit a visual cacophony as loud and as ostentatious as anything found in the United States, with its vast stretches of unregulated commercial strips.[6] Visually, it is a stark departure from the traditional French cultural presentation, generating a landscape that would almost never be encountered by foreign tourists visiting France. Indeed, American

---

5. *"Faubourg,"* a late fifteenth-century French term for settlement outside the walls of the town, derived from the Latin (foris) and Frankish (bourc) for "outside of the town"; later altered to faux bourg (or false town) in the folk idiom.

6. The embodiment of promotional hyperbole in the design of commercial structures has been regarded as one of the virtues of American forms of "postmodern" architecture. See Robert Venturi, Denise Scott Brown, and Steven Izenour, *Learning from Las Vegas: The Forgotten Symbolism of Architectural Form* (Cambridge, MA: MIT Press, 1977).

tourists coming upon a French commercial zone might regard the scenery as atypically despoiled or contaminated by commercial excess, viewing it as visually disastrous, a "cultural Chernobyl."[7]

On one level, commercial zones populated by big box chain stores can be seen as *non* places, to the extent that they are distinctive for their *lack* of distinction. This is partly due to the chain character of the retail businesses occupying these zones, whose form must have a certain uniformity for customers to be able to identify particular brands, in order to make them recognizable to customers in Metz, or Biarritz, or Yvelines, while simultaneously (and paradoxically) their building structures must stand out, visually, to allow for clear recognition from a distance and at high speeds, since establishments in these zones are basically only accessible by automobile. Visual uniformity and exaggeration, or hyperbole, are thus key principles of the design of building structures. Since these are areas that tend to attract the same or similar collections of businesses, the development of commercial zones can be seen to contribute to dissolution of the distinctiveness of place. Moreover, it is more than a little ironic that as French suburban spaces increasingly came to resemble American suburbia, in the United States a new design paradigm was taking hold in residential and commercial construction that explicitly advanced the "European town square" as the anchor and centerpiece of a "New Urbanist" model of suburban development![8]

In France the *périurbain* fringe has been developed as a space distinct from the traditional *banlieue*, with its historic identification as a stronghold of the industrial working class and its more recent identification with marginalized immigrant populations. Originally formed in the 1870s alongside the rapid development of the metal and chemical industries, *les banlieues*

---

7. This resonant characterization was offered by Ariane Mnouchkine, a French theater director, with regard to the introduction of Euro Disney outside of Paris. See Richard Kuisel, *The French Way: How France Embraced and Rejected American Values and Power* (Princeton: Princeton University Press, 2012), p. 168.

8. "New Urbanism" has been a design model developed in reaction to critical works like Jane Jacobs's *The Death and Life of Great American Cities* (New York: Random House, 1961) and William S. Kowinski's *The Malling of America* (New York: Morrow, 1985). In reaction to problems of suburban sprawl, architects and urban planners have sought design models to minimize the necessity of the automobile, while encouraging human-scale, low-rise, and mixed-use development conducive to face-to-face interactions. See Charles C. Bohl, *Place Making: Developing Town Centers, Main Streets, and Urban Villages* (Washington, DC: Urban Land Institute, 2002) and Peter Katz, *The New Urbanism: Toward an Architecture of Community* (New York: McGraw Hill, 1994).

stretched out along the waterways and railroad lines that extended from the urban core.[9] With industry expanding and the population quadrupling over the course of the next century, growing numbers of workers were housed in close proximity to industrial areas, in the roughest of conditions. The situation of the working-class *banlieue* was a bleak one and remained so even with the construction of low-cost, cheaply made housing subdivisions (*lotissements*) in the decade after World War I. These densely packed clusters of private housing estates often lacked basic utilities, sanitary facilities, and sidewalks.[10] After 1955, massive public housing projects were constructed in the banlieues, termed "*grands ensembles*," with large numbers of tenants concentrated in housing estates begun as hopeful symbols of working-class stability but soon devolving into dreaded, stigmatized spaces of immigrant dispossession and chronic unemployment.[11]

In contrast to the earlier process of the *banlieue*, which had taken place as an extension of industrial expansion and concentration, the process of suburban development termed "pèriurbanisation" was driven by a decentralization of industry, along with a rise in individual home ownership, and the increasingly heavy use of automobile travel. In other words, it was animated by some of the same factors that, decades earlier, had made the postwar development of the U.S. suburbs possible. In the United States, the privately owned detached house, located in new suburban housing developments (made possible by government-subsidized mortgages and prefabricated production techniques), had been the centerpiece of postwar suburbanization, facilitated by mass automobile ownership and huge federal investments in highway construction.[12] In France, in 1970, only 33 percent of households had lived in individual detached houses (*les pavillons*), but by 1985 the percentage had risen to 54 percent (and the percentage of French households living in apartments had fallen from 67 percent to 46 percent in the same

---

9. See John Merriman, ed., *French Cities in the Nineteenth Century* (New York: Holmes and Meier, 1981) and John Merriman, *The Red City: Limoges and the French 19th Century* (New York: Oxford University Press, 1985).

10. Tyler Stovall, *The Rise of the Paris Red Belt* (Berkeley, CA: University of California Press, 1990), pp. 38–40.

11. Bernard Dézert, Alain Metton, and Jean Steinberg, *La Pèriurbanisation en France* (Paris: SEDES, 1991), pp. 43–44; Loïc Wacquant, *Urban Outcasts* (Malden, MA: Polity Press, 2008), pp. 170–173.

12. See Kenneth T. Jackson, *Crabgrass Frontier: The Suburbanization of the U.S.* (New York: Oxford University Press, 1985) and Robert A. Beauregard, *When America Became Suburban* (Minneapolis: University of Minnesota Press, 2006).

period).[13] While the growing popularity of home ownership was led by a "new middle class" (of technicians, engineers, managers, professionals, etc.), it also drew from the ranks of a financially "solvent" proletariat, or stably employed skilled workers for whom migration to "new villages" in the outer suburbs represented a certain expression of social mobility.[14]

Périurbain development in the outer suburbs and semirural areas was made possible by an expansion of the highway system and increasing rates of automobile ownership (in 1970, 58 percent of French households owned a car, a percentage that would increase to 73 percent by 1985), and, in the French cultural imagination the automobile was fast becoming a physical embodiment of modernity itself.[15] Between 1962 and 1977 the population of the Paris suburbs had grown 41 percent (from 5,679,000 to 7,977,000), while the population of Paris proper had decreased by 20 percent (from 2,790,000 to 2,226,000).[16] Moreover, from the late 1960s through the 1970s rural migration from large metropolitan areas was supported by an ideology promoting a "return to the country" and a nostalgia for "homecoming" (to the family village of origin), and this, combined with an increase in middle-class acquisition of secondary homes in rural villages and provincial towns, encouraged relocation from urban centers to restyled French suburban and exurban spaces.[17]

The expansion of the *périurbain* fringe required a substantial amplification of commercial activity. Indeed, to supply the daily, practical household needs for vast tracts of newly built single-family housing developments

13. Gérard Mermet, *Francoscopie: Les Français: Qui sont-ils? Où vont-ils?* (Paris: Librarie Larousse 1985), p. 126.

14. A tendency that was more than disconcerting to the French Communist Party, which still held electoral power throughout much of suburban France (as well as the loyalty of a large portion of the working class) as it struggled to refine a perspective on individual housing, and especially individual home ownership. See Jean-Claude Boyer, "Les Conséquences socio-spatiales de l'accession à la propriété en banlieue ouvrière," *Espaces et Sociétés*, no. 5, 1987, pp. 109–129.

15. G. Mermet, *Francoscopie*, p. 188; J.-M. Normand, "Les Français utilisent de plus en plus leurs voitures particulières," *Le Monde*, December 22, 1995, p. 9; and see Kristin Ross, *Fast Cars, Clean Bodies: Decolonization and the Reordering of French Culture* (Cambridge, MA: MIT Press, 1995).

16. A. Metton, *Le Commerce et la ville en banlieue parisienne* (Coubevoie: Alain Metton, 1980), pp. 517–518.

17. Michel Forsè, Jean-Pierre Jaslin, Yannick Lemel, Henri Mendras, Denis Stoclet, and Jean-Hugues Dèchaux, *Recent Social Trends in France 1960–1990* (Montreal: McGill-Queen's University Press, 1990), p. 250; B. Dézert, A. Metton, and J. Steinberg, *La Périurbanisation en France* (Paris: SEDES, 1991), pp. 44–51.

necessitated a veritable "commercial revolution" in the French suburbs.[18] The driver of new commercial development was often the *hypermarché*, a big box "superstore" combining a supermarket and a department store within a single structure of from three thousand to over ten thousand square meters in size, located in an area where land was inexpensive relative to urban centers, and accessible by automobile, facilitated and supported by parking spaces for up to two thousand vehicles. The first *hypermarché* was introduced in the Parisian suburb of Sainte-Geneviève-des-Bois in 1963 by Carrefour, a company that in recent years has become the largest retailer in Europe and the second largest retailer in the world (behind Walmart). The first to adopt the "American model" of retail food distribution in France, the founders of Carrefour were inspired by what they had learned in Marshall Plan productivity missions, visiting supermarkets and food distribution outlets in the United States, as well as by attending trade fairs and conferences organized by trade groups, like AIDA (Association Internationale de la Distribution des Produits Alimentaires).[19]

Basic "self-service" techniques were introduced in France in 1948, but the practice of "*libre-service*," the ability to roam freely to shop for items in a store, was largely unknown to most French consumers until 1960, when the Carrefour chain opened the first of its many supermarkets in France.[20] The cofounders of Carrefour had previously studied American retail methods from a Colombian-born American named Bernardo Trujillo, a management employee of the National Cash Register Company. Trujillo was a celebrated figure who was variously called "The Prophet of Selling," "The Oracle of Distribution," and a "Retail Guru" for his role in disseminating American commercial methods abroad. His seminars on "Modern Shopping Methods" held at the company headquarters in Dayton, Ohio, were well attended

---

18. The term was invoked by A. Metton in "L'Expansion du commerce péripherique en France," *Annales de Géographie*, no. 506, XCI année, July–August 1982, pp. 463–479.

19. The AIDA was an international trade organization in the food products industry that had been created by the president of the American trade journal *Super Market Merchandising* and by the head of *Docks de France*, a French food distribution company, organizing trade fairs to promote the supermarket model of food distribution. See Jean-Marc Villermet, "Histoire des 'grandes surfaces': Méthodes américaines, entrepreneurs européens," *Entreprises et Histoire*, 1993, no. 4, pp. 41–53. Marshall Plan productivity missions extended beyond issues of technological development in basic industries to encompass the customs, habits, and attitudes of the service sector. See Anthony Carew, *Labour under the Marshall Plan: The Politics of Productivity and the Marketing of Management Science* (Detroit, MI: Wayne State University Press, 1987), p. 165.

20. Villermet, "Histoire des 'grandes surfaces,'" pp. 42–43; and see J. Bombal and P. Chalmin, *L'Agro-alimentaire* (Paris: Presses Universitaires de France, 1980), p. 83.

by French businessmen from the retail sector.[21] Trujillo presumably proselytized in the hope of selling cash registers to foreign purchasers abroad, for his seminars brought over eleven thousand foreign businessmen, including three thousand from France, to Dayton to instruct them in the logistics and methods of large-scale retail selling. As one commentator put it, "He teaches the doctrine of rapid turnover, of large shops with a wide range of goods, and of the loss-leader, or as he puts it 'islands of loss in an ocean of profit.'"[22] As another scholar has noted, Trujillo preached an aesthetic vision of retail sales to his students that stressed "cleanliness, refinement, aestheticism, and an emphasis on beautifying commercial space, highlighting new forms of architectural design. The use of varied materials and colors which, combined with the floor, the walls and the shelves, all contributed to the creation of an 'atmosphere' of a new kind, an aesthetic that was being expressed by the Pop Art movement. What Americans call 'showmanship,' the art of *mise-en-scène*, would be generalized to all developed countries and become one of the essential elements of commercial promotion."[23]

Like a magician, Trujillo mesmerized his students with tales, not only of the profits that could be had but of the dazzling powers of transubstantiation to be attained with his approach to marketing and selling mundane

21. Villermet, "Histoire des 'grandes surfaces,'" p. 45. Tracie McMillan in *The American Way of Eating* (New York: Scribner, 2012), p. 105, notes that several of the earliest initiatives to export the U.S. supermarket form to Europe in the 1950s had largely failed because the two main ingredients of American supermarket success were not yet in place: residential suburbs and industrial agriculture. By the mid-1970s both had been developed in France.

22. Quoted in J. Ardaugh, *The New French Revolution* (London: Secker and Warburg, 1968), p. 106; J.-B. Duval, "Bernardo Trujillo, 'Le Prophète de la distribution,'" *LSA: Commerce and Consommation*, no. 2306, February 13, 2014 (online version, no page nos.).

23. Villermet, "Histoire des 'grandes surfaces,'" p. 45. Not only did the founders of Carrefour (Fournier and Defforey) learn from Trujillo but others who would later become leaders in the French supermarket and hypermarket industry participated in his seminars, including Bernard Darty (Darty); Gérard Mulliez, the father of Gérard Mulliez (Auchan); Paul Dubrule and Gérard Pélisson (Accor); and Edouard Leclerc (E. Leclerc). It was not until the 1960s that French business leaders were able to receive institutionalized "management" education in France, when INSEAD (Institut Européen d'Administration des Affaires) was created by former students of the Harvard Business School who, with American foundation support, provided courses in English, taught by American professors, using the Harvard Case Method to bring an American style of management education to France. See Ibrahim Warde, "Irrésistibles 'Business Schools,'" *L'Amérique dans les têtes*, Manière de Voir 53, September–October 2000, pp. 83–86 (edition published by Le Monde Diplomatique, Paris). Also see Luc Boltanski, "Visions of American Management in Postwar France," *Structures of Capital: The Social Organization of the Economy*, ed. S. Zukin and P. DiMaggio (Cambridge: Cambridge University Press, 1990), p. 359.

retail goods. But as Marcel Mauss once explained, magic is fundamentally a social phenomenon and so the powers of the magician are not primarily vested in the magician's skills or sleight of hand but in the beliefs of his audience and, indeed, in the entire field of social action within which the magician performs his magic: "A magician does nothing, or almost nothing, but makes everyone believe that he is doing everything, and all the more so since he puts to work collective forces and ideas to help the individual imagination in his belief. The art of the magician involves suggesting means, enlarging on the virtues of objects, anticipating effects, and by these methods fully satisfying the desires and expectations which have been fostered by entire generations in common."[24]

Young people in France (and internationally) were drawn to American cultural iconography like moths to a flame, in a domain in which American mass cultural forms and practices were often considered to be "coolness" personified; while French entrepreneurs were hypnotized by the dazzlingly innovative business techniques of American capitalism, attracted by the Midas-like powers that it promised. For French adolescents and their peers who were dazzled by the "coolness" of American things and the "cutting-edge" qualities of American mass cultural practices, as well as for French entrepreneurs and their peers who were dazzled by ostensible managerial successes and technical innovations of American business practices, "Americanism" represented a potent form of symbolic capital that could be parlayed into cultural or financial profits. It was just such a "magical" belief that prompted French businessmen to stretch the framework of high-volume selling beyond the scale of the supermarket to gargantuan proportions, in the creation of the *hypermarché.*

The French *hypermarché* was an unusually concentrated commercial space, so that a store of nine thousand square meters equated to three hundred traditional shops (of thirty square meters) in a town or a city. Between 1963 and 1972, 176 hypermarkets were opened in France, more than in any country outside of the United States, and by 1980 there were 71 hypermarkets implanted in the Paris region alone.[25] Overall, between 1962 and 1977, there was a seventeen-fold increase in the number of square meters of selling space in the Paris suburbs.[26] Increasingly, hypermarkets were planned and

24. Marcel Mauss, *A General Theory of Magic* (London: Routledge, 1971), pp. 174–175.
25. Villermet, "Histoire des 'grandes surfaces,'" p. 46; Metton, *Commerce et la ville*, p. 423.
26. Metton, *Commerce et la ville*, p. 518. This figure is for growth in all forms of grandes surfaces (large retail establishments) and not only hypermarkets.

designed in structures that were physically attached to other shops, often including auto centers, garden supply stores, and restaurants, and in some cases owned, marketed, and managed as a single unit; or in other words, as a shopping center, or *centre commercial*. In 1968, and for the very first time, a *centre commercial* of 15,000 square meters, with 1,200 parking spaces, was built around a 5,630 square meter "*Euromarché*" hypermarket, with an attached arcade of twenty-five small shops in the Paris suburb of Saint-Michel sur Orge.[27] Moreover, forty-five such *centres commerciaux* were opened between 1972 and 1974 in the Paris region, a further manifestation of the "commercial revolution" under way—a revolution largely based on selling methods and technical innovations that had proven themselves in the U.S. market, and whose principles and mechanisms had been imparted to French businessmen through study trips sponsored by the Marshall Plan.[28]

Who were the consumers who shopped in these new "selling factories"? According to a marketing survey of the clientele of eighty-five hypermarkets between 1974 and 1978, the customer base was not markedly different than the early market for American-style fast food in France. The predominant age bracket of shoppers in hypermarkets was eighteen to thirty-five years, a group that comprised 51 percent of all customers of hypermarkets but only 19.2 percent of the French population as a whole.[29] More specifically, the shoppers in hypermarkets were typically made up of young households with between one and three children. The socioeconomic status of these consumers was heavily weighted toward a broad "middle class" of professionals, senior executives, middle managers, and office and clerical employees. While industrial workers also shopped in the hypermarkets, they did so at no more nor less than their proportion in the French population; while just 4 percent of the heads of industrial and commercial businesses were found to shop in the suburban hypermarkets. According to Metton, the socioeconomic distribution of the clientele may have reflected, as much as anything else, the placement of hypermarkets in the outer suburbs where there was a higher concentration of those from middle-level occupations, as well as owners of private homes.[30]

27. A. Delobez, "The Development of Shopping Centres in the Paris Region," in J. A. Dawson and J. D. Lord, eds. *Shopping Centre Development: Policies and Prospects* (London: Croom Helm, 1985), p. 129.

28. This was the case with the most basic levels of service innovation, like all "large self-service shops" and supermarkets. See Delobez, "Development of Shopping Centres," pp. 144–145.

29. Metton, *Commerce et la ville*, p. 439.

30. Metton, *Commerce et la ville*, p. 440.

Although it varied considerably by social class, in 1970 relatively few French households owned such domestic appliances as a dishwasher (2.4 percent), color television (7.7 percent), or freezer (10.1 percent); while 56.9 percent owned a washing machine and 57.6 percent an automobile.[31]

The new forms of retail commerce that were being introduced into newly re-formed French suburbs (areas that would become home to many McDonald's fast-food drive-in outlets) were bringing significant changes to French commercial culture. It was then a new thing for French people to shop by automobile and the new hypermarkets and shopping centers were in locations only accessible by car, with parking lots that made them accessible.[32] This entailed a significant change in French consumption practices. Among other things, it created new opportunities for shopping in the evenings and on Saturdays and at almost any time. By opening their doors at nine or ten in the morning and remaining open until ten or eleven at night, the hypermarkets were open nearly twice the number of hours of traditional French stores, thus reconfiguring how weekly shopping might be reorganized and contributing to a developing "commercial comportment."[33] Within these new retail spaces, the French customer had to adapt to the depersonalization of store personnel, fewer of whom would be on site, and who would be deployed differently than in traditional French shops, where a certain commingling of formality and familiarity had always characterized the interaction of customers and store clerks. New interactional dynamics created a new customer experience, as well as new experiences for retail workers, as cost-saving efficiencies in the grandes surfaces were reshaping the nature of retail work, with the "*palettisation*" of stocks, the necessity of internal surveillance of store activities, and increasingly computerized systems of store management making it possible to deploy just one worker for twenty-five square meters of selling area, a ratio one analyst termed "*une remarquable économie de personnel*" relative to traditional retail practices.[34]

---

31. *La France des commerces 1991*, published by the French Ministère de l'Artisanat, du Commerce et de la Consommation (Paris, 1991), p. 76.

32. In 1970 only 57.6 percent of French households even owned an automobile, in contrast to 82.5 percent of U.S. households—rates that would increase to roughly 75 percent in France and 88 percent in the United States by 1990. (Sources: Insee, cited in *La France des commerces* and U.S. Department of Transportation, Federal Highway Administration website: www.fhwa.dot.gov/planning/census_issues/ctpp/data_products/journey_to_work/jtw1.cfm.

33. Metton, *Commerce et la ville*, pp. 448–449.

34. Metton, *Commerce et la ville*, p. 449. The big box retail stores also tended to draw upon a workforce that was more feminized, more part-time, and paid wages at the lower end of the retail workforce scale. See G. Cette, *Le temps partiel en France* (Paris: La Documentation

The new scale of retail trade generated resistance in France, and not just from trade unions and retail workers but from many small shopkeepers, who were well organized in local communities and in administrative positions at the regional level. By 1969 pressure was being put on local councils to deny planning permission and building authorization for large-scale commercial development, an effort that was then extended to the national government where protection against the advance of the "commercial revolution" was offered by the Royer Law. Eventually passed at the very end of 1973, the Royer Law had been initially prepared by the Finance Minister, V. Giscard d'Estaing (while adopting the name of his successor, Jean Royer). The law included sixty-five articles touching on many aspects of commercial life in France, but most relevant to the forms of new commercial development was its attention to retail and retail planning, including a strengthening of the role of local planning commissions to give them decision-making power (and not simply a consultative role) in the development of new grandes surfaces.[35] According to Delobez, while the Royer Law contributed to a slowing of the rapid explosion of shopping centers, hypermarkets, and other forms of large-scale retail development, the saturation of local markets and easing of population growth were also cooling off this market.[36]

Retail trade became a battleground for struggles over the place of commerce in French society, often played out in disputes about regulation of new retail sectors. For example, for two decades French unions waged an ongoing fight to restrict the ability of retail stores to open on Sunday, in an effort to preserve the customary day of rest for workers and their families, against retail interests seeking to overturn what they argued were anachronistic regulations limiting consumer convenience. So, in 1979, a month after the minister of commerce had summoned professionals, unions, and organizations representing consumers to brief them about a proposed law

---

Française, 1999), p. 196 (a publication of the Conseil d'Analyse Économique, Office of the Premier Ministre); E. Caroli and J. Gautié, *Low-Wage Work in France* (New York: Russell Sage Foundation, 2008), p. 43.

35. Delobez, "Development of Shopping Centres," p. 150; and see "La Réforme de l'urbanisme commercial" (no author), *L'Actualité Juridique-Droit Administratif*, October 20, 1996, pp. 754–761; and "Lois," *Journal Officiel de la République Française*, July 6, 1996, pp. 10199–10207; and also see Metton "L'Expansion du commerce," pp. 463–479.

36. Delobez ("Development of Shopping Centres," pp. 151–153) explained that while the effect of the law may have been "broadly dissuasive," limiting "risky and anarchic enterprises" from making applications, "barely one-third of applications have been turned down by administrative bodies" in any event.

to liberalize Sunday shopping restrictions, unions held a demonstration of ten thousand in Paris to demand the withdrawal of the proposed law. Then, in 1988, two companies (IKEA and Leroy Merlin) opened two of their stores on Sunday in defiance of legal restrictions. In 1991, the results of a Harris poll were publicized indicating that 56 percent of the French favored opening stores on Sunday, sparking a renewal of the initiative in the French parliament. The press headlines read, variously: "A Schizophrenic Day: Depending on whether One Is a Consumer or a Worker the Opening of Stores on Sunday Does Not Mean the Same Thing" (*Libération*); "The French Want Stores to Open on Sunday" (*Le Journal du Dimanche*); "Not the Night, nor Sunday" (*L'Humanité*). In 1993 a new Virgin Megastore on the Champs-Élysées opened on Sunday in defiance of the law, with its CEO, Richard Branson, announcing that if it were prevented from opening on Sundays in the future, he would completely halt his investments in France, warning "We could open thirty stores in France."[37] Strongly encouraged by a group of big box retail chains (the home improvement stores Saint-Maclou, Leroy Merlin, and Mondial Moquette, along with the furniture chain, Conforama) who had indicated their intention to open a dozen of their stores on Sunday, the Virgin Megastore and the Disney Store were granted a legal exception to be open on Sundays within certain specified locations likely to attract tourists, such as the Champs-Élysées. It marked an important change, in symbolic terms, by cracking what, for a century, had been an inviolable seal protecting a part of every week from the intrusion of commercial activities. Following the initial change, a varying mix of exceptions to the Sunday-closing rule were gradually allowed, including all "tourist areas" during "tourist season" in the centers of the largest cities, in supermarkets during morning hours, and at some of the large suburban retail stores. While "*le commerce dominical*" remained formally sacrosanct for some years, in practice it was becoming increasingly possible to shop on Sundays.[38] For many French people the lure of "convenience" competed with the strongly held belief that workers and their families deserved one day per week free from work. This had been a widely accepted notion, not just for workers but also for small shopkeepers who feared that they would

---

37. "VIRGIN REVIVES THE BATTLE OF SUNDAYS" ("Virgin relance la bataille du Dimanche") read the headline in the daily newspaper *Libération* of August 6, 1993.

38. From "Shopping in France" on the About-France.com, available at http://about-france .com/shopping-in-france.htm. It remained forbidden for stores to be open twenty-four hours a day, however.

not be able to maintain sufficient staff levels to remain open seven days per week and thus would lose out to the large chains, and so they often resisted longer opening hours.[39]

Although the commercial revolution that had been inundating French *périurbain* space had begun to cool by 1974, it left a deep impression on French society. Not only had it introduced new forms of retail trade and new modes of shopping, along with a new commercial infrastructure, but also a new conceptual vocabulary. That is, the language of the mass market had put into circulation terms that signified new ways of thinking about commercial activity and assessing it in the context of large-scale retail trade. Terms like "discount," "merchandising," and "sourcing" were part of a new and distinctive language of *grande distribution* (mass-market retail trade), within which were inscribed new measures for determining value and calculating worth.[40] Basic terms like "turnover" (*chiffre d'affaires*), "sales area" (*surface de vente*), and "employment rate" (*le nombre d'employés*) were increasingly familiar references for the French, speaking to a new framework for retail commerce—an emergent logic based on high volume, low cost, and a rapid turnover of merchandise. Indeed, in 1991 the Ministry of Arts and Crafts, Trade, and Consumer Affairs of the French government published a glossary of French translations of foreign commercial terms that had, since 1973, been officially decreed as mandatory for use in official documents and educational manuals. Included were the following:[41]

Centre auto: Auto Center
Centre d'affaires international: World trade center
Centre commercial: Shopping center
Couponnage: Couponing
Crédit permanent: Revolving credit
Franchisage: Franchising
Jardinerie: Garden center

39. See M. S. "Sometimes on Sunday: Stores' opening hours in France," *The Economist*, December 2, 2013, available at http://www.economist.com/blogs/schumpeter/2013/12/stores-opening-hours-france.

40. Metton, *Commerce et la ville*, pp. 46–48.

41. The list was based on official decrees put forward between 1973 and 1991 by the Ministère de l'Artisanat, du Commerce et de la Consommation as "l'Enrichissement du Vocabulaire Commercial" and published in the document, *La France des commerces édition 1991* (Paris: Direction Commerce Intérieur, 1991), p. 77. It is noteworthy that virtually all of the "foreign" terms listed for translation were English terms.

Magasin d'usine: Factory outlet
Maisonnerie: Home center
Marchandisage: Merchandising
Mercaticien: Marketing specialist
Mercatique: Marketing
Minimarge: Discount house
Parrain: Sponsor
Payer-prendre: Cash and carry
Sourcage: Sourcing

Food as an Industry

The new selling domain of the grandes surfaces, which included super-markets, hypermarkets, shopping centers, and various other big box chain stores, were incubators for a new conceptual vocabulary, where traditional industrial principles of high volume, efficiency, and standardization were applied to the practices of retail trade.[42] Of course, the institutions, methods, and concepts of capitalist industrialization had been fully developed in France by the decade of the 1970s, including within the realm of food production.[43] At a basic level, *l'industrie agro-alimentaire* (the French equivalent of "agri-business" or the food-processing industry) has been that sector of the French economy engaged in transforming agricultural products to supply the dietary needs of consumers and includes all facets of the production, processing, and marketing of food.[44] The range of its activities is broad:[45]

> A. Production: seeds, planting, fertilizer, animal selection, livestock feed, veterinary products, farm machinery, operating equipment,

---

42. Indeed, the grandes surfaces were termed "les usines à vendre" (selling factories) by many analysts and commentators. See Metton, *Commerce et la ville*, p. 438; and Villermet, "Histoire des 'grandes surfaces,'" p. 46. For the expanding application of new forms of retail commerce in the domain of the food trade in France, see F. Amand and C. Laguzet, "Les grandes tendances de l'évolution des différentes formes de commerce, par marche, de 1980 a 1990," *Revue Française du Marketing*, no. 135, Cahier 5, 1991, pp. 5–12.

43. Until the oil crisis of 1973, the French economy was still enjoying the "Trente Glorieuses," the three decades of rapid economic "catch up" that followed a long period of relatively slow growth that France (and Europe) experienced through the first half of the twentieth century. See J. Fourastié, *Les Trente Glorieuses* (Paris: Fayard, 1979) and T. Piketty, *Capital in the Twenty-First Century* (Cambridge, MA: Harvard University Press, 2014), p. 87.

44. L. Mallassis, *Économie agro-alimentaire* (Paris: Éditions Cujas, 1979), p. 12.

45. This list was adapted from the map of the "Agro-alimentaire complex" by J. Bombal and P. Chalmin, in *L'Agro-alimentaire*, p. 11, and translated by the author.

farm buildings, cereals, plants, fruits, vegetables, wine growing, sugar production, milk, meat, animal husbandry, seafood, and so on.

B. Processing: crushing of seeds into oils, milling grains for bakeries and patisseries, malting for bars and brasseries, starch and glucose production, sugar processing for candies and distilleries, slaughterhouses, meat cutting, meat curing, canning of fruits and vegetables, frozen foods, precooked foods, and so on.

C. Distribution: for export and domestic markets, retail outlets, packaging, restaurants (traditional restaurants, chain restaurants, new restaurant forms), institutional catering, and so on.

The French industry of agro-alimentaire has been engaged in all of these activities, but its development followed by several decades the emergence of a food-processing industry in the United States, where technological innovations in production, transport, and conservation had been introduced earlier, largely driven by the size of U.S. markets and the economies of scale that they permitted.[46] In addition, as a heavily agricultural society with virtually year-round southern growing seasons, France had been somewhat slow to develop the institutional infrastructure for a heavily industrialized food-processing system.[47] Perhaps equally important was that the traditional French cultural predisposition toward and appreciation for *artisanal* food preparation had tempered the development of industrial techniques in the realm of foodways. As one observer noted, "The processing industry has been late to develop in this nation of fastidious eaters who prefer the taste of fresh food. French values of farm-fresh quality, so closely related to the

---

46. Manifested in such things as mechanized slaughterhouses, refrigerated rail transport, and specialized train cars built to transport animal carcasses. See P. Saunier and B. Schaller, "L'évolution technico-économique des industries alimentaires 1896–1987," in *La Grande Transformation de l'agriculture*, ed. G. Allaire and R. Boyer (Paris: Economica, 1995).

47. As Giorgio Pedrocco ("The Food Industry and New Preservation Techniques," in *FOOD: A Culinary History from Antiquity to the Present*, ed. Jean-Louis Flandrin and Massimo Montanari (New York: Columbia University Press, 1999), pp. 487–489, explains, American firms, aided by technical innovations in refrigeration techniques, were able to successfully enter the European market during the agricultural depression of 1873, exporting substantial quantities of fresh and processed foods. The mass production of preserved foods had begun in the United States in the 1860s, with canning techniques and factory production that had been rapidly developed in response to the outbreak of the Civil War, along with advertising techniques perfected in the United States by Campbell and Heinz and Borden. Thus industrial and advertising innovations combined to permit U.S. firms to establish markets for processed foods in Europe.

genius of French country cooking, are at the opposite end of the scale from industrial values of packaged efficiency."[48]

Others indicated the role of traditional culinary practices in slowing the development of industrial food-processing techniques: "In the context of global food, the situation of France is very paradoxical. First, the international reputation of French gastronomy, with its famous products and indisputable prestige, and on the other hand production structures that often still rely on craft techniques and demonstrate very uneven success as exports (excluding the export of unprocessed agricultural products)."[49]

Although France has been known as an agricultural nation that had long exported high-quality wines, spirits, and cheeses, until 1968 France actually had a net trade deficit in food and drink. Within only a decade, however, that deficit was essentially reversed as a great burst of productivity in the industry of agro-alimentaire produced a trade *surplus* of 8 percent in food and drink.[50] In the face of both European economic integration and the challenges posed by American multinational corporations, French farmers had begun to realize the tangible economic benefits of processing their own products. This was encouraged by several French government initiatives, including (1) the creation of large provincial agricultural markets, in close proximity to railway hubs, and (2) assistance to farmers in organizing agricultural collective societies to increase their leverage in relation to large corporations, while implementing strategies to maintain prices during periods of glut (with plans, for example, to divert part of their produce to their own canning and deep-freezing plants).[51] Although French farmers' cooperatives had existed for nearly a century, in the decade between 1970 and 1980 they "expanded tenfold, notably on the food-processing and marketing side, galvanized by the challenge of what they tend to see as their natural enemy: American capitalism!"[52] Farmers had feared that U.S. agribusiness companies would enclose them in a web of dependency in which agricultural commodity prices would be determined by huge foreign corporations whose vertical integration would severely restrict the farmers' ability to market their products elsewhere. To support French farmers, the French

48. J. Ardagh, *France in the 1980s* (Harmondsworth, U.K.: Penguin Books, 1982), p. 227.
49. Bombal and Chalmin, *L'Agro-alimentaire*, p. 70. Translated by author.
50. Ardagh, *France in the 1980s*, p. 227.
51. These organizations, called "Sociétés d'Intérêt Collectif Agricole" (SICA), were often quite successful, although more so in some regions than others. See Ardagh, *France in the 1980s*, p. 225.
52. Ardagh, *France in the 1980s*, p. 226.

government tacitly promised to impose restrictions on American agricultural investment if farmers would develop their own processing operations. So, for example, after Libby's had built a tomato canning plant near Nîmes, putting local growers under contract, a regional farmer's cooperative was organized to supply its own peach- and pear-canning factory, which would later grow to become "one of the largest and best of its kind in Europe—much bigger, in fact, than the local Libby's plant."[53]

French agricultural cooperatives were essentially revivified in reaction to the influx of American food-processing firms in the 1960s and 1970s, providing French farmers with an ability to retain a degree of control over the price and disposition of their products through the various stages of production, processing, marketing, and distribution. Some cooperatives were able to build enormous food-processing operations that rivaled the largest private firms. Thus giant dairy cooperatives like Union Laitière Normande and SODIMA had sales of 5.4 and 5.2 billion francs in 1978 (roughly $912 million, and $872 million, respectively); while in that same year the meat cooperative, Socopa France had a turnover of 1.9 billion francs ($322 million). This equaled some of the largest private French companies in agro-alimentaire, companies with names like BSN-Gervais-Danone (7.9 billion francs in dairy products and other foods—$1.3 billion), Beghin-Say (5 billion francs in sugar—$833 million), Pernod-Ricard (4.5 billion francs in spirits—$750 million), Sopad-Nestlé (3.5 billion francs in dairy and other foods—$583 million), Moët-Hennessy (1.9 billion francs of wines and liquors—$316 million), Perrier (1.5 billion francs in drinks and other foods—$250 million), Bel (2.5 billion francs in cheeses—$416 million), Bongrain (1.9 billion francs in cheeses—$380 million), Morey (1.1 billion francs of meats and cured meats—$183 million), Rousselot (1.4 billion francs in livestock feed—$233 million).[54] These were firms that operated on the basis of capitalist principles and were often modeled, in organizational terms, after the largest and most successful U.S. companies.[55]

Indeed, within the industry of agro-alimentaire (again, a term corresponding to the concept of agribusiness or food-processing industry), the United States was the uncontested leader, worldwide. Accordingly, sixteen of the twenty-five largest firms in the world were U.S.-based companies,

53. Ardagh, *France in the 1980s*, p. 226.

54. Companies listed in "French food-processing companies of over 1 billion francs, 1978," Table 12, in Bombal and Chalmin, *L'Agro-alimentaire*, p. 76.

55. D. Galliano, "Modèles de groupes et dynamiques industrielles: Cas des IAA" [Industries Agro-Alimentaires], in Allaire and Boyer, *La Grande Transformation*, p. 204.

with the balance being British (six), French (one), Swiss (one), and Japanese (one).[56] The largest of the firms were American, so that in 1977 the largest French firm, BSN-Gervais-Danone, was ranked twenty-first in the world with a turnover of $3.1 billion, while the largest American food company that year, Beatrice Foods (dairy products), had a turnover of $7.4 billion, over double the size, and was not even ranked among the top thirty largest U.S. corporations at the time.[57] In other words, in the mid-1970s U.S. corporations were gargantuan relative to European firms, and U.S.-based multinationals in food processing tended to thoroughly dominate world markets, including the French market. French farmers' fears of U.S. dominance would thus seem to have had a material basis.

Through the 1970s the French food-processing industry was developing alongside the suburban-based commercial "revolution," in which new modes of retail production and consumption were introduced, and at the moment when a market for American-style fast food was beginning to emerge in French cities. The various social factors that social science and marketing research had identified as contributing to changes in French eating habits, and thereby creating a foundation for the development of fast food in France, were also underwriting the cult of consumer "convenience" reflected in the growing industrie agro-alimentaire and the expansion of the grandes surfaces, or big box supermarkets and hypermarkets. Changes in French family life, including the growing number of women in the labor force, an increase in spendable income of adolescents, and a weakening of family ties that was placing less emphasis on family meal times, were unfolding along with changes in the realm of work that contributed to new patterns of eating. Observers noted that American influence on French business practices had included expansion of the "*journée continue*" (workdays without extended meal breaks) which, along with an increasing availability of workplace canteens and cafeterias, an increase in urban traffic congestion, and thus suburban commuting time, all contributed to a decline in the traditional practice of two-hour midday meal breaks.[58]

Alongside the growth of commercial forms driven by the principles of the mass market, a new consumer comportment was forged that privileged

---

56. "Ranking of the 25 largest global agribusiness firms," Table 3, in Bombal and Chalmin, *L'Agro-alimentaire*, p. 36.

57. Agribusiness reportedly accounted for 15 percent of industrial production in the United States in 1975, Bombal and Chalmin, *L'Agro-alimentaire*, p. 39.

58. See J. Ardagh, *The New French Revolution* (London: Secker and Warburg, 1968), pp. 267–269.

convenience and frugality over custom and convention. That could only be accomplished if the traditional French antipathy to industrially produced foods were overcome. As two analysts observed: "French consumers want natural products, not industrial, and if possible fresh. A demand for this grows when financial resources permit, to reject industrial products in favor of non-standardized products made in an artisanal way. . . . This gastronomic conception of food is deeply rooted in the spirit of the French consumer, and explains the delay in the industrialization of food products in certain sectors."[59]

To a large degree, in the realm of French gastronomy the rules of mass markets were introduced in practice, through such prosaic activities as eating (fast food), shopping (in big box stores), and purchasing the foods produced and marketed by the food-processing industry (l'industrie agro-alimentaire). During periods of economic slowdown French consumers would become particularly observant students of the logic of mass markets, as the companies themselves recognized, for when faced with budgetary constraints consumers tended to be "more attentive to the quality-price ratio of artificially differentiated products . . . particularly concerning food purchasing," and the supermarkets responded with marketing strategies to emphasize product prices and the low-cost retail or store brands, rather than highlighting the traditional producers of the products, particularly when these goods were not of a clearly superior quality.[60] In other words, consumers were weaned away from traditional or customary methods of shopping and increasingly directed toward heavily promoted lower price "discount" brands. The offer of discounts soon came to be expected and the purposeful search for discounts and low prices ("bargain hunting") gradually became a common practice. The main point, however, is that it was in the very prosaic activity of normal, everyday food shopping that the values of convenience and efficiency (and "productivity") were absorbed by French consumers who were trained to seek out "bargains" in ways that resembled the drive for efficiency and productivity at work.

Shopping was thus a key portal through which the postwar logic of the mass market was introduced into the domain of gastronomy. It proceeded somewhat more slowly in France than in the United States, where industrial modernity had been able to advance relatively unimpeded. In

---

59. Bombal and Chalmin, *L'Agro-alimentaire*, p. 81.

60. Quoted on p. 26 of R. Perez, "Les stratégies des firmes multinationales alimentaires," in *Économie Rurale*, vol. 231, January–February 1996, pp. 21–28.

1980 there were still only 109 fast-food restaurants in France, compared to many thousands in the United States; the big box stores (grandes surfaces) had only just begun expanding across the French landscape, while already firmly entrenched in the United States; and prepared and frozen foods were just entering the French market when they were already a common feature of the U.S. diet (in 1976 per capita frozen food consumption in France was less than one-quarter of what it was in the United States).[61] In France, the decade of the 1970s was a key period in the industrialization of the French gastronomic field.

With the explosion of retail innovations under way, a common set of references and conventions had to be forged, not only for consumers but among French businessmen as well. The proliferation of methods, styles, and technologies of selling that were being implemented were essentially matched by the proliferation of magazines and trade journals providing their readers with information about emerging business trends and technical innovations, as well as about the multitude of companies, services, suppliers, and equipment involved in facilitating the new business strategies and practices. Periodicals such as *La Revue de l'industrie agro-alimentaire*, and *Magazine LSA* (Libre Service Actualités), founded in 1953 and 1958, respectively, were important trade organs oriented to the management of food-processing companies; while *Néorestauration* magazine was begun in 1972 as a key publication for the managements of chains of commercial and collective restaurants, with a particular attention to the developing trends and innovations in *restauration* (from fast-food chains, to takeaway restaurants, to theme restaurants, etc.). Dozens of related trade publications appeared, with some focusing on the managers responsible for specific elements or stages in food-processing practices, such as technologies, transport, frozen foods, food additives, or vending opportunities; with others oriented to the management of specific foods or food groups (breads, dairy, baked goods, sugar, drinks, meats, fruits, vegetables, etc.); and still others geared to employment and human relations and career development within the industry. These were published in various forms, including glossy magazines, newspapers and newsletters, and later websites; provided a range of various services to their readers, such as marketing studies, reports of emerging (and fading) trends in production, consumption, and distribution processes, and legal

---

61. Per capita consumption of frozen foods was 23.5 kilos in the United States and 5.4 kilos in France in 1976–1977, according to J. Bombal and P. Chalmin, in *L'Agro-alimentaire*, p. 68.

and scientific developments; and were funded by the industry trade groups and advertising space that was purchased from those hoping to sell a wide range of products, services, and supplies.

"Americanism" as Symbolic Capital

At the institutional level, the newly developed business models that accompanied (and enacted) this industrialization tended to share family lines. Not only did they speak the common language of mass markets and share a business orientation based on the lure of discount pricing, high-volume retail selling, and aggressive marketing but they also shared a common ancestry in the "American" roots of their business practices. Indeed, having an American lineage could serve as a key source of legitimacy, if not sanctification, when it came to business methods viewed as innovative departures from traditional French industrial practices, characterized by a combination of industrial planning, nationalized enterprise, and private entrepreneurship.[62] The association of the United States with industrial modernity had long held a powerful symbolic place in the European (and French) social imagination, as the wellspring of the most advanced industrial technologies, managerial methods, and organizational innovations. Although French corporations flourished through the last decades of the nineteenth century, competing with the traditional family-owned firm, at least as far back as the 1920s French businessmen were looking with approval toward American business, admired for the application of innovative "scientific" principles of management, including a high degree of professionalization, the specialization and separation of distinct managerial spheres, and the development and application of industrial psychology.[63] After the war, American mana-

---

62. See R. Kuisel, *Capitalism and the State in Modern France* (Cambridge: Cambridge University Press, 1981). As David Landes has noted, before World War II in France, "the model enterprise was family-owned and operated, security-oriented rather than risk-taking, technologically conservative and economically inefficient. . . . Both big and small enterprises were abetted in this comfortable stalemate by the state and society, which took stagnation for granted, looked on most forms of competition as *déloyale*, and preferred the social criterion of contribution-by-work to the market criterion of contribution-by-efficiency." D. Landes, *The Unbound Prometheus: Technological Change and Industrial Development in Western Europe from 1750 to the Present* (Cambridge: Cambridge University Press, 1969), p. 528.

63. Modern corporate methods were not necessarily incompatible with the existence of family firms and were implemented earlier in France than has often been acknowledged. See C. E. Freedeman, *The Triumph of Corporate Capitalism in France, 1867–1914* (Rochester, NY: University of Rochester Press, 1993), p. 129. For an analysis of the sources of admiration for American methods, see, J. Gillingham, "Background to Marshall-Plan Technical Assistance:

gerial practices would represent the main inspiration for post–World War II economic planning in France. The postwar program had been designed to both attract American aid in the rebuilding and modernization of the French economy and break with models of socialist planning championed by French socialists and communists in the 1930s.[64] Jean Monnet, chief planner of French postwar economic reconstruction and the key architect of postwar European unity, had reportedly been powerfully influenced by his experience in Washington during the war, where he had been sent by the British to negotiate for war supplies and where he immediately became an informal adviser to FDR. For Monnet, who "acted as the self-proclaimed trustee of American economic policy," American methods of economic modernization were embodied not just in specific technologies or particular management systems but principally in a "state of mind" and a "dynamic attitude"; for him, economic planning was a "psychological exercise" in which "French industry needed to adopt the American business psychology and particularly its attitude to growth and constant change."[65]

Monnet's principal economic development strategy for postwar France (and Europe) had been to stimulate a consciousness of productivity, inspired by the American model. Indeed, French "productivity missions" to the United States, organized under the auspices of the Marshall Plan, were mostly effective in transmitting a spirit of productivity, or a belief that everything should be put in the service of productivity. Indeed, when asked to identify the main advantage of the United States over France in economic terms, the chief government official responsible for organizing the Marshall Plan "productivity missions" to the United States asserted: "More than anything else, the American industry is pressured by a spirit of competitiveness and the productivity spirit. Also, the idea that the market was not a given

---

Productivism as American Ideology," in *Catching Up with America: Productivity Missions and the Diffusion of American Economic and Technological Influence after the Second World War*, ed. D. Barjot (Paris: Presses de l'Université de Paris-Sorbonne, 2002), p. 55.

64. R. Kuisel, *Capitalism and the State*, pp. 224–225. As Djelic has written, "The institutionalization of the French productivity effort thus coincided with increasing American intervention. The USA came to finance a large proportion of the productivity effort through the technical assistance program and American productivity experts were soon touring French factories, companies, farms, and administrations. . . . An increased familiarity with the American model combined with the dependence of French productivity institutions on American funds to bring the French productivity discourse fully into line with the American tradition." See M.-L. Djelic, *Exporting the American Model* (New York: Oxford University Press, 1998), p. 148.

65. Quotes from R. Kuisel, *Capitalism and the State*, pp. 226, 232, and from Carew, *Labour under the Marshall Plan*, p. 215.

but could be expanded through effort was quite new. Then the practical work that underpinned management, especially in marketing, was particularly impressive."[66]

With the Marshall Plan as the central vehicle of transmission ("an agency of propaganda" as one analyst noted[67]), an identifiable "American model" was constructed within the French (and European) imagination that represented the direct antithesis of traditional artisan practices. According to Jonathan Zeitlin, "the 'American model' meant above all mass—the high-volume manufacture of standardized goods using special-purpose machinery and predominantly unskilled labor—together with the host of 'systematic' management techniques, organizational structures, and research and marketing services developed for its efficient administration and effective exploitation."[68]

There was nothing magical about American business practices, for it was only that they had largely been implemented and tested under the favorable conditions of a rapidly expanding postwar economy, along with an industrial base that had been not only untouched by the war but greatly expanded by furnishing the materials of war. The effect was that postwar economic growth in Europe proceeded with American business essentially setting the terms.[69] The general situation for postwar business development was less constrained in the United States than it had been in France where "free enterprise" had never been an object of reverence and where protectionist impulses had traditionally served to temper the "competitive spirit."[70] Adding to American authority within the domain of French business and industry was the fact that alongside the growth of American mass production had been the corresponding growth of mass consumption. This could be viewed as having been as much a cultural-psychological process as a structural-economic one: "In the US, two nearly simultaneous

66. Interview with Rotislaw Donn in T. Hara, "Productivity Missions to the United States: The Case of Post-War France," in Barjot, *Catching Up with America*, p. 177.

67. Carew, *Labour under the Marshall Plan*, p. 137.

68. J. Zeitlin, "Introduction," in *Americanization and Its Limits: Reworking US Technology and Management in Post-War Europe and Japan*, ed. J. Zeitlin and G. Herrigel (New York: Oxford University Press, 2000).

69. See G. Lundestad, *The United States and Western Europe since 1945* (Oxford: Oxford University Press, 2003), p. 64; V. R. Berghahn, ed. *The Americanization of West German Industry, 1945–1973* (Cambridge: Cambridge University Press, 1986); and Marie-Laure Djelic, *Exporting the American Model: The Postwar Transformation of European Business* (Oxford: Oxford University Press, 2001).

70. Kuisel, *Capitalism and the State*, p. 275.

trends appeared to create a consumer society: while an emerging mass-production economy produced a need for mass markets, the erosion of the ascetic Victorian personality created an American psyche susceptible to the appeals of merchandisers. Economic concentration, rapid transportation, capital intensive production and mass communications made national advertising a vital tool for creating wants to which Americans were especially receptive."[71]

There was nothing "magical" about U.S. business, in the sense that its authority had largely derived from concrete and demonstrable historical processes. However, in another, more anthropological sense, there *was* something quite magical about U.S. business in its ability to charm. Drawing from the perspective of Marcel Mauss, one can understand the magician as succeeding not as a result of their specific skills or conjuring tricks but as a consequence of performing in the context of the *collective belief of the group*.[72] Following Mauss, Bourdieu referred to magic as a "collective misrecognition, collectively produced and maintained, which is at the source of the power that the magician appropriates."[73] Viewed this way, magic can be seen as depending on and contributing to a tacit complicity of all the participants in a system of symbolic production, wherein the system acts to "screen" the magician and the object of their magic, making it difficult for the audience (of producers or consumers) to perceive the act of magic, as magic. As we saw in the previous chapter, for French youths American styles and American cultural goods were endowed with enhanced symbolic value (i.e., were considered *la mode*, "cool") precisely when they were considered authentically "American" and were thus decidedly "not French." Across a broad spectrum of cultural goods, including fast food, American goods were endowed with considerable symbolic capital for French youths. In a

---

71. G. Cross, *Time and Money: The Making of Consumer Culture* (London: Routledge, 1993), p. 156. Further, the construction of a consumer society in the United States was aided by a considerable amount of intellectual labor. See D. Horowitz, *Consuming Pleasures: Intellectuals and Popular Culture in the Postwar World* (Philadelphia: University of Pennsylvania Press, 2012).

72. What I have in mind is the social production of magic, as outlined by Marcel Mauss in *A General Theory of Magic* (London: Routledge, 2001). Bourdieu often drew upon this conception of magic to understand the operation of art markets, the consecrating power of the state, and the symbolic power of fashion designers. See, for example, P. Bourdieu and Y. Delsaut, "Le Couturier et sa griffe, contribution à une théorie de la magie," in *Actes de la Recherche en Sciences Sociales*, no. 1, 1975, pp. 7–36. An outline of this article in English can be found in "Haute Couture and Haute Culture," in *Sociology in Question*, ed. P. Bourdieu (London: Sage Publications, 1993), esp. pp. 136–138.

73. P. Bourdieu, *The Rules of Art* (Stanford, CA: Stanford University Press, 1995), p. 169.

parallel fashion, within the economic field, American business practices, management techniques, and styles were endowed with the symbolic capital able to "magically" induce a suspension of belief on the part of French businessmen, state officials, or journalists.[74] In the arena of youths and consumption a "magic of Americanism" was at work, partly represented by the visual hyperbole of the fast-food outlet; and in the field of economic practices, a comparable "magic" of "Americanism" held sway, with the visual hyperbole of the fast-food outlet an expression of the brash, aggressive promotional style of American business practices more generally.

The "American model" would thus come to be embedded in the realm of French gastronomy, although not in its most rarified regions where three-star restaurants and the artistry of grand chefs were the central symbols of French cultural supremacy. Rather, the American model tended to be most enthusiastically received and applied in the industrializing sector of the gastronomic field, a region where standardization and high-volume production processes were combined with low-cost, mass-market consumption, and facilitated by advanced marketing strategies. The soil where the American model took root and flourished in the gastronomic field was among commercial restaurant chains and institutional catering operations, which, although largely invisible in symbolic terms, to the French and others, actually came to overshadow French haute cuisine in material terms.

Structure of the Industrial Sector

Inside the industrial regions of French cuisine two broad categories are employed to designate restaurants: *restauration commerciale* and *restauration collective*. The former denotes eating establishments that are open to the broad public and are also sometimes referred to as *restauration grand public*. They include all manner of public restaurants, including local independent restaurants and bistros, hotel restaurants, chain restaurants, and fast-food companies. In France, roughly 80 percent of commercial restaurants are independently owned by individuals or families, while 20

---

74. It was just this reciprocally confirming process of collective belief that led French (and American) public officials, journalists, and business figures in the 1980s and 1990s to misconstrue the U.S. economy as the "Great American Jobs Machine." See R. Fantasia, "Dictature *sur* le prolétariat: Stratégies de répression et travail aux Etats-Unis," in *Actes de la Recherche en Sciences Sociales*, no. 138, June 2001, pp. 3–18.

percent are owned and operated by corporate chains (a percentage that is increasing).[75] The other broad category of restaurants, *restauration collective* (or sometimes *restauration sociale*), are basically institutional catering establishments, such as cafeterias and canteens, in which access is generally reserved for those who are attached to the institution (to schools, workplaces, hospitals, retirement homes, prisons, the military, airlines, etc.). Approximately 20 percent of these kitchens are managed and run by a branch of the State or by nonprofit associations connected to the institutions themselves, while the other 80 percent are subcontracted to external catering companies.[76] Altogether, the restaurant, catering, and food service industry employed about 700,000 workers in some 174,000 establishments in 2002, distributed in the following manner (see Table 4.1).

TABLE 4.1 DIVISION OF FRENCH RESTAURANT INDUSTRY BY SECTOR (2003)

Sector	# Establishments by Sector	# Employees by Sector
Traditional restaurants	55,099	293,663
Hotels with restaurant	17,383	145,928
Fast food	16,364	105,061
Workplace canteens and cafeterias	14,970	73,669
Cafés and bars	9,081	42,073
Institutional caterers	2,346	24,067
Independent caterers	1,755	14,859

Source: GIRA-SIC Conseil, "Les Chiffres Clés de la RHD en France et en Europe," published by the trade magazine *Néorestauration* (in collaboration with the food service marketing firm, GIRA-SIC Conseil), November 2003, p. 22. The employment figures cited are consistent with the official French government sources cited in S.-A. Mériot, *Le Cuisinier nostalgique*, p. 55.

75. The findings of an industry study showed the number of chain restaurants growing at 6 percent between 1994 and 1998, set on a steady upward trajectory. Reported in S.-A. Mériot, *Le Cuisinier nostalgique: Entre restaurant et cantine* (Paris: CNRS Editions, 2002), p. 54n4.

76. Mériot, *Le Cuisinier nostalgique*, p. 54. While there are dozens of such companies, three are dominant. In a profile of thirty-seven leading companies within this sector, from 2008, Groupe Sodexho, Elior (formerly Avenance and Eliance, respectively), and Compass Group France accounted for over three-fourths of the employees (76,000), three-fourths of the restaurants (12,721) and together had an annual turnover rate (4.7 billion euros) triple the amount of the thirty-four other firms combined. Source: "Dossier restauration collective: Le classement des opérateurs en France," *Néorestauration*, no. 463, April 2009, p. 27.

The industry sources that provide figures on the numbers of restaurants do not differentiate on the basis of qualitative criteria, so that the number of traditional restaurants (55,099) includes tens of thousands of independent restaurants and bistros; several thousand corporate-owned chain restaurants, many organized according to particular formulas or themes; as well as 500-plus Michelin-starred restaurants, recipients of the highest forms of symbolic consecration in the field of gastronomic practices.[77] In the industrial region of the field it is basically only size that matters. The standards employed and the factors brought to bear when conferring value on the actors in this domain are based solely on quantitative measures. These include *volume*, measured in *chiffre d'affaires* (annual revenue or turnover); *size*, measured in number of "*unités*" (number of restaurants or business establishments, and sometimes the number of employees); *trend* (movement upward or downward from the previous year with regard to volume and size); and *rank* (where the company stands in relation to other companies in annual revenue).[78] Under the terms of these factors the structure of the catering industry has been relatively stable over the past several decades in France, with the leading companies generally able to maintain their relative position and ranking (see Table 4.2).

Some firms listed among the top ten commercial restaurants owned and managed a single brand and single type of restaurant, while others listed were restaurant conglomerates that owned multiple restaurant chains. So whereas in 2010 McDonald's owned 1,195 McDonald's fast-food outlets in France, France Quick SAS owned 371 Quick fast-food outlets, and Buffalo Grill held 327 of its own chain restaurants, Agapes Restauration was the parent company of 454 restaurants consisting of a variety of different chain businesses, including 234 Flunch (cafeteria-style self-service restaurants), 44 Pizza Paï (Italian family-style pizzerias), and 13 Amariné (seafood

---

77. As we noted previously, *Michelin*-starred restaurants are themselves highly stratified, so that in any given year there are roughly four hundred to five hundred restaurants with one *Michelin* star, seventy to ninety restaurants with two stars, and about twenty-five restaurants awarded three stars in the *Michelin Guide*. Other significant, but lesser, forms of recognition are used by the *Michelin Guide* (restaurants designated with "toques" and "fourchettes"), and restaurants and chefs are also ranked in the *Gault-Millau* guide and in various other sites of gastronomic recognition (see Chapter 2).

78. The principal trade magazine of the industry, *Néorestauration*, publishes an annual dossier on the state of the catering industry that ranks the top eighty or one hundred companies in *restauration commerciale* and in *restauration collective* for France and for Europe by volume, size, and growth trends.

TABLE 4.2 RANK OF PRINCIPAL CORPORATE ACTORS IN THE
FRENCH CATERING INDUSTRY (2010)

Rank/Name of Company	CA*	# of Establishments	Previous Rankings
1. McDonald's France	3,900	1,195	2006: 1 2000: 1 1993: 1
2. Agapes Restauration	880	454	2006: 3 2000: 3 1993: 4
3. Quick France	811.9	371	2006: 2 2000: 2 1993: 5
4. Elior (previously Eliance)	646.1	776	2006: 4 2000: 4 1993: 9
5. Groupe Flo	570.8	280	2006: 7 2000: 6 1993: 7
6. Buffalo Grill	550.3	327	2006: 6 2000: 7 1993: 8
7. Le Duff	504.1	437	2006: 8 2000: 10 1993: 15
8. Servair	501	11	2006: 5 2000: 5 1993: 6
9. Casino Restauration	323.9	287	2006: 9 2000: 9 1993: 2
10. Yum! Brands	320	118	2006: 13 2000: — 1993: —

*Figures on *chiffres d'affaire* (CA), or sales turnover, are in millions of euros.
Source: Rankings and numbers have been drawn from the annual dossiers (industry profiles) of the French catering industry published by *Néorestauration* magazine for selected years.

restaurants), along with breweries, cafés, and chains of salad bars.[79] This is not an unusual pattern of ownership in this region of the field. Twenty years earlier, in 1990, the three leading restaurant *groupes* in France were (1) Casino, (2) McDonald's, and (3) Accor. McDonald's owned 150 of its

---

79. The 2010 list is compiled in "Le Classement 2010 des opérateurs de la restauration commerciale," *Néorestauration*, no. 486, May 2011.

own fast-food outlets; while the Casino Groupe owned 139 cafeterias, 132 Quick fast-food outlets, and 16 Hippopotamus chain restaurants, among others; while Accor owned 259 restaurants that included 12 different brand names of chain restaurants and fast-food companies. Twenty years later, McDonald's was the largest commercial restaurant company, by far, with an annual turnover rate over four times the rate of the next largest firm (see Table 4.2); but Casino had sold off a number of its restaurants (though it remained France's largest chain of supermarkets and hypermarkets); and in 2010 Accor was a major owner of hotel and motel chains but had fallen to 22 on the list of the largest commercial restaurants, retaining just two significant food-related holdings, a line of gourmet bakeries and chocolate shops, and a company that supplied the catering for the French train system. Between 1990 and 2010 some of the large food groups grew substantially by thoroughly reconfiguring their portfolios of brands and companies, while others grew by maintaining a similar mix of companies, but increasing the number of their holdings of these companies.[80]

So while there has been a measure of stability to the structure of ownership within this region of the field, both single-chain companies (like McDonald's and Buffalo Grill, etc.) and the parent companies of different restaurant chains (like Agapes Restauration, Groupe Flo, Groupe Le Duff, etc.) have been in a fairly constant state of change, ever expanding or reducing the number of restaurants in a specific chain, buying new chains, and selling off or closing others. Among other things this seems to indicate little commitment to any particular brand, or company, or type of cuisine offered. As chains, they strive for standardization and replication in order to produce at a high level of volume. As business firms, they operate fully and exclusively on the basis of profit and loss. Decisions about growth, contraction, and trajectory are made solely with regard to profitability. In this domain, there is very little room for sentiment, or venerability, or artistry in managerial strategies or valuation and, in fact, an agent or institution is regarded as a leader and is considered successful on the basis of completely different, even opposing principles. While they may (and do) acquire and accumulate a measure of symbolic value, it is symbolic value bestowed on

---

80. Groupe Flo, which had owned just 8 classic bistros in 1990, went on to acquire 280 chain restaurants from a variety of chain companies, while Groupe Le Duff maintained ownership of 156 chain restaurants, cafés, and fast-food viennoiseries but acquired more of the same chains, as well as a chain of pizza restaurants. Data for 1990 and 2010 data are presented in "Les 50 Premier Groupes," *Revue Technique des hôtels et restaurants*, March 1991, p. 61, and "Les Classement 2010 des opérateurs."

the basis of high volume production, operational efficiency, and ascending growth.

These are companies that are led NOT by chefs de cuisine, who have been cultivated for a particular culinary métier after a long period of apprenticeship in a great restaurant, but by *chefs d'entreprise*, men trained in and by the business world. While the data available is not as systematic as one might wish, such evidence as there is indicates that the great majority of the corporate heads in the industrialized regions of the gastronomic field entered their firms as industrialists or as professional business managers, after having trained in business schools, law schools, as engineers, or by having risen from the ranks of lower management in the food service or hotel industry.[81] This is suggested in the background information provided on seven of the P-dg's (*Président directeur-général*) within the ten largest commercial restaurant firms in 1990. Of these seven, it seems that only one had been trained for a career as a chef. Jean-Paul Bucher, the head of Groupe Flo in 1990, was the son of a restaurateur and studied for a *Baccalauréat Technologique Hôtellerie* (BTH) before apprenticing at the restaurant of a grand hotel in Mulhouse, followed by cooking jobs at three notable Parisian restaurants. He went on to become the proprietor of several Parisian brasseries, which were brought together under the umbrella corporation, Flo Prestige, a catering/chain restaurant firm. Bucher became PDG of Groupe Flo in 1977, managing the acquisition of numerous bistros and restaurants over the course of the 1980s.[82] But Jean-Paul Bucher was the exception

81. Besides information on individual corporate executives gleaned from industry trade magazines and various editions of *Who's Who in France*, I have relied on a published compendium of "the principal actors" of "*commercial et collective restauration*" in France. Published in 2003 by *Néorestauration* magazine, in collaboration with the publishing firm Philippe Hersant and Partners, *L'Annuaire de la restauration 2003–2004* (Paris: Éditeur Groupe Industrie Services Info, 2003), the document was designed to be a comprehensive index of all commercial and collective catering companies, listing company information, professional organizations (training organizations, professional associations, unions, state organizations, etc.). In addition, and of particular value, is a 200-page section entitled "The Book" (in English) that provides the CVs of some 460 members of what the publisher terms the "top management" of *commercial et collective restauration*. While the criteria for inclusion is not fully specified, and while it does not appear to be comprehensive (it excludes a fair number of prominent managers), and the CVs presented are of variable degrees of detail, it nevertheless provides a useful survey of the career trajectories of a significant segment of managers in the French catering industry.

82. Through the 1980s, Groupe Flo purchased several venerable Parisian restaurants and bistros, including La Coupole and Julien, and opened a number of their own bistros (Flo Barcelone, Flo Prestige Opera, Flo Prestige Daumesnil, among many others), as well as creating Japon de Flo in Japan. Source: see entry for Jean-Paul Bucher, in *Who's Who in France 1990–1991: Dictionnaire biographique*, 22nd ed. (Paris: Editions Jacques Lafitte, 1990), p. 356.

among this group of corporate leaders, most of whom had been trained for the world of business rather than the world of cuisine.

Much more typical in this region of the field were Paul Dubrule and Gérard Pélisson, copresidents of Accor. Dubrule, the founder of Accor, was the son of an industrialist and studied at l'Institut des Hautes Études Commerciales, an elite business school at the University of Geneva, after which he held internships at the Swiss Bank Corporation and the Chemical Corn Exchange, before spending 1962–1963 in Dayton, Ohio, as an assistant to Bernardo Trujillo, the Prophet of Selling (as noted above). In 1963, at the age of 29, Dubrule cofounded Novotel, a hotel chain, which would later merge with Jacques Borel International, owner of a chain of restaurants and fast-food companies, to form Accor in 1983.[83] Gérard Pélisson, Dubrule's copresident at Accor, studied engineering in Paris and then earned an MS in Industrial Management at the Massachusetts Institute of Technology (MIT). He worked for eight years as an industrial engineer in logistics, systems analysis, and strategic marketing at IBM Europe, before cofounding Novotel with Paul Dubrule.[84] Besides the fact that (like most of their peers) they had been prepared for business careers rather than for careers as chefs or other culinary occupations, like many (if not most) of their peers, they also spent significant portions of their working lives "suckling at the tit" of the American model of business. What this means is not just that they had spent time working and studying in the United States, although French businessmen in this industry often did just that, but that they adopted or embraced an outlook or set of perspectives on business methods that had been commonly practiced in U.S. industry and that they could bring back to implement in France as business innovations. For example, in an early interview in *Néorestauration* magazine, Louis Le Duff, the head of Groupe Le Duff, was asked about what he had learned from his three years of working for restaurant chains in the United States:

> During my stay across the Atlantic, I discovered that catering [*restauration*] was a true industry in the noble sense of the term and that against what has often passed in the French university, that it can attract young university graduates in the same way as electron-

---

83. Sources: Profile of Paul Dubrule in "The Book," in *L'annuaire de la restauration 2003–2004*, p. 161, and in *Who's Who in France*, p. 615.

84. Sources: Profile of Gérard Pélisson in "The Book," in *L'annuaire de la restauration 2003–2004*, p. 249, and in *Who's Who in France*, p. 1285.

ics, distribution, or banking. . . . Henceforth, the image of catering has evolved in France; the sector has gained acclaim and with that a need for higher education training in catering and hotel management, implemented by the creation of, notably . . . the Cornell-Essec à Cergy-Pontoise program.[85]

In the United States where restaurants in the catering industry were managed as businesses, Le Duff seemed to have absorbed a measure of confidence in the professional status and legitimacy of catering *as an industry*. Within two years of his return to France, at age twenty-eight, Le Duff created a management company for institutional catering (Restaurel) based in Brittany, and one year after that, in 1976, founded La Brioche Dorée a franchise fast-food company that sold croissants and pastries and that has grown steadily over the course of subsequent decades.[86] Observing the U.S. fast-food industry up close gave the young French businessman a vantage point from which to learn how he might apply industrial methods to the production and distribution of artisanal foods: "La Brioche Dorée is more innovative with regard to the way the product is sold than on the product itself. In truth, in a certain sense we have industrialized the management and selling methods of a product normally fabricated in artisanal fashion."[87]

The institutional catering sector in France, called *collective restauration*, has maintained an industry structure similar to *commercial restauration*, to the extent that it has been controlled by just a few firms and, within that small group, the largest has held its dominant position for over a quarter century. Sodexho became Groupe Sodexho France (and later, Sodexo) as it expanded its operations internationally in the 1990s to become the largest institutional catering company in the world. Sodexo is the parent of several firms that, taken together, are twice the size of the two next largest

85. Author translation. The reference to Cornell-Essec Cergy-Pontoise refers to a joint MBA program in "hospitality management" that existed between Cornell University (most likely its Hotel management school) and ESSEC (Ecole Supérieure des Sciences Économiques et Commerciales) an elite French business school, located in the Paris suburb of Cergy-Pontoise. Source: *"Invité d'honneur 81: Louis Le Duff, un marqueur de buts"* [trans.: Louis Le Duff, goal scorer], *Néorestauration*, no. 109, December 1981, p. 47.

86. *Néorestauration*, no. 109, p. 47. Groupe Le Duff had 109 *Brioche Dorée* [trans.: "Guilded Brioche, or Bun"] outlets in 1990, 235 in 1998, 315 in 2002, and 349 in 2008. Sources: "Les 50 Premier Groupes," in *Revue technique des hôtels et restaurants, Collectivités, Equip' Hôtel*, no. 496, March 1991, p. 61; and from dossiers in the following issues of *Néorestauration* magazine: no. 354, May 1999, p. 45; no. 398, May 2003, p. 60; and no. 464, May 2009, p. 45.

87. *"Invité d'honneur 81,"* p. 48.

companies (Groupe Elior and Compass Group France). These three companies are themselves three times the size of the next forty-seven companies combined.[88] These companies are the organizations that daily feed the French population at schools, in universities, in hospitals, in prisons, and in workplace canteens, with most (80 percent) as profit-making corporations operating along capitalist principles, like the conglomerates that own chains of commercial restaurants (noted above).

Like those chain restaurant companies, the institutional catering firms tend to be headed by managers who have been prepared for the world of business, and not cuisine. While it may or may not be the case at the smallest operations, the corporate heads of the largest institutional catering firms have profiles very similar to those of the heads of the largest commercial restaurant *groupes*. Thus, Pierre Bellon, the founder, longtime CEO, and current chairman of Sodexo (and among the richest men in the world), is the son of an industrialist, graduating from the elite business school, l'école des Hautes Études Commerciales (HEC); while the copresident of Groupe Elior, Francis Markus, trained as an engineer, worked for IBM Europe and a New York–based engineering firm, before beginning a thirty-year career in management at Générale de Restauration (formerly owned by Accor, and which later became Groupe Elior); and his copresident, Robert Zolade, studied economics and law before serving as director of Development and Acquisitions for General Mills (Europe) and working in other senior management positions for various commercial restaurant chain companies. And though Compass Group France is not a French- but a British-owned conglomerate (formerly Eurest in France), its upper-level French managers all seem to have been prepared for the business world rather than for the culinary world.[89]

88. For at least the past fifteen years these three companies, together, have been larger than the next *forty-seven* institutional catering companies combined (many of which specialize in one or another form of institutional catering). In 2001 their combined figures in turnover (3 billion euros), number of restaurants (9,000), employees (55,000), meals served (740 billion) and numbers of central kitchens (558) were all at least three times larger than the figures for the next forty-seven firms combined. Source: *"Dossier: La restauration collective, le top des opérateurs en France," Néorestauration,* no. 386, April 2002, p. 66.

89. For example, Alain Dupuis, the executive director, received an MBA at INSEAD, an elite business school, and a law degree; the chief executive of the Western Europe Division, Antoine Cau, studied management at a business institute in Grenoble and was president and vice president of Hertz International, before Compass Groupe. A possible exception is Thierry Durecu, regional director of Eurest France (Compass Groupe France) who studied at a school of hotel management before being hired at the management level at Eurest (a possible

The Structure of Industrial Kitchens

This, of course, has not been the case for those who work as cooks and servers in the kitchens of the chain restaurants and the institutional catering firms run by these managers. The workers are a sizable sector of the French labor force, and in the late 1990s there were some 450,000–500,000 skilled cooks, assistant (or apprentice) cooks, and servers in France.[90] Most of the cooks working in the industrial regions of the French gastronomic field began their careers by seeking a basic qualification or credential in a culinary trade, the same route also taken by many of the most highly recognized French chefs. These were young workers entering various vocational school programs to learn a culinary trade. While about one-third of the cooks in institutional catering establishments and commercial chain restaurants show no formal school qualifications, 57 percent have either the CAP (*Certificat d'Aptitude Professionelle*) or BEP (*Brevet d'Études Professionelles*), secondary vocational diplomas that represent the customary route into the skilled crafts in France. With these diplomas recipients are deemed qualified for a specific métier within the culinary field.[91] In addition to vocational schools, attendance at a private or public hotel school has been another means of entrance to the cooking profession, and both have been roads taken by many of the most highly venerated French chefs. Data col-

exception because one can be trained for a culinary career at hotel schools. Sources: "The Book," in *L'annuaire de la restauration*, pp. 130, 164.

90. Various sources slice this labor force in various ways and at various points in time. Although she used 1998 figures, Mériot (*Le Cuisinier nostalgique*, p. 75) estimated 444,900 for this subgroup (servers, skilled and assistant cooks/chefs) a figure that rises to 832,000 when the kitchen staff of hotel restaurants, independent restaurants, and cafés are included (p. 55). Mériot's figures are drawn from the primary official government source, Insee (Institut National de la Statistique et des Études Économiques). Rather than using current statistics, it seems much more appropriate to use figures roughly consonant with the state of the industry in the period of interest, roughly between 1980 and 2000. The larger figure cited above is not so far off of the industry-generated figure of 781,425 for 2002, published in "Les chiffres clés de RHD en France et en Europe," produced jointly by the industry marketing firm Gira Sic Conseil and *Néorestauration*, November 2003, p. 22.

91. See Mériot, *Le Cuisinier nostalgique*, pp. 78–79. A vocational diploma serves as the primary passkey for entrance to the culinary professions. According to Isabel Terence in her analysis of the scholastic-culinary landscape in France, the following number of diplomas were granted in 1985: 22,397 pupils received a CAP diploma (in one of various culinary fields); 4,143 received the BEP (in *Hôtellerie-Cuisine*); 1,092 students received the BT (*Brevet de Technicien*); and 423 students the BTS (*Brevet de Technicien Supérieur*), which is basically equivalent to a community college program in the United States. See I. Terence, *Le Monde de la Grande Restauration en France* (Paris: L'Harmattan, 1996), p. 36.

lected for this study indicate that of the most highly consecrated French chefs at work throughout the 1990s (identified in Chapter 2, above) two-thirds had received a secondary vocational diploma, either CAP or BEP (or BTH), or had attended a vocational hotel school, while the other third had no formal training at all.[92] Of the 244 other highly recognized French chefs considered for this study (and identified by the leading organ of the chef profession as "noteworthy," "important," or "up and coming" chefs, see Chapter 2), 42 percent were recipients of a vocational diploma or had attended a vocational hotel school.[93] While the diploma offers a recognized form of basic training into the profession it does not ensure advancement. A more indispensable experience for the young chef wishing to achieve culinary stardom has been to serve an apprenticeship in a significant restaurant alongside an already-consecrated chef de cuisine. In other words, the acquisition of symbolic capital through apprenticeship to a recognized chef has been an important element, separating the trajectory of the future grand chef from that of the merely competent skilled cook. The latter may be capable of translating his cooking skills into steady work and a modest standard of living, but without a measure of recognition from the profession itself he or she will be destined for a career in the more industrialized regions of the gastronomic field.

Just how good of a living would one have been able to enjoy in this region of the field? The occupations comprising the culinary field have not generally been particularly well paid in France. In traditional restaurants the pay of a cook (cuisinier) has normally been less than half of the pay of the head chef (chef de cuisine), and slightly more than the pay of a junior cook (*commis de cuisine*).[94] However, the salary of a chef is highly dependent on the size and profitability of the restaurant where he or she works, so that the head chef of a restaurant with a very high annual turnover rate may be paid twice the salary of the head chef of a small restaurant with a low turnover rate; and a cook at a restaurant with a high-turnover would be paid about one and a half times that of a cook working in a modest restaurant.[95] Cooks'

---

92. The BTH refers to *Baccaulauréat Technologique Hôtellerie*, and is, reportedly, no longer granted.

93. These were chefs who were profiled by *Le Chef* magazine.

94. For example, the mean monthly salary of a cook (cuisinier) was 5,885 francs in June 1998 (just prior to the change to the euro), the monthly salary of a head chef was 10,265 francs, and the salary of a junior cook (*commis de cuisine*) was 5,865 francs (see Mériot, *Le Cuisinier nostalgique*, p. 81).

95. The salary ranges for eleven different culinary occupations were compared at commercial restaurants that had annual turnover rates under 4 million francs with those that had over 8 million francs in a report (dossier) entitled "Les Salaires dans la profession,"

salaries depend not only on the profitability of the restaurant but also on whether or not it is independent or part of a chain, whether it is a commercial or an institutional (*collective*) restaurant, as well as whether it is self-managed (by the institution) or subcontracted out to a private institutional catering firm. For example, in 1998 the mean monthly salary of a cook in an independent commercial restaurant was 5,885 francs, or 79 percent of the mean monthly pay of a cook in a *collective* restaurant (institutional kitchen), which was 7,440 francs per month.[96] Though highly dependent on the specific work situation, the pay of a French cook has been modest, though generally above the minimum wage and, relative to many of his or her contemporaries working in the food-processing sector, in bakeries, and in supermarkets and hypermarkets, a cook has not been considered a particularly low-wage occupation.[97]

Like material compensation, the symbolic status of the cook has also depended on the specific work situation. In her study of the profession of cuisinier within the world of institutional catering in France, Sylvie-Anne Mériot has shown that there are important differences between cooks in commercial restaurants and those in institutional catering establishments. The lore of the *grand chef* in France has permitted cooks in commercial restaurants to maintain an elevated conception of their profession (and thus of themselves) as a creative and skilled métier, one that is widely celebrated and highly valued, even as the rapid industrialization of culinary practice has substantially narrowed the scope of innovation and creativity in the work itself. With the growth of the chain restaurant industry, including chain "family restaurants" (like Hippopotamus, Buffalo Grill, Pizza Paï), as well as the chain cafés (Flunch) and fast-food restaurants (McDonald's, Brioche Dorée), the repetitiveness and rationalization of kitchen work, the increasing use of centralized kitchens, the standardization of menus, and the use of preprepared foods have drastically reduced the skill requirements

---

produced by the trade magazine *Revue Technique des hôtels et restaurants*, no. 500, June 1991, pp. 79–89.

96. Mériot, *Le Cuisinier nostalgique*, p. 81. Mériot's analysis shows that the monthly mean salary for cooks in self-managed institutional kitchens was slightly less at 7,215 francs per month.

97. Nearly a quarter of the workforce in the food-processing sector was classified as low wage in 1995, though eight years later the proportion of low-wage workers in food processing had dropped to 11.6 percent, due to an increase in the minimum wage and the introduction of the 35-hour workweek. See E. Caroli and J. Gautié, eds., *Low-Wage Work in France* (New York: Russell Sage Foundation, 2008), esp. chaps. 2 and 3.

of the cooking profession.[98] This has produced among cooks what Mériot has termed a "nostalgic syndrome," or a kind of collective cognitive dissonance between the mythology surrounding culinary work in French society and the *"cuisson minute,"* or "short-order cooking," that has become its actual practice. The central place of gastronomy in French culture has served as a powerful lure enticing generations of young French workers to enter a profession that demands extremely hard work and long hours. According to Mériot, their endurance has been buttressed by the dreams and aspirations nurtured in the training process itself, which emphasizes the artistry of culinary creativity and inventiveness that is only actually found in the most rarified kitchens of the most highly consecrated restaurants.[99] As Mériot noted, many of the cooks working in the kitchens of institutional catering companies have taken jobs out of economic necessity and not professional enhancement, with many having previously worked in commercial restaurants. These cooks are doomed to spend their careers in a state of longing for a return to the craftsmanship and professional recognition that they once aspired to and from which they are now largely excluded: "Catering is thus an economic alternative to social prestige, always looking but temporarily excluded."[100] The supreme irony of this situation is that although the cooks in the institutional catering sector bear the psychic scars of their stigmatized status within the profession, in practice they are often able to exert more creativity and independence in the actual cooking process than do cooks working for commercial restaurant chains, whose autonomy has been greatly restricted by a severe industrial/technological discipline.[101]

Of course, this should not be surprising in an industrial realm where the "bottom line" is the "bottom line" of profitability and "market share" rather than the quality of the ingredients, the culinary prowess of the chef, the flawlessness of service, and exquisite artistic presentation on the plate. The industrial region of the gastronomic field is populated by a large number of social actors, both individual and institutional, all more or less animated by a similar ethos. Here success is largely determined by quantity, and so those wishing to operate successfully in this domain must accede to the logic of ever-increasing productivity and technological efficiency, to high-volume production lines to produce low-cost goods for mass markets that privilege

98. Mériot, *Le Cuisinier nostalgique*, pp. 291–292.
99. Or "artistic" cuisine, as André Grelon notes in his preface to Mériot, *Le Cuisinier nostalgique*, p. 10.
100. Mériot, *Le Cuisinier nostalgique*, p. 34.
101. Mériot, *Le Cuisinier nostalgique*, p. 292.

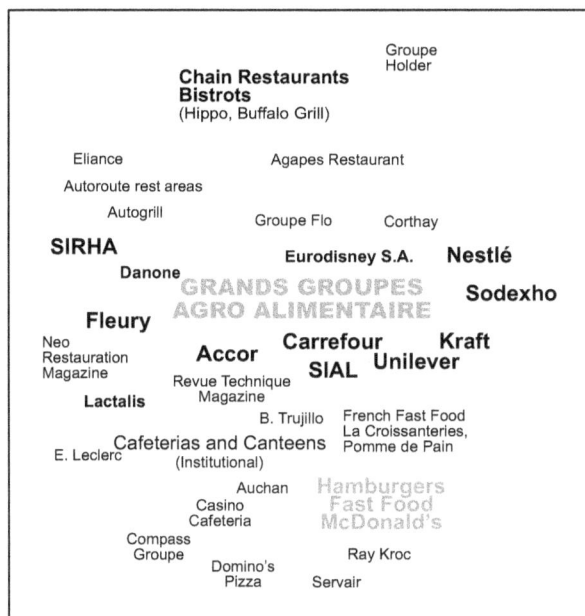

Figure 4.1 Institutional Components of the Industrial Food Sector in France, 1990

convenience, simplicity, and informality. If one could have frozen the domain of industrial cuisine at the moment when the major industrial players who had emerged in the 1960s and 1970s had taken their place more or less fully formed on the French market, the configuration would have looked like Figure 4.1.[102]

The combination of restaurant, fast-food and supermarket chains, food-processing companies, and magazines that represent them to themselves and beyond, tend to share a set of family ties with each other. They operate as a relatively cohesive cluster of organizations involved in the mass production and distribution of foods. Their activities are animated and directed not primarily by the aesthetic and artisanal skills of the most talented cooking professionals but by the commercial concerns and interests of shareholders and corporate managers. They share a common logic that differs sharply from the logic we considered previously, in the practice of haute cuisine, that characterizes the

---

102. The diagram is designed to be a rough and partial illustration of the major institutions active within the industrial sphere of the French gastronomic field in about 1990. The relative material weight of the institutional actors (annual turnover rates—*chiffres d'affaires*—and the size of the workforce) are approximations, represented by the size of the font, and the relative symbolic weight of the various institutions and actors are expressed in the relative boldness of the type. Since the early 1990s, several companies and institutions have disappeared or been merged with other firms, while others have appeared.

more artisanal regions of the gastronomic field and that represents French gastronomy to itself, to its practitioners, to France, and to the entire world.

If the actors in the industrialized regions of the field share certain family ties with each other, they can also be seen to have shared American roots. This has not meant that their origins have necessarily been "American" in a literal sense but that they have often looked to American forms of business as models. In other words, for French businessmen in a number of areas, and particularly in the activities of food processing, mass distribution techniques, and management of chain restaurants, those firms that have often dominated international markets, have set productivity standards, and have led in the introduction of technological innovations have often been American multinational firms. This should not be surprising, given that U.S. firms have been able to develop and refine their operations within a huge and varied domestic market in a relatively un (or de)-regulated economic environment at home, while playing an outsized political role in setting the terms of the international economic order.[103] So as American food-processing firms began operating in France, and as fast-food companies began to appear, and French investors and entrepreneurs considered investing in supermarket chains and shopping malls, their model and inspiration tended to be American.[104]

With a recognition of *two* very different regions within the field of gastronomic practices in France, several fundamental questions emerge. For not only do these practices appear incompatible and contradictory but from an aesthetic, cultural, and social perspective they would seem to operate in a perpetual state of mutual repulsion. What has been the nature of the relationship between an American-inspired sphere of industrial practices, on the one side, and the "very French" world of haute cuisine on the other? Can they coexist? Has the rise of the one hastened the demise of the other? Which will prevail? The following chapter examines the terms of existence by which the two main regions of the gastronomic field have subsisted, and considers the trajectory and dynamics of their relationship and its expansion into new domains of gastronomic practice.

---

103. Indeed, American capitalism had been able to create "A World After Its Own Image," as Leo Panitch and Sam Gindin have masterfully demonstrated in their book *The Making of Global Capitalism: The Political Economy of American Empire* (London: Verso, 2012), chap. 11.

104. It is for this reason that Ray Kroc, the founder of the McDonald's Corporation, has been included in the diagram above. In my interviews with French entrepreneurs in the French fast-food industry, both Kroc and his company served as an outsized inspiration, for the foundational myths surrounding Kroc's individual entrepreneurship and for the massive worldwide success of McDonald's.

5

Conflicts of Interest

A Cultural Field in Transformation

An Analytic Construction of the Gastronomic Field

With the previous chapters I have sought to present the key players in the field of gastronomic practices in France, with the intention of demonstrating the range of different and competing institutions that have entered the field over the course of the past half-century, along with the distinct logics and practices that they brought with them. As I indicated previously, in taking Bourdieu's approach I refer to a field as a distinctive social microcosm that develops its own characteristic practices, principles, rules, forms of authority, and standards of evaluation that develop over time and can also decline over time. A field is a relatively autonomous social universe, which means that it is more or less able to shield itself from the influences of neighboring or intruding fields, by upholding its own criteria of evaluation against the logic of these external influences.[1] There are several reasons why the concept of field has seemed analytically valuable: (a) it provides for a radical contextualization of the social object under investigation; (b) it obliges theoretical and empirical consideration of the relational character of that social context, with attention to the process

---

1. This rather rough definition of "field" is drawn from Loïc Wacquant, whose brief distillation of the concept is a particularly clear one in L. Wacquant, "Pierre Bourdieu," in *Key Sociological Thinkers*, ed. R. Stones (New York: New York University Press, 1998).

by which groups and institutions come into being and engage in practices in relation (and in reaction) to one another; (c) fields are highly differentiated (and hierarchical) social formations; (d) analysis of a field requires attention to classification as a central social act by which groups are symbolically "made" and "unmade"; it thereby draws our attention to a key symbolic mechanism by which groups fortify their dominant position in relation to other groups.

To visualize the social microcosm of French gastronomic practices it can be helpful to construct a social "map" of the field. The following diagram is the generic framework that has been employed in this analysis but could very well have been used in an analysis of any cultural field (see Figure 5.1). The key axes are production practices along the horizontal axis and consumption practices on the vertical axis. The production practices range from the *artisanal* (on the left), referring to a reliance on traditional methods and techniques of production, utilizing craft skills that have been acquired over relatively long periods of time and that produce unique, non-standardized cultural goods in small batches, to *industrial* practices (on the right), which rely on modern techniques and technologies, seek to produce in the shortest time possible, and rely on highly standardized production techniques to produce uniform goods in high-volume production cycles. Consumption practices are indicated along the vertical axis, and range from mass-market consumption patterns at the bottom of the diagram, which tend to be based on the values of convenience, simplicity, informality, low-cost, and thus broad inclusivity. At the other end are restricted (or luxury) consumption practices, which are calculatingly exclusive and require a measure of cultural sophistication and discernment and a recognition of the formal rules of consumption, as well as the financial means to invest in expensive cultural goods.

So if we consider the grouping of food-processing companies and related institutions of industrial cuisine that were presented together in Figure 4.1 (see Chapter 4), it appears as the industrial sector (at the southeast quadrant) of the French gastronomic field in the following way (see Figure 5.2).[2] Together, the institutions and figures provide a schematic representation of the industrial region of the field. The relative size of each institution (based on approximate turnover rate) and its symbolic importance (based on the estimated frequency of mention and treatment in the principle industry

---

2. American and French flags are meant to signal which culinary and gastronomic practices have generally been associated with which region of the French gastronomic field.

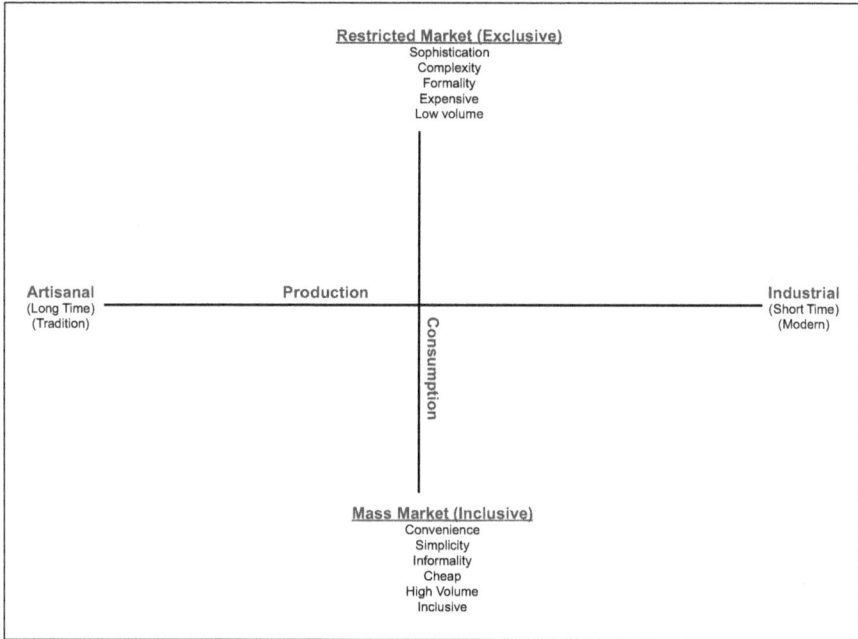

Figure 5.1 Generic Diagram for a Cultural Field

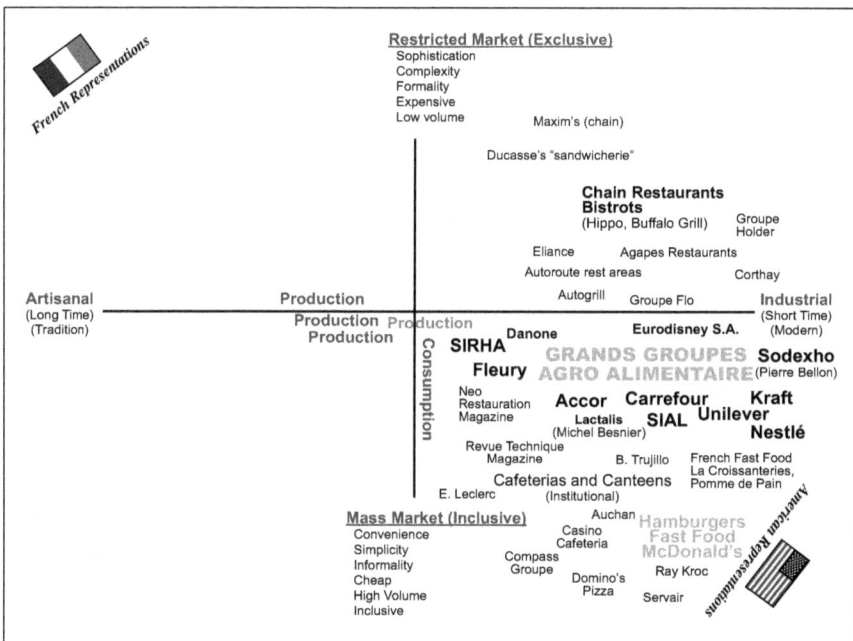

Figure 5.2 Industrial Region of the French Gastronomic Field, 1990

trade magazines) are represented by the size and boldness of the typeface. The industrial region of the French gastronomic field is occupied by institutions that have employed advanced industrial techniques, that have been the key players in the mass production and distribution of culinary goods, and that are oriented to or entail consumption practices based on convenience, simplicity, and low cost. As was illustrated in Chapters 3 and 4, this is an area of the field where U.S.-based corporations have dominated, historically, based on their size, sales volume, and market share, as well as their innovative application of industrial technologies. Within the industrial regions of the gastronomic field, where the industrial model is practiced unreservedly and has been highly valued, U.S.-based corporations have enjoyed a particularly high degree of recognition and appreciation. In other words, for French businessmen and industrialists, American business has held considerable symbolic capital within the economic domain.

What is so obviously missing from this map of the field is the sector that has been overwhelmingly central, in symbolic terms, both for the French and for the rest of world, namely French haute cuisine (or *grande cuisine*, or *haute gastronomie*). It is this region that has been symbolically central to the gastronomic field in France and has furnished it with its founding point of view, its *nomos*, or the core principles of vision and division with which the field has traditionally defined itself.[3] The most important institutional and individual actors occupying French haute cuisine in the 1990s are indicated in the northwest quadrant of the diagram in Figure 5.3.

Traditionally, French gastronomy had functioned largely as a world unto itself, as a relatively autonomous universe of culinary practices that operated on the basis of its own rules and regulations, its own forms of authority, and its own methods and standards of evaluation.[4] Gastronomy not only has been one of the main pillars of the French cultural patrimony but for generations France set the standard for gastronomic excellence at the international level, serving as Mecca for an international network of culinary

---

3. Bourdieu referred to the idea of nomos across his various analyses of fields, but his most focused discussion, and the one that seems most appropriate here, is a section in his analysis of the field of art entitled "The *nomos* and the question of boundaries," in P. Bourdieu, *The Rules of Art: Genesis and Structure of the Literary Field* (Stanford, CA: Stanford University Press, 1995), pp. 223–227; also see P. Bourdieu, *Pascalian Meditations* (Stanford, CA: Stanford University Press, 2000), pp. 96–97.

4. These were examined in Chapter 2, "The Symbolic Economy of French Gastronomy."

French Representations

Ducasse
Escoffier
Troisgros Bocuse Guide Culinare

Restricted Market (Exclusive)
Sophistication
Complexity
Formality
Expensive
Low volume   Maxim's (chain)

3 MICHELIN STARS

Academie Robuchon "Thuries" **Grands Bistrots &**
Culinaire de Blanc Magazine **Brasseries**
France Pacaud Vergé (La Coupole, Lipp, Le Balzar)

Ducasse's "sandwicherie"

Claude Terrail La Taillevent Restaurant
(La Tour d'Argent Loiseau Legendre Senderens Lameloise
Restaurant) Lorain Boyer Guerard
Conseil National PIC
Des Arts "Le Chef" Foundation Trama Savoy
Culinaires Magazine Brillat-Savarin Rostang
MOF Veyrat Chapel **Guide Michelin** Gault-Millau Magazine

**Chain Restaurants
Bistrots**
(Hippo, Buffalo Grill) Groupe Holder

Eliance Agapes Restaurants
Autoroute rest areas Corthay

Les Trois Alsaciens Huguet Mazere
Artisanal (Jung, Westermann, Haeberlin) Passard
(Long Time) Production
(Tradition)

Autogrill Groupe Flo
Industrial
(Short Time)
(Modern)

Consumption

SIRHA Danone Eurodisney S.A.
GRANDS GROUPES Sodexho
Fleury **AGRO ALIMENTAIRE** (Pierre Bellon)

Neo Restauration **Accor Carrefour Kraft**
Magazine Lactalis SIAL **Unilever**
(Michel Besnier) **Nestlé**

Revue Technique
Magazine B. Trujillo French Fast Food
La Croissanteries,
Cafeterias and Canteens Pomme de Pain
E. Leclerc (Institutional)

Mass Market (Inclusive) Auchan
Convenience Casino Hamburgers
Simplicity Cafeteria Fast Food
Informality Compass McDonald's
Cheap Groupe Ray Kroc
High Volume Domino's
Inclusive Pizza Servair

American Representations

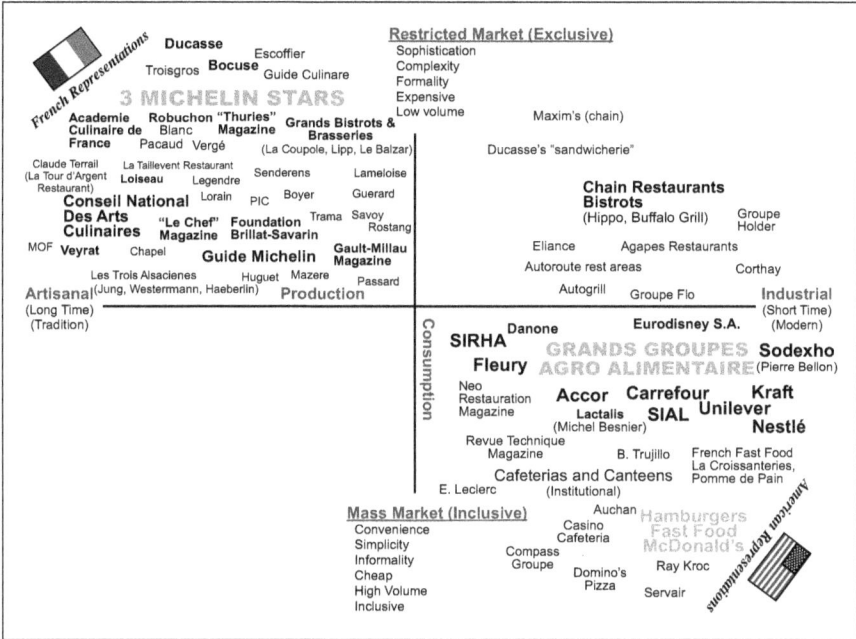

Figure 5.3 Principal Regions of the French Gastronomic Field, 1990

practitioners, observers, and critics.[5] As we noted previously the autonomy of the gastronomic field was achieved over the course of the nineteenth century, with *grands chefs* taking their place at the center of the emerging field, against the industrial practitioners of industrial cuisine and as professional male artisans over female domestic cooks.[6] The hierarchical social differentiation of culinary practice was made possible by the development of a system for the production and reproduction of belief in the virtuosity of the grand chef and the cultural meaning of haute cuisine. Through a collective system of competitions, awards, schools, culinary guides, trade

5. See, for example, A. Lazareff, *L'exception culinaire française* (Paris: Albin Michel, 1998); and A. Drouard, *Le Mythe gastronomique français* (Paris: CNRS Editions, 2010).

6. See Chapter 1, and Vicki A. Swinbank, "The Sexual Politics of Cooking: A Feminist Analysis of Culinary Hierarchy in Western Culture," *Journal of Historical Sociology*, vol. 15, no. 4, December 2002, p. 469. According to Goody, traditionally, across different cultural settings, male cooks have appropriated women's recipes for everyday cooking, using them in aristocratic cuisine (Jack Goody, *Cooking, Cuisine, and Class* [Cambridge: Cambridge University Press, 1982], p. 101). The traditional expression "La femme naît cuisinière, l'homme le devient" ("the woman is born a cook, the man becomes one") seems to capture this process, in J.-C. Ribaut, "Cuisine au féminin," in *Le Monde*, June 15–16, 2003, p. 18.

journals, journalists, and food critics, including both the established actors and institutions and the rebels, the principles of gastronomic excellence were established and maintained. Although they may seem peripheral to the cooking process in the kitchen, they have been central to the social production of belief in both the power of the grand chef and the power of grand cuisine as a cultural object. Until the 1970s the integrity of this system, and thus the relative autonomy of the gastronomic field, was upheld by a sort of protective "firewall" that repelled intrusions from the outside (like economic logic), thereby shielding French gastronomy from the logic of industrial practice, as shown in Figure 5.4.

By firewall, I have in mind a social partition maintaining both a *symbolic* boundary or divide between different or opposing mental constructions (aesthetic, linguistic, technical, etc.) and a *material* divide between different or competing structural patterns (class association, institutionalized powers of consecration, the degree of embeddedness of institutions, etc.). In the case of gastronomy this firewall served to protect the traditional logic of artisanal excellence, culinary perfection, and the perpetual aim of attaining an aesthetic manifestation of the sublime, against the economic logic of efficiency, productivity, mass markets, and profit maximization. This was not so much a "symbolic boundary" as it was a boundary in which both the material and the symbolic were interpenetrated, mutually reinforcing processes.[7]

The operation of a firewall has been manifest throughout the entire edifice of French gastronomy, where the system of consecration, the production of belief, and the practice of social exclusion and exclusivity have sustained it as a world apart (and above) the mundane exercise of cooking and eating. Thus, a kind of mental firewall was evident in the earliest interviews for this book, with both the president of the Académie culinaire de France, a gatekeeper of haute cuisine, and the president of SNARR, the fast-food employer's association. Neither viewed fast food as operating within the same cultural universe as French gastronomy, and both denied seeing it as a po-

---

7. Although the concept of "symbolic boundaries" would seem appropriate here, as a concept it has been more concerned with subjective boundaries (categories) than structural, material processes. Indeed, it was explicitly advanced to counter the structural emphasis in comparative research. As Michèle Lamont has written, "most recent comparative research has centered on structural, i.e., economic and political, phenomena. Focusing on symbolic boundaries can renew interest in properly cultural comparative work and in the comparative stratification research that to date has tended to analyze transfers of social position rather than the broad features of status systems." See M. Lamont, *Money, Morals, and Manners: The Culture of the French and the American Upper-Middle Class* (Chicago: University of Chicago Press, 1992), p. 8.

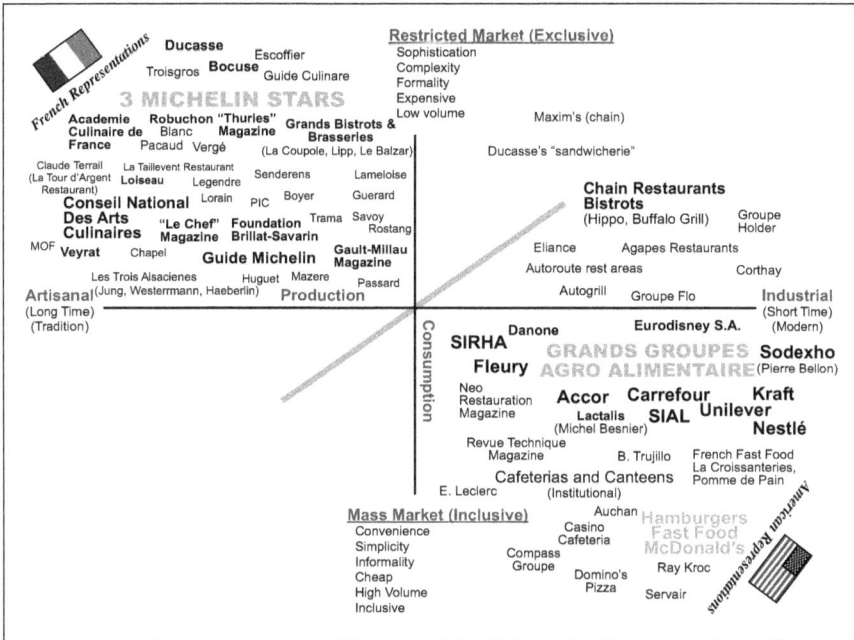

Figure 5.4 Firewall Separating Principal Regions of the Field, 1990

tential threat because, at the time, any relationship at all between fast food and French gastronomy was inconceivable.[8] But the French gastronomic field has not been a static universe, and the growth and expansion of industrial organizations and practices began to show their effects across the entire field.

Breach of the Firewall

It seems that the first of the grand chefs to venture across the firewall and enter the domain of the industrial was the *grand chef de cuisine* Michel Guérard. His restaurant, Les Prés d'Eugénie, in southwest France, had held the highest ratings in the three principle gastronomic guides (three stars in the *Michelin Guide*, a rating of nineteen and a half out of twenty in *Gault-Millau*, and four stars in *Bottin Gourmand*). Well known for being one of the leading lights of French "nouvelle cuisine," Guérard was the author of a best-selling cookbook, *La Grande Cuisine minceur*, published in 1976, and in that same year Guérard signed a contract with the Nestlé Corporation.[9]

---

8. See Chapter 3.
9. "Minceur" means slimness, or slenderness, but the term is often used to refer to "low-calorie" cuisine.

In an issue of *Gault-Millau* announcing the "Eight Best Chefs of France," Michel Guérard's "breach of the firewall" was described under the heading, "The first French chef to go slumming with an industrial corporation":[10]

> Yet it was his low-calorie cuisine that would bring him to discover another universe. In 1976, he was contacted by the chief of the Nestlé Group, who was seeking someone able to infuse some creativity into one of their brands, "someone who would bring romanticism to Frozen food." Michel Guérard signed up right away, "I would have been crazy not to agree to take these steps. I thought I had a lot to learn. That's how I became the first French cook to go slumming with an industrial corporation. It was a respectful and unequivocal partnership."

Guérard's was a momentous act within French gastronomy. According to the trade magazine, *Néo Magazine* (which would later become *Néorestauration*), it was the first time that a French grand chef had become associated with an industrial food corporation. The contract was for Guérard to furnish the company with "know-how, imagination, and refinement" as Nestlé International sought to follow its American branch by launching a line of "light cuisine" foods in France under the mark of Findus Restauration.[11] It was the beginning of a long collaboration for Guérard, who noted, "At first I did not feel at all prepared; I had to learn many things, but in recent years, I have come to feel like a fish in water."[12]

In an important way, by entering the domain of industry Guérard had violated sacred principles of grand cuisine and, as a result, endured a torrent of scorn and criticism: "All of the Chefs screamed 'treason' and Guérard was vilified by his peers, even in these pages," according to the account in *Gault-Millau*. However, that magazine also quickly defended Guérard's act as an expression of the magazine's own culinary wisdom, noting that "he was performing one of the '10 Commandments of Nouvelle Cuisine,' set forth three years earlier, 'to always be searching for new techniques.'"[13]

---

10. S. Demorand, "Michel Guérard: L'empereur de génie" in *Gault&Millau*, no. 337, Winter 1999–2000, pp. 51–52. Author's translation of "Le premier chef français à s'encanailler avec un industriel."

11. F. Cordier, "Michel Guérard: Comme un poisson dans l'eau dans l'industrie," in *Néorestauration*, no. 199, June 1989, p. 36.

12. Cordier, "Michel Guérard," p. 36.

13. Demorand, "Michel Guérard: L'empereur" p. 51. *Gault-Millau* is well-known for having "created" nouvelle cuisine in France, a point that is further explored below.

Once breached, the traditional firewall between the artisanal and the industrial became increasingly porous as the trickle of chefs stepping over into the industrial realm would become a steady stream. As *Néorestauration* magazine recalled on the occasion of its thirtieth anniversary: "Michel Guérard was one of the first leaders to succumb to a partnership with a major group of the food processing industry, and his example was followed by many others, such as Paul Bocuse, Bernard Loiseau, Guy Martin and Joël Robuchon," all who were among the leading chefs at the time.[14] It seemed telling that the magazine focused exclusively on the ways in which the culture of the grand chefs had changed the food-processing industry, and not at all on whether or how industrial practices and principles might have changed the artisanal culture of the grand chefs.[15]

The first chefs to sign contracts with the large food-processing companies were the most highly consecrated since they could potentially provide companies with the most symbolic capital.[16] That is, by hiring chefs who had achieved significant recognition conferred by the gastronomic field, industrial corporations could indirectly purchase recognition to enhance or sanctify the image of their brand or company. Most contracts were for consulting services so, for example, Alain Senderens, the celebrated chef de cuisine at Lucas Carton ("a monument of Parisian gastronomy") and the long-running recipient of three *Michelin* stars, who was the former president of the Syndicat de la haute cuisine française, and who had been considered "one of the popes of nouvelle cuisine," was hired by the industrial food group, Guyomarc'h, to assist their research and development arm, France Restauration, a consulting firm through which Senderens would work for Carrefour, the supermarket chain, as well as for various food-processing companies.[17] According to one account, Senderens had not previously

14. D. Sicot, "La culture des chefs transforme l'industrie" in the special issue, "30 Ans de Restauration," *Néorestauration*, no. 385, March 2002, p. 22. At the time, Bocuse, Loiseau, and Robuchon were among the most highly consecrated French chefs, and Guy Martin was amply consecrated with a three-star *Michelin* rating.

15. Sicot, "La culture des chefs": "The industries are restoring the chefs in the universe of fresh and frozen products for all the preparations, from entrees to pastries and dishes" (p. 22).

16. By symbolic capital I refer to, after Bourdieu, a capital of recognition, garnered by those who have gained recognition in a field. The specific qualities and forms that symbolic capital takes tend to be specific to particular fields of human activity.

17. B. Balayé, "Alain Senderens," a profile published in *Thuriès Magazine*, no. 29, May 1991, p. vii; F. Cordier, "Alain Senderens toutes réticences vaincues," *NéoMagazine*, no. 206, January 1990, p. 36; G. Golan, "Le Courage de regarder le futur," *Le Chef,* no. 36, October 1990, pp. 18–19.

been known as "a warm supporter" of the food industry and had had to overcome considerable doubts to do this work: "He wages war against standardization in excess, against the monotony of profitmaking, and against pre-prepared meals which, in his view, cannot maintain freshness."[18] When asked why he had agreed to commit such a "sacrilege" by collaborating with an industrial firm like France Restauration, Senderens replied, "Because this company cares about raising the level of quality of its dishes, and will be a winner in the future since this is an initiative that corresponds to a general effort to improve taste."[19]

By overcoming his reticence Senderens provided the justification for other highly consecrated chefs to consider similar moves, encouraging others to join him on the far side of the firewall. One of the first was Paul Bocuse, a French chef with a gigantic personality who, at a young age, had been a helper and an apprentice to both Mère Brazier and Fernand Point, two legendary figures of French gastronomy, and who, himself, would later come to personify French gastronomy and represent it to the world.[20] With three *Michelin* stars for his restaurant in Collonges au Mont-d'Or, outside of Lyon, and as recipient of the coveted Meilleur Ouvrier de France (MOF) and the French Legion of Honor medal, Bocuse was among the most highly consecrated chefs (and cultural figures) in France when he began to trade his stock of symbolic capital with the industrial firms. Over the course of his career he would sign contracts with several food-processing companies, cookware companies, and champagne and wine distributors; would open a chain of French bakeries, a cooking school, and two restaurants in Japan; and would sign a contract with the Disney Corporation for the French restaurant at Epcot Center in Orlando, Florida.[21] In addition, Bocuse would eventually open five relatively inexpensive bistros in and around the city of Lyon to trade on his name and his celebrated three-star restaurant.

---

18. F. Cordier, "Alain Senderens," p. 36.

19. F. Cordier, "Alain Senderens," p. 36; Golan, "Le Courage," p. 19.

20. Bocuse has often been considered the foremost "ambassador" of French gastronomy, having opened restaurants at Disney's Epcot Center in Orlando, Florida, and in Japan, and as founder of the Bocuse d'Or, an annual competition for chefs from around the world. See c no. 2, September 1988, pp. 7–17; G. Golan, "Paul Bocuse: Le parrain, le combattant et le sage," in *Le Chef*, no. 119, December 1999, pp. 18–23; R. Chelminski, "Le Bocuse d'Or," in *Smithsonian Magazine*, May 2001, pp. 72–80.

21. Balayé, "L'Album du chef"; G. Golan, "Paul Bocuse: La gastronomie comme un humanisme," *Le Chef*, no. 83, December 1995, pp. 18–21; M. Lansard, "Tsuji/Bocuse: Le savoir-faire rhônalpin exporté au Japon," *Figaro du Samedi*, June 30, 1990, pp. 72–74; J.-F. Mesplède, "Paul Bocuse au sommet de la cuisine," *L'Hôtellerie Restauration*, no. 2928, June 9, 2005, pp. 2–4.

For the *grands chefs*, like Bocuse, this was essentially an act of transubstantiation in which they were able to convert their accumulated symbolic capital into economic capital, as industrial companies began lining up to enter the market to purchase the symbolic capital that they could never earn themselves.[22] A particularly notable example of this transaction occurred when Sodexho, the massive institutional catering firm, purchased the "signatures" of six prominent grands chefs to expand a program to enhance the skills and the self-esteem of Sodexho's cooks and kitchen managers. For several years, Marc Veyrat, who was then known as a young, brash chef with a three-star Michelin restaurant in the Haute-Savoie region, had started working for Sodexho as a consultant, advising the company on a "school for chefs" in which Sodexho chefs and cooks would participate in a series of two-day training sessions at an inn near Annecy.[23] In 1999 this program was being expanded with Veyrat and five other highly consecrated grands chefs: Michel Bras, Jacques Chibois, Jean-Michel Lorain, Alain Passard, and Olivier Roellinger.[24]

The magazine, *Le Chef*, responded to the Sodexho initiative in an editorial entitled "*REVOLUTION IN THE KITCHENS*" by posing the rhetorical (and sociological) question of whether the "Group of Six" grands chefs had "sold their artistic image to the giant of mass catering?" The response by the editors to this question was to unambiguously assert that by signing on to train the industrial leaders responsible for serving so much of the French population, the grands chefs were making a significant contribution to improving the "conditions of French taste." For the editors, such a partnership was "a real feat that deserves to be welcomed," "an intelligent symbiosis between qualitative and quantitative," and "the best response to the danger of drifting toward the fast food lying in wait for the American population."[25] The article about the Sodexho program in the same issue of *Le Chef* (also written

---

22. Trade magazines would often display advertisements and make announcements about new contracts between chefs and the food industry, like for Joël Robuchon's line of frozen casserole dishes with the firm Fleury Michon, and Bernard Loiseau's line of signature soups with Unilever, Michel Oliver's line of precooked foods for the cafeterias of a large supermarket chain, and so on.

23. G. Golan, "L'École des chefs: L'air des cimes pour Sodexho," *Le Chef*, no. 82, November 1995, pp. 34–35; and G. Golan, "La Gastronomie, bureau de recherche de la restauration collective," *Le Chef*, no. 122, April 2000, pp. 20–21.

24. At the time, four of these chefs had restaurants with three *Michelin* stars and the other two had restaurants with two *Michelin* stars each.

25. G. Golan and F. Luzin, "Révolution dans les cuisines," *Le Chef*, no. 122, April 2000, p. 4.

by one of the editors) not only revealed how permeable the wall separating the artisanal and the industrial had become by the 1990s in French gastronomy but also exposed its own complicity in the process:[26]

> Fourteen years ago *Le Chef* launched the idea of a *rapprochement* between haute gastronomy and the industry of institutional catering. This concept, which was considered funny at the time, has since taken shape and today chain restaurant companies have become more and more appealing to the *grands chefs.* . . . Pierre Bellon, the CEO of Sodexho (with almost 60 billion francs in sales) is an experienced gastronome . . . his firm is the world leader in mass catering. . . . Over the past seven years his teams have created, surprisingly, a school for chefs with Marc Veyrat . . . although this once seemed incongruous, today the results of the partnership cannot be questioned.

It should be remembered that this initiative was developed to provide training sessions for cooks and managers of institutional kitchens, including those working in retirement homes, school cafeterias, workplace canteens, and so on, including massive centralized kitchens used to preparing up to two thousand meals per day to supply the canteens and cafeterias of institutions. The potential difficulties of bringing these two worlds together, *haute gastronomie* and industrial cooking, was obvious and was explicitly addressed by the magazine, which questioned whether chefs "who can be difficult to please and who guard their independence and their artistic image, will be able to live in a partnership with a company that has often been attacked by critics opposed to mass cuisine."[27]

In addition to acquiring the symbolic capital of grands chefs directly, industrial groups also sought to purchase the venerability of the most venerable of historic Parisian bistros. Thus Groupe Flo, the corporation that owned various restaurant chains and bistros, purchased Le Balzar and La Coupole. Groupe Bertrand (which has owned Quick fast-food outlets, cafés, cafeterias, and restaurants) purchased Brasserie Lipp, and developed it as an international chain; while Maxim's, a historic Belle Époque restaurant located at the Place de la Concorde near the U.S. Embassy, a magnet for celebrities and politicians in the 1960s, was bought by the fashion designer

---

26. Golan, "La Gastronomie, bureau de recherche," p. 20 [author's translation].
27. Golan, "La Gastronomie, bureau de recherche," p. 21.

Pierre Cardin and turned into an international brand of chain restaurants, shops, and merchandise.[28]

During this period the grands chefs sought to enter the industrial domain from various angles, not just by signing contracts and leasing their signatures to frozen food companies, supermarkets, and restaurant chains but by drawing upon the high rankings that their primary restaurants had received in the *Michelin, Gault-Millau*, and *Bottin Gourmand* guides to open less expensive, more informal bistros nearby. This was referred to as "*l'annexité*" in the industry and served as a way for a grand chef to trade on the symbolic value that his name and/or his restaurant had been accorded by opening a more accessible restaurant for tourists and for those unable to afford the expense of a three-star restaurant (and which might very well require a reservation several months in advance). The wave of *l'annexité* swept over French gastronomy in the 1990s. Besides Paul Bocuse's four bistros, other three-star chefs who opened multiple small restaurants included Georges Blanc (4), Gérard Boyer (2), Bernard Loiseau (3), and Guy Savoy (7), while often, many other three- and two-star grands chefs would open a single bistro near their principal restaurants.[29] In certain respects, Alain Ducasse was a case apart for his ability to exchange the considerable symbolic capital he had accumulated in the French gastronomic field for worldwide celebrity and a substantial degree of wealth.

Like Bocuse, Ducasse had been a culinary prodigy, receiving his first *Michelin* three-star rating in 1990, at the age of thirty-four for the restaurant

---

28. "Le roi de la brasserie règne sur la Coupole," *Néorestauration*, no. 183, February 1988, p. 5 (no author listed); and A. Gopnik, "Saving the Balzar," *New Yorker*, August 3, 1998, pp. 39–42. In 1999, Groupe Bertrand CHR was the twenty-third largest commercial restaurant group in France, owning nine restaurants (including Brasserie Lipp), with an annual turnover rate of 34 million euros. "Les 80 leaders en France," *Néorestauration*, no. 376, May 2001, p. 45. In 2000 the Eliance Groupe, which owned 666 chain restaurants, including many fast-food restaurants, also owned a Maxim's restaurant at Orly Airport (Maxim's Orly Ouest), see listing for Eliance in "Les 80 leaders en France," a commercial restaurant ranking published in *Néorestauration*, no. 387, May 2002, p. 62.

29. This included Michel Rostang and Jean-Paul Lacombe, both two-star chefs at the time, who opened six and seven bistros, respectively, over the course of the 1990s. Other three-star chefs opening a bistro or brasserie were: Michel Guérard, Michel Lorain, Jacques Pic, Pierre Troisgros, and the brothers Jacques and Laurent Pourcel; and the following two-star chefs opened a bistro near their principal restaurants: Jean-Pierre Billoux, Gérard Bonnefoy, Richard Coutanceau, and Olivier Roellinger. Other chefs very likely opened an "annex" restaurant as well, but these are the chefs whose ownership could be verified, through an analysis of chef profiles collected for this study, as well as from the following sources: G. Pudlowski, "Le Syndrôme de 'l'annexité,'" *Le Point*, no. 1455, August 4, 2000, pp. 58–59; and "Dossier restauration commercial: Les 80 leaders en France," *Néorestauration*, no. 365, May 2000, pp. 51–58.

Louis XV at l'Hôtel de Paris in Monte Carlo, and then a second three-star rating in 1998 at the age of forty-two for his restaurant, Alain Ducasse in Paris.[30] His name had become widely recognizable, not just throughout France but within the gastronomic circles of international capitals like London, New York, and Tokyo, where there seemed to be voracious markets for French haute cuisine and where Ducasse would make a series of audacious business moves. Functioning with the aggressive comportment of a corporate chief, Ducasse opened almost simultaneously his first New York restaurant, at the Essex House on Central Park, in London the second of three bistros (Spoon, Food and Wine had already opened in Tokyo and l'Île Maurice in Mauritius), and in Monaco a "Bar and Boeuf" brasserie, all while moving his Parisian three-star restaurant, Alain Ducasse, to the Hôtel Plaza Athénée in Paris.[31] These were moves made within just the first decade of his investiture into the inner sanctum of French gastronomy, when he received his first three-star rating in the *Michelin Guide*.[32]

Although it was something new in the gastronomic domain, selling one's "signature" was not at all unique to the culinary world. It was what leading sports figures and famous film stars had done for some time, and for decades it had been a standard practice within the fashion world, where the most highly consecrated designers had sold their names and their labels for the production and distribution of various (and more or less mass-market) fashion "accessories." The parallels between fashion and haute cuisine have been recognized for the ways in which mass-market principles were being applied to luxury foods, with the example of the refurbishing of Fauchon, a "venerable Parisian purveyor of fine foods" employing a business model based on fashion houses and luxury goods companies. As the firm's managing director noted, "business and creation have to jibe. . . . We need to manage this brand like a luxury brand. . . . Here, Fauchon is a *'griffe*

30. See J.-F. Mesplède, *Trois Étoiles au Michelin: Une histoire de la haute gastronomie française* (Paris: Éditions Grund, 1998), p. 184.

31. B. Thiault, "Ducasse superstar," *Néorestauration*, no. 356, July–August, 1999, p. 14; G. Spitzer and B. Thiault, "Ducasse à la conquête de Londres et New York," *Néorestauration*, no. 365, May 2000, p. 18; and A.-C. Sanchez and S. Chayet, "Alain Ducasse: Un chef-cuisinier conquiert le monde," *Le Point*, no. 1455, August 4, 2000, pp. 52–57.

32. Ducasse would later open a cooking school in Paris and would continue to open other restaurants, at various levels, in New York and in other parts of the world. See P. Fedele, "Alain Ducasse ouvre une école à Paris," *Néorestauration*, no. 462, March 2009, p. 21; N. Lemoine, "Rech, une brasserie tout poisson pour Ducasse," *L'Hôtellerie Restauration*, no. 3029, 18 May, 2007, p. 6; N. Demorand, "Alain Ducasse: ducasse.com," *Gault-Millau*, no. 337, Winter 1999–2000, pp. 41–47.

alimentaire' or a food label"[33] For Bourdieu the fashion world provided the quintessential model for analyzing the production of symbolic goods more generally, and specifically for understanding the production of value in the world of art. In an early article about the fashion world, Bourdieu wrote, "It is the rarity of the producer (which is to say the rarity of the position that he occupies in the field) that makes the rarity of the product."[34] For Bourdieu, this was fundamentally a social process in which the creator was symbolically created, through "an operation of symbolic transubstantiation, irreducible to a material transformation," in which the signature of the designer (or artist, or grand chef) "transforms in an almost magical way the status of the marked object."[35] For Bourdieu, the collective production of belief in the symbolic power of the signature represented an expression of collective misrecognition that required powerful institutional ballast:[36]

> The power of words lies not in the words themselves but in the conditions that give power to the words by producing collective belief, which is to say the collective misrecognition of the arbitrariness of the creation of value accomplished by a determined use of words. The imposition of value that symbolizes the "signature" is a special case of all operations of the transference of symbolic capital (i.e., prefaces written by a famous author for the first book of an unknown writer, the imprint of a prestigious publishing house) in which an agent or, more accurately, an institution acting through the intermediation of a duly mandated agent, invests value in a product. It is in the very structure of the field or, what amounts to the same thing, in the laws that command the accumulation and circulation of symbolic capital, rather than in any particular instance or in any particular agent or even a combination of unique factors (agents, instruments, circumstances) that resides the conditions of possibility of the social alchemy and of the transubstantiation that it realizes.

---

33. K. Weisman, "Culinary Haute Couture: The Designing of 'Concept' Foods," *International Herald Tribune*, October 8, 2004, p. 13. Also see D. Thomas, *Deluxe: How Luxury Lost Its Luster* (New York: Penguin Press, 2007).

34. Page 21 in P. Bourdieu with Y. Delsaut, "Le Couturier et sa griffe: Contribution à une théorie de la magie" [The designer and his signature: Contribution to a theory of magic] in *ACTES de la Recherche en Sciences Sociales*, no. 1, January 1975, pp. 17–36. This was the first edition of ACTES, the journal that Bourdieu would direct over the course of the rest of his career.

35. Bourdieu with Delsaut, "Le Couturier," p. 22.

36. Bourdieu with Delsaut, "Le Couturier," pp. 23–24. Translated by the author.

By the 1990s the exchange of the symbolic capital of the grands chefs for the economic capital of industrial corporations was an increasingly common and regular transaction, but it was still largely concealed from the French cultural imagination by the thick "veil of belief" that enveloped haute cuisine. For the chefs who had garnered a fair measure of recognition within the profession, the possibilities for such new arrangements were becoming increasingly available. Of the various publications of French gastronomy, *Le Chef* had been among those most fully engaged in the business of chef recognition, and so it was both ironic and significant that *Le Chef* had become a key player in reporting the social transformations that it was simultaneously and subtly helping to usher in. The complicity could be seen in persistently "sensible" and "balanced" editorial positions that it took with respect to the increasing presence of the grands chefs in the industrial regions of the gastronomic field, while being fully cognizant of the violation that this might represent for the integrity of the chef profession. Through its *reportage* that chronicled these changes it was simultaneously participating in them. Thus, in the issue of *Le Chef* magazine in which Alain Ducasse was named "Chef of the Year" in 1990, his award was underwritten by five industrial food companies (Sopad-Nestlé, Eurest, Molteni, Volailles de Challans, and Griottines) with an entire page of the magazine reserved for testimonies of top executives from each of these companies, who had been asked to "explain their partnership."[37] Characteristic was the following, by Jean-Pierre Houbre of Sopad-Nestlé: "As manufacturers we have a role in the development of the culinary arts. Especially in the elaboration of our products in partnership with the chefs. We are listening to their needs. Jointly the chefs bring us their talent, their creativity, and such synergies can only contribute to the dynamism of the profession." Moreover, in this same issue in which Ducasse was bestowed with the "Chef of the Year" award, *Le Chef* magazine also announced the awards given to food-processing companies at the fourteenth meeting of the international food exposition, SIAL (Salon International de l'Alimentation). The "lauréats" of the food-processing companies included the Bonduelle company (for "cooked vegetables in frozen packets"); Darégal (for "frozen aromatic herbs"); Mikogel (for "mini-bavarian desserts"), and Sopad-Nestlé (for "uncooked flan desserts").[38] See Figure 5.5 and 5.6.

---

37. "Ils sont les partenaires des chefs," *Le Chef,* no. 38, December 1990, p. 19.

38. "Les Industriels à l'honneur," *Le Chef,* no. 38, December 1990, p. 26. Here, the principal trade magazine for professional chefs was collaborating with industrial food companies by promoting their goods. Some years later the collaboration was reciprocated when *Néorestauration,* the trade magazine for the industrial food companies, published an issue with a

Figure 5.5 Alain Ducasse named "Chef of the Year" in December 1990 issue of *Le Chef* Magazine

Figure 5.6 Corporate Executives Awarded for Industrial Cuisine in December 1990 issue of *Le Chef* Magazine

That the premier magazine of the chef profession would serve as a medium for bringing the industrialized world of food processing together with the world of haute cuisine and French gastronomy in this manner was really quite remarkable. Two decades earlier such a symbolic connection would have essentially been a social and cultural impossibility, but over the course of the 1990s these sorts of oxymoronic expressions and associations would gradually help to wear away the firewall separating the two worlds. Thus, when *L'Hôtellerie* magazine published the image of Pierre Bellon, CEO of Sodexho, the corporate giant, alongside Claude Terrail, the prominent longtime proprietor of la Tour d'Argent, a venerated Parisian restaurant considered among the most elegant and well regarded in France, it seemed to signify open acknowledgment of the new arrangement within the gastronomic field itself, with the magazine's cover reading, "Journey of two men, animated by the same passion: restaurant catering."[39] See Figure 5.7.

In its representations to the outside world, French gastronomy continued to cloak itself in the venerability and integrity of haute cuisine. This took several narrative forms, including highlighting the lines of descent operating from the top of the chef profession ("Roger Verge begat Alain Ducasse, who begat Alain Solivérès," etc.), a fascination with the cross generational ties linking family "dynasties" of grands chefs (such as the multigenerational lines of the chef-families Troisgros, Pic, Blanc, and Lorain), and by fostering a veritable cult of reverence for the entire domain of *haute gastronomie*. Yet, in spite of the incessant talk devoted to gastronomy, which served to perpetuate belief in its cultural value, what was under way in the gastronomic field was the erosion of its autonomy as a field—in other words, a gradual wearing down of the field's capacity to preserve the traditional criteria by which value was determined and evaluated, along with its ability to shield itself from the powerful influence of the economic field. Thus despite all appearances, from the mid-1970s onward French gastronomy had become a site where symbolic capital could be converted into economic capital, so

---

Michelin three-star chef, Jacques Pourcel, as guest editor. In the issue, Pourcel, who shares the three stars with his twin brother, Laurent, both *chefs de cuisine* and owners of the three-star Le Jardin des Sens restaurant in Montpellier, published articles about his career as a chef, about his consulting business, his various "annexes," and about the day-to-day experience of editing *Néorestauration* magazine. In addition to being an act of collaboration between the artisanal and the industrial sides of the gastronomic field, it was also a transparent manifestation of self-promotion. See "Un Chef à la rédaction," *Néorestauration*, no. 458, November 2008.

39. *L'Hôtellerie*, no. 2634, October 7, 1999.

Figure 5.7 Major
Industrialist and
Venerable Restau-
rateur, Together

that once a chef was anointed by the appropriate institutions of consecration, his name was—Midas-like—granted the power to turn accumulated
symbolic capital into economic gold. Under these emerging conditions it
became increasingly possible for a Paul Bocuse, a Bernard Loiseau, or a
Guy Savoy, and for dozens of other highly consecrated chefs, more or less
well-known, to apply their signatures to all manner of goods, from pots and
pans, to aprons, tableware, cookbooks, and inexpensive bistros, to consulting contracts, and to international restaurant ventures. Through this process the grands chefs were not only generating considerable economic profits
for themselves but creating space in the imaginations of all French chefs to
include economic wealth as a goal to be pursued in charting one's career
trajectory. With economic capital beginning to flow from the *grands groupes
industriels* into the domain of the grand chefs, in exchange for the symbolic
capital that the grands chefs had accumulated, the mutual repulsion that
had historically characterized relations between these two regions of the
gastronomic field was becoming increasingly untenable. See Figure 5.8.

French Representations

Ducasse

Troisgros **Bocuse** Escoffier
Guide Culinare

3 MICHELIN STARS

Academie Robuchon "Thuries" Grands Bistrots &
Culinaire de Blanc Magazine Brasseries
France Pacaud Vergé (La Coupole, Lipp, Le Balzar)

Claude Terrail La Taillevent Restaurant
(La Tour d'Argent Loiseau Legendre Senderens Lameloise
Restaurant)
Conseil National Lorain Boyer Guerard
Des Arts PIC Trama Savoy
Culinaires "Le Chef" Foundation Rostang
MOF Magazine Brillat-Savarin
Veyrat Chapel **Guide Michelin** Gault-Millau
Magazine

Les Trois Alsaciennes Huguet Mazere
Artisanal (Jung, Westermann, Haeberlin) Passard **Production**
(Long Time)
(Tradition)

Restricted Market (Exclusive)
Sophistication
Complexity
Formality
Expensive
Low volume Maxim's (chain)

Ducasse's "sandwicherie"

Chain Restaurants
Bistrots
(Hippo, Buffalo Grill)
Groupe
Holder
Eliance Agapes Restaurants

Autoroute rest areas Corthay

Autogrill Groupe Flo **Industrial**
(Short Time)
(Modern)

Economic Capital

Symbolic Capital

Consumption

Danone Eurodisney S.A.
SIRHA **GRANDS GROUPES** **Sodexho**
Fleury **AGRO ALIMENTAIRE** (Pierre Belon)

Neo
Restauration **Accor Carrefour Kraft**
Magazine Lactalis SIAL **Unilever**
(Michel Besnier) **Nestlé**
Revue Technique
Magazine B. Trujillo French Fast Food
La Croissanterie,
Cafeterias and Canteens Pomme de Pain
E. Leclerc (Institutional)
Auchan
Mass Market (Inclusive) Hamburgers
Convenience Casino Fast Food
Simplicity Cafeteria McDonald's
Informality Compass
Cheap Groupe Domino's Ray Kroc
High Volume Pizza Servair
Inclusive

American Representations

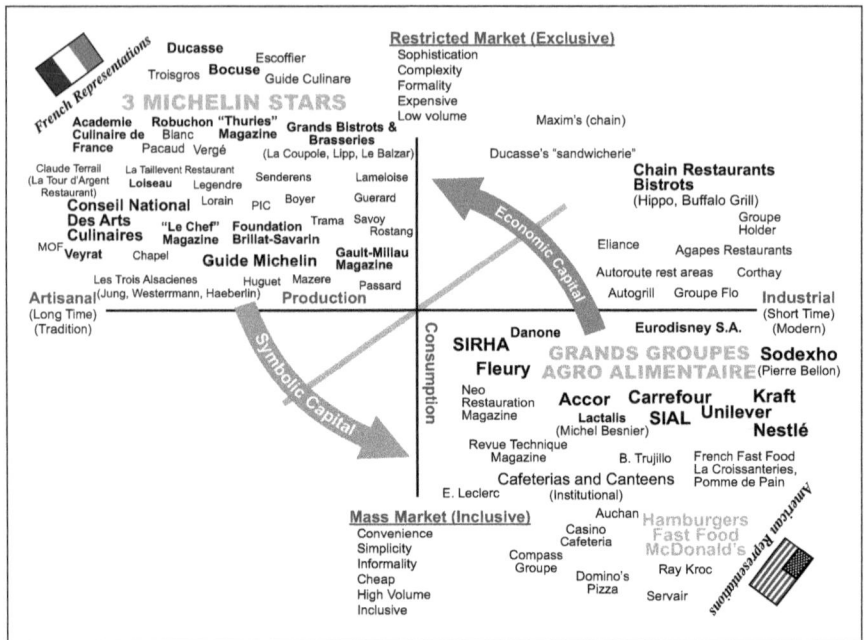

Figure 5.8 Direction of Capital Flows in the Principal Regions of the French Gastronomic Field

It was striking how the rhetoric of the grands chefs could change once they had achieved their third *Michelin* star, shifting from a discourse of "excellence" and "exclusivity" to one of "democracy" and "accessibility"— that is, from the public stance of Ducasse asserting "no expense should be spared to secure the absolutely finest ingredients possible" to the notion that "everyone must be given an opportunity to experience the wondrous creations of our kitchens".[40] In the thirtieth anniversary issue of the magazine a journalist for *Néorestauration* noted, with respect to the inexpensive bistros ("annexes") opened by the grands chefs, "These institutions have conquered the public by offering quality food at affordable prices in a friendly atmosphere. Although once viewed as being a fleeting or ephemeral style, the bistros of the chefs are permanently inscribed in the landscape of the contemporary restaurant world and one does well to emulate them."[41]

The grands chefs tended to describe the new business ventures not prin-

40. B. Thiault, "Alain Ducasse: 'Je veux rendre accessible notre savoir-faire culinaire,'" in *Néorestauration*, no. 350, January 1999, p. 53.

41. P. Cecconello, "De grands chefs . . . d'entreprise," *Néorestauration*, no. 385, March 2002, p. 13.

cipally as profit-making activities but as means of diffusing their artistry to a wider public. Thus, after signing contracts with Sodexho, three-star chefs Alain Passard and Michel Bras each referred to their new business activities as opportunities to spread the gospel of good taste:[42]

"Thanks to this partnership we are able to pass something to our children, like our grandparents did, bringing gastronomy to communities. This is a very good time for French taste with regard to the table and we can thus contribute to its maintenance and its development. With our expertise there is a real complementarity with that of Sodexho." [**Alain Passard**]

"I would like to bring to this partnership with Sodexho a little of my experience and what I have lived. Experience, because every year I discover school children in my area who have no opening to a universe of taste which they did not know existed. . . . with Sodexho I would like to contribute to the growth of a world of connoisseurs of good food, which is to say a better world." [**Michel Bras**]

For Guy Savoy, business activities served as both a means of realizing creative impulses and distributing them more widely:[43]

When I created my first Bistro, I had no particular strategy in mind. When the formula worked I didn't hesitate to turn myself into a businessman because I like the teamwork. My first motivation is not to do business, but to give life to projects that inspire me. . . . I look less to diversify than to find other forms of expression in my profession. I like working with new themes, looking for new ideas, renewing myself. The important thing, in my eyes, is to make every place a quality kitchen. . . . In the future I hope to continue to juggle all my activities and to maintain intact the passion and enthusiasm that can grow and that will last. I am happy to demonstrate that one can have both a gourmet restaurant at a high level of excellence, while transferring expertise to other places without tarnishing them.

---

42. G. Golan, "Dossier gastronomique et collectivités," *Le Chef,* no. 122, April 2000, p. 21.
43. P. Cecconello, "Transposer son savoir-faire sans le galvauder," *Néorestauration,* no. 385, March 2002, p. 13.

In this new situation the means of converting symbolic capital into economic capital could be facilitated more easily than ever before, but it was neither guaranteed nor irreversible. In the case of three-star chef Anne-Sophie Pic, the ability to convert a significant accumulation of social and symbolic capital was slowed both by a loss (twice) of a *Michelin* third star and, quite possibly, by her status as the only female chef/owner of a three-star restaurant. Anne-Sophie Pic was the scion of an illustrious family of grand chefs. Her grandfather, Andre Pic, son of a restaurateur himself, had moved his Restaurant Pic to Valence, on the Paris–Côte d'Azur national motor route in 1934, after having received three *Michelin* stars. Although he lost one of its stars, it was later recovered in 1973 by his son, Jacques Pic (Anne-Sophie's father), a grand chef who had gained considerable standing in the world of French gastronomy, until his death in 1992 when his daughter took over the family restaurant.[44] The restaurant again lost its third star in 1995, but was able to recover it twelve years later under the direction of Anne-Sophie, who quickly moved on a string of business initiatives. Within a year of recovering her third star she opened the first of a chain of gastronomic restaurants, at the Beau Rivage hotel in Lausanne, Switzerland, after having just constructed a luxury hotel at the family restaurant in Valence; which was followed by the opening of a bistro, 7 par Anne-Sophie Pic, a cooking school, and a cookbook project.[45] This series of business ventures suggests that the gastronomic field had been sufficiently conditioned, at its very center, to quickly create economic opportunity out of symbolic recognition, thereby offering a means of (economic) capital accumulation that had been unavailable in an earlier period of French gastronomy.

The rapid pace by which Anne-Sophie Pic was able to begin to cash in, economically, on her store of symbolic (and social) capital, was rivaled by the speed at which Joël Robuchon was able to accumulate symbolic capital early in his career as a chef. After receiving the Meilleur Ouvrier de France award, Robuchon collected *Michelin* stars in rapid succes-

44. Working with her brother, Alain, Anne-Sophie Pic lost her third star in 1995, before recovering it in 2007. See J.-F. Mesplède, "Anne-Sophie Pic: Au nom du père," *L'Hôtellerie* magazine, no. 2590, December 3, 1998, pp. 4–7; "Jacques Pic: L'Album du chef," *Thuriès* magazine, no. 14, November 1989, pp. i–vii; F. Fabricant, "The Latest Woman to Join a Very Exclusive Club," *New York Times*, February 28, 2007, p. D2.

45. "Anne-Sophie Pic: Dans la cour des grands" (no author), *LTI: Les Tendances Internationales*, no. 4, May 2007, pp. 14–16 (a magazine published by Groupe Food); M. Luginsland, "Chef: Anne-Sophie Pic s'internationalise," *Néorestauration*, no. 458, November 2008, p. 20; P. Fedele, "*Une aventure Suisse en forme de challenge*," *Néorestauration*, no. 464, May 2009, p. 15.

sion (his first in 1982; his second in 1983; and his third star in 1984) thus identifying him as a veritable *wunderkind* in French gastronomic circles.[46] But in 1996 Robuchon astonished the French gastronomic world by closing his three-star restaurant in Paris and, after a seven-year hiatus, opened the first of six bars/bistros that explicitly sought to break down the distinction between haute cuisine and pub food.[47] Robuchon had released himself from the pressures of managing a three-star restaurant, although with the knowledge that his considerable symbolic capital would sustain his standing at the top of the field and provide a foundation of support (symbolically) for whatever business activities he might enter in the future.

For the grands chefs, the situation was not a simple one. Those staying with their original restaurants, serving only those able to afford very expensive meals, faced a difficult financial struggle.[48] For example, in the mid-1990s Bernard Loiseau claimed that the "signature" dish at his la Côte d'Or restaurant was bringing in just $1.20 in profit, for a dish that cost about $60 ("Frogs legs with garlic and parsley puree"), while the three-star chef, Jean-Michel Lorain, reported an overall profit margin of zero after having invested $5 million in his hotel and restaurant declaring, "Basically, I work for the banks and the government."[49] As one former two-star chef explained to a journalist:[50]

---

46. B. Balayé, "Joël Robuchon: L'album du chef," *Thuriès Magazine*, no. 8, April 1989, pp. I–IX; G. Golan, "Joël Robuchon: Le début d'un mythe," *Le Chef,* no. 43, June–July, 1991, pp. 16–18: G. Golan, "La Nouvelle Cuisine de Joël Robuchon," *Le Chef,* no. 67, March 1994, pp. 28–30.

47. R. W. Apple Jr., "Out of Retirement, into the Fire," *New York Times*, May 2, 2003, p. D1; and J. Sigal, "The Chef: Joël Robuchon," *New York Times*, March 28, 2007, p. D1.

48. In the 1990s the restaurant industry in France lobbied ferociously for a reduction in the VAT (Value Added Tax on consumption) on restaurant meals. The rate had been at 19.6 percent and industry representatives sought to lower it to 5.5 percent, the same rate as "take-out" foods, which included fast-food restaurants, complaining that this had amounted to an unofficial state subsidy to the fast-food industry in France. In 2008, the industry received its VAT rate reduction to 5.5 percent from the French government, under Nicolas Sarkozy, in an effort to boost the restaurant industry and to encourage employment. Sarkozy raised the rate to 7 percent in 2010, and under Francois Hollande the rate was raised again to 10 percent. M. Saltmarsh, "France to Lower Tax to Entice Diners to Restaurants," *New York Times*, April 28, 2009; H. Samuel, "French Fury at VAT Restaurant Raise," *Daily Telegraph* online edition, November 6, 2012, available at http://www.telegraph.co.uk/news/worldnews/Europe/france/9659243/.

49. C. R. Whitney, "Gloomy 3-Star Chefs Say the Fault Is Not Theirs," *New York Times*, November 24, 1995, p. A4; R. Chelminski, *The Perfectionist: Life and Death in Haute Cuisine* (New York: Gotham Books, 2005), p. 258.

50. Chelminiski, *Perfectionist: Life and Death*, p. 259.

As soon as I got my second star, I never made any money from the restaurant, anymore. . . . After all the investment you put into the place, and the cost of the personnel, on those winter evenings when you've got two or three clients, a business like that is like a vacuum cleaner for your money. You might do OK on the weekend, but then, come Monday and Tuesday—no one, not even a rat, but you've still got the fixed charges to pay. . . . So what do you do to survive? You do things on the side. You open a bistro next door. You write books. You endorse products. You do special gastronomic weeks. That's how I got by in Auch.

Two three-star chefs saw their restaurants close in 1996. For Pierre Gagnaire it was reportedly because his restaurant was located in an industrial city with few tourists and few residents able to afford to eat there, and for Marc Veyrat the debts incurred from substantial renovations to his restaurants forced him to briefly close one of them.[51] A thoroughly remodeled restaurant had become essential for three-star consideration by Michelin, and with renovations costing half a million to 1 million euros, it was crucial for chef-owners to maintain a strong relationship with their banker. When asked what advice he would give to up-and-coming young chefs, Marc Veyrat was explicit: "They should create restaurants in their own image and should consider bankers as allies, not as adversaries—I have renegotiated my loans and they should do the same to be better able to face the future."[52]

To seek financing for his future bistro projects, Bernard Loiseau entered the Paris stock market in 1998, noting, "Over the years I have worked to obtain my third Michelin star; and now my goal is to be able to operate at the level of the stock market."[53] For Loiseau, the interplay between symbolic and economic capital can be seen to have operated in a relationship of mutual constitution, so that as his professional recognition increased, he was able to "capitalize" by investing in business deals and, in turn, to a certain degree, his public recognition was enhanced by the publicity surrounding

---

51. M. Steinberger, *Au Revoir to All That* (New York: Bloomsbury, 2009), p. 76.

52. Quoted in J.-F. Mesplède, "Paul Bocuse et Marc Veyrat, "L'union sacrée," *L'Hôtellerie*, no. 2570, July 16, 1998, p. 3; The trade magazine, *Néorestauration*, explicitly listed the "10 Keys for Seducing Your Banker," in P. Fedele, "Comment financer son project," *Néorestauration*, nos. 405, 406, January–February 2004, pp. 38–41.

53. T. Noisette, "Bernard Loiseau parie sur la Bourse," *Néorestauration*, no. 346, September 1998, p. 22.

his business deals. At the same time, however, to fully maintain the recognition that made his business opportunities possible, Loiseau had to be able to entrust a certain amount of control of the day-to-day work in the kitchen to others (in his case to Patrick Bertron, his longtime *second de cuisine* at his la Côte d'Or restaurant), while being careful to maintain a sufficient personal presence in the kitchen to demonstrate (or certify) the authenticity of the cuisine.[54]

In addition to la Côte d'Or, in which he reportedly invested some $10 million in renovations over two decades, and which always comprised the largest part of his economic activities, Loiseau had opened a boutique across from the restaurant (selling various souvenirs, including foods, cookbooks, kitchen products, etc.), opened a branch of his restaurant in a Sheraton Hotel in Japan (which closed after three years due to an earthquake), and opened three bistros in Paris.[55] By the end of 1998, his company, Bernard Loiseau S.A., was listed on the Paris stock exchange, a first within the world of French gastronomy, and within the following months sales turnover (*chiffre d'affaires*) grew 54 percent to $3.4 million (22.2 million French francs) with the company's business activities divided up as shown in Table 5.1. Three years later, and one year prior to his suicide, the portion of Loiseau's business activities occupied by his original la Côte d'Or restaurant in Saulieu had dropped from 58 percent to 42 percent as shown in Table 5.2.

The shift can be viewed as a reflection of the effects of diversification and the diminishing importance of la Côte d'Or in relation to the overall configuration of Loiseau's business activities. The public offering had raised about $4.5 million and, according to William Echikson, was used by Loiseau to pay off debt and to acquire two Paris bistros (Tante Marguerite and Tante Jeanne, followed soon by a third, Tante Louise), as various additional business ventures presented themselves.[56] With some sixty-five employees, la Côte d'Or restaurant had been the anchor of Loiseau's business activities and was a substantial operation, but it was still just a small business, struggling with the same relatively narrow profit margins as other small, independent French businesses. The cost and the time required to produce haute cuisine

---

54. This observation was made by Isabel Terence in her study of starred French chefs, *Le Monde de la grande restauration en France* (Paris: L'Harmattan, 1996), p. 21.

55. Echikson, "Death of a Chef."

56. For example, in 2001, Loiseau signed a consulting agreement to provide management services to a restaurant hotel project being built in Toulouse (Florence Jacquemond, "Projet de Bernard Loiseau en Haute-Garonne," *Néorestauration*, no. 378, July–August 2001, p. 14) and see Echikson, "Death of a Chef," p. 65.

TABLE 5.1 BUSINESS HOLDINGS OF BERNARD LOISEAU (1999)

Business Activity	% of Bernard Loiseau S.A.
La Côte d'Or (restaurant)	58
Relais and Château (hôtel)	19
Tante Louise (the first Paris bistro)	12
Consulting services	6
Boutique in Saulieu	5
Total	100

Source: "Le Rêve du businessman," *Le Chef,* no. 117, October 1999, p. 8.

TABLE 5.2 BUSINESS HOLDINGS OF BERNARD LOISEAU (2002)

Business Activity	% of Bernard Loiseau S.A.
La Côte d'Or (Saulieu)	42.0
Hôtel in Saulieu (Relais and Château)	18.0
3 Paris bistros (Les Tantes)	30.0
Consulting services (BLO)	6.4
Evénementiel (events, catering)	0.6
Boutique in Saulieu (incl. mail order)	3.0
Total	100.0

Source: Website for La Côte d'Or, March 16, 2004: http://www.bernard-loiseau.com/.

presented challenges for restaurant owners, and the state-mandated reduction in working hours had been a particular concern and point of contention.[57]

What about the food? Did the opening of the gastronomic field to economic logic and practice diminish the quality of food served in three-star restaurants? First, the focus of this analysis has been on changes in relations

---

57. The "Loi d'orientation et d'incitation à la réduction du temps de travail" [trans.: The Orientation and Incentive toward Reduction of Working Time Law] was passed in 1998, mandating a gradual process of reducing the French workweek to 35 hours in enterprises with more than 20 workers and providing state assistance to businesses to ease the process. The policy pushed against traditional conventions of the organization of labor in the restaurant business and so was a major topic of debate, discussion, and contention across the industry. A significant counterbalance to the reduction in working time (and the related adjustment of the minimum wage) has been a movement in the European Union for a substantial reduction of the TVA (value-added tax) on traditional restaurant meals from 19 percent to 5.5 percent (for all member states). For industry accounts, see Christel Reynaud, "Les 39 heures, mission impossible?" *Le Chef,* no. 118, November 1999; Patrice Fleurent, "2002: Euro, RTT . . . Mais à quand la TVA?" *Néorestauration,* no. 383, January 2002, p. 3; and "TVA: Une première victoire pour la restauration," *L'Hôtellerie,* no. 2830, July 17, 2003, p. 22.

within French gastronomy as a cultural field, and not on the quality of the food produced by chefs and cooks in France. Second, and more significantly, there is simply no way to assess the quality of the meals served in three-star restaurants, or any restaurants for that matter, in an objective way. That is, there is no culinary guide or food critic or food journalist able to evaluate this cultural object from a neutral or an objective standpoint, since all food critics, and journalists, and guides are implicated in the collective construction of belief in the value of French cuisine. In other words, all the players on the field have a stake in the game, whether the established voices or the insurgents, and all have been drawn into the vortex of belief in French gastronomy, while simultaneously producing collective belief in its value. Thus it is impossible to know with certainty how the quality of French cuisine has been affected by the sorts of changes we have been describing. As the changes unfolded, there was a good deal of anxiety and speculation about the future of the field, from positions within it, with the theme of the "crisis of gastronomy" becoming a fairly regular focus of conjecture and commentary.[58]

While it is difficult to objectively judge a cultural object whose value is maintained by the judges themselves, it is not impossible to see ways in which the new undertakings may have shaped the practice of chefs in their craft. Above all, the amount of *time* they could actually spend in the kitchen was necessarily reduced—greatly for some—and this was an issue that generated a considerable amount of attention and criticism, and particularly after Bernard Loiseau's suicide.[59] Time, which represents the virtual leitmotif of all artisanal practice, had to be constricted to accommodate the many additional business activities. For the grands chefs this meant less time to cultivate relationships with food suppliers, less time to experiment and in-

---

58. Some examples from *Le Chef* magazine: G. Golan, "Alain Senderens: Le courage de regarder le futur," no. 36, October 1990, pp. 18–19; G. Golan, "Interrogations sur la cuisine française" no. 36, October 1990, pp. 21–22; G. Golan, "La Crise du restaurant gastronomique," no. 54, October 1992, pp. 24–26; G. Golan, "Crise de la Gastronomie?" no. 84, January–February 1996, pp. 36–38; G. Golan and F. Luzin, "Regards sur la cuisine française," no. 93, January–February 1997, p. 38; and from *Néorestauration* magazine: J.-C. Schamberger, P. Cecconello, E. Bravo, P. Fedele, and J.-F. Vuillerme, "Les Chefs face à leur avenir," no. 400, July–August 2003, pp. 31–43; D. P. Fedele, "La fin d'une époque," no. 464, May 2009, p. 3.

59. Some of this attention was prompted by the suicide of Bernard Loiseau in 2003, and especially because it was widely reported that the director of the *Michelin* guide had earlier warned Loiseau that he risked losing a star if he did not "stay in your kitchen" and spend so much time on business. He did not lose his third star, but the pressure from the guides was viewed as a possible factor in his suicide. See M. Steinberger, *Au Revoir to All That*, p. 70; Chelminski, *Perfectionist: Life and Death*; and see Chapter 1.

novate, and less time to teach one's skills to secondary chefs and commis in the kitchen. One reaction to the new demands on a chef's time, articulated by Alain Ducasse, has been to amend the traditional role of the chef, from being the supreme authority at the center of a working kitchen to representing a spiritual figure who lends his "spirit" and "philosophy" to a restaurant: "The role of the chef is to train people to take care of the clients, who live in the spirit which he develops over the years . . . the walls of the restaurant sweat his philosophy."[60] Of course, when one is involved in a dozen or more various restaurant projects on several continents, there is little time to lend much more than one's philosophy or spirit to a restaurant. By contrast, a more traditional chef's perspective on time and the kitchen has been offered by Benoit Guichard, who worked in the kitchens of several three-star chefs and is a recipient of the MOF. He lamented the new arrangement:[61]

> We are in a society where everything has to go fast, so that by the age of 26 one should already be a chef and have published his book. This attitude is the communications business, it is not cooking. I refuse to enter into this race. It no longer allows the time to cook and to learn. We must all follow the rising chefs-of-the-year and appear in all the magazines . . . [but] if one is passionate about cooking, 90% of the time should be devoted to cooking. Do we cook because we love it or do we cook because cooking is a way to satisfy the ego?

While change in the quality of the food on the plate cannot be judged easily or objectively, the breakdown of the traditional divide between artisanal and industrial practice in the French gastronomic field has led to short cuts being taken that were previously unthinkable. In the 1990s the press reported examples of the dough for *baguettes* being produced in centralized industrial bakeries and delivered to *boulangeries* for baking, while adulterated with additives to make the bread rise more effectively, last longer, and come out whiter, and this practice led to government regulations stipulating that to be recognized as a genuine *boulangerie* the dough must be made, kneaded, and baked on the premises.[62] Meanwhile, in a survey of its members, the National Union

---

60. Ducasse quoted in J. Wadler, "Building an Empire on Gastronomic Memories," *New York Times*, July 20, 2000, p. A22.

61. G. Golan, "Le Fond prime sur la forme," *Le Chef*, no. 168, May 2005, p. 39.

62. A. Breeden, "Decrees Governing France's Bakeries Prompt a Wider Debate on Work Rules," *New York Times*, February 11, 2015, p. A6; and H. La Franchi, "France Moves to Protect Revered Part of Life—and Its Reputation," *Christian Science Monitor* online edition,

of Hotel, Restaurant, and Café Operators, found that at least a third of the restaurants in France were using industrial frozen foods produced in centralized kitchens, leading to a parliamentary initiative to specifically designate "artisan restaurants" as those that prepare all their dishes on the premises.[63] The obvious lure of industrial practice is the savings that it can yield, in time and thus in money, as one journalist recounted: "A chunk of tuna cooked Provencal style with an attractive ratatouille on the side . . . can be bought in a restaurant-supply factory for $4, stored in the freezer indefinitely and sold to a diner for $17 after three minutes in the microwave."[64] Among other things, what the increasing industrialization of French gastronomy accomplished was a gradual reduction of the stigma attached to frozen and preprepared foods for the average French consumer (per capita frozen food consumption rose from 4 lbs. to 66 lbs. between 1960 and 2001) as well as for at least some French chefs.[65] The leading test chef for Picard, France's best-known frozen food retail chain, recalled, "When I first came to work here, my fellow chefs turned their backs on me. . . . Now more of my old friends are calling. Very quietly, they ask 'So, well, how can I use this frozen food?'"[66]

The changes that occurred saw the logic of the economic field gradually imposing itself on the fundamental logic, or nomos, of the gastronomic field.[67] A veritable "symbolic revolution" was under way in French gastronomy, a field that had been represented (and had represented itself) through the cultural language of haute cuisine, and where space was now carved out for practices driven primarily or partly by economic interest rather than

---

September 1, 1993, available at http://csmonitor.com/layout/set/print/1993/0901/01032.html.

63. Since the survey depended on self-reporting by restaurant owners, the figure was very likely much larger than one-third. This use of industrial frozen food in French restaurants has occurred in the "low to mid-level of the Paris food chain," rather than in the most highly consecrated restaurants, according to G. Viscusi, "Dirty Secret of French Restaurants Out as Food Origin Sought," in *Bloomberg* news, June 26, 2013 (online), available at www.bloomberg.com/news/print/2013-06-26/dirty-secret-of-french-restaurants-out-as-law-seeks-food-origin.html.

64. E. Cody, "French Restaurants Acknowledge Serving Factory-Frozen Food," *Washington Post*, July 9, 2013 (no page number).

65. E. Sciolino, "Foie Gras in the Freezer? Just Don't Tell Anyone," *New York Times*, December 19, 2002, p. A4; L. Alderman, "France, of All Places, Finds Itself in a Battle against Processed Food," *New York Times*, January 30, 2014, p. B1; M. Bittman, "French Food Goes Down," *New York Times*, July 23, 2014, p. A25.

66. Quoted in E. Scolino, op. cit. p. A4.

67. In Bourdieu's formulation the nomos refers to the principle vision and division of the field, the founding vantage point from which the field has been constituted and that defines the right of entry into it; see P. Bourdieu, *The Rules of Art* (Stanford, CA: Stanford University Press, 1996), p. 223.

by the pursuit of culinary perfection and the goal of realizing the sublime. Whatever material effects these changes may have had, the most consequential effect was to make the symbolic edifice of French gastronomy more precarious and unstable. That is, if the increasing interpenetration of the artisanal and the industrial meant that symbolic consecration of the former enabled access to the economic capital of the latter, it also made for a more precarious structure since the symbolic aura of haute cuisine was put in danger of being perforated and potentially destroyed by too obvious an embrace or association with economic practices, preoccupations, and interests.[68]

The gastronomic field in France was not destroyed by the advance of neoliberalism, but it was forced open to influences and practices that have eroded its autonomy as a cultural field.[69] The influence of economic capital and the institutional forces that surround it have been felt not only within the relatively small, but symbolically important, circle of restaurants and grands chefs and food guides located at the geographic center of French gastronomy (Paris, but also Lyon and the Côte d'Azur) but extending *outward* from the large cities into rural France, and thus *inward* into the cultural heart of "*La France profonde.*"

Reign of *Le Terroir*

If the frog legs that Bernard Loiseau had served at his la Côte d'Or restaurant yielded as small a profit as he had claimed, it would have been at least partially the result of the domestic frog shortage, caused by the gradual loss of marshland in France, thus requiring Loiseau and other chefs to purchase

---

68. This has obviously been true not only in the French gastronomic field but in all cultural fields where the logic of the economic field has intruded, reconfiguring or confounding the principle vision and division upon which it was founded (cinema, literature, painting, publishing, higher education, sports, etc.). Some, such as Jean-Claude Marcel, have argued that French gastronomy had already essentially been destroyed by its association with industrial and, specifically American, foodways. See J.-C. Marcel, *La Sale Bouffe* (Paris: Éditions Bernard Barrault, 1990).

69. This is an important part of the argument advanced by Alexandre Lazareff in *L'Exception culinaire française: Un patrimoine gastronomique en péril?* (Paris: Albin Michel, 1998). While I referred (above) to the process as an unfolding "symbolic revolution" in the gastronomic field, (in other words, a transformation in the vision of the world by participants in a social universe tied closely to changes in the categories of belief and perception that are then used, imperceptibly, by the participants to comprehend that world) what was taking place might be more accurately referred to as a "symbolic *counter-revolution*" that was eroding the autonomy of the French gastronomic field. See Pierre Bourdieu: *MANET: A Symbolic Revolution* (Medford, MA: Polity Press, 2017).

imported frog legs from various Eastern Europe countries, as well as from Texas and Cuba.[70] The situation of agriculture has been an important aspect of the gastronomic field. How changes in the field reverberate through French agriculture, and how agricultural practices contribute to changes in the gastronomic field, are not marginal concerns. By 1970 France had become Western Europe's principal agricultural society, the third largest producer of agricultural products in the West, as the variation of its soils and climates were able to produce a wide variety of fruits, vegetables, wines, cheeses, and most basic dairy and meat staples.[71] France arrived at a position of agricultural supremacy following what was termed a "rural revolution" in the postwar decades, driven by a rapid and massive mechanization of the agricultural sector. This mechanization was characterized by a "tractor craze" that swept through French agriculture in the 1950s, in which the number of farm tractors increased from 37,000 in 1945 to 230,000 in 1954, and then to 625,000 in 1959; while the number of harvesters increased from 250 to 42,000 in that same period.[72] While the increasing mechanization generated steady and substantial productivity increases overall, there were regional disparities that saw substantial increases in peasant indebtedness, the uneconomical mechanization of farms too small to benefit, and, accordingly, a 27 percent decline in the number of farms between 1963 and 1975, with a corresponding exodus from the land, as the French workforce engaging in agriculture declined from over 20 percent in 1963 to about 8 percent in 1978.[73] According to one analyst, "For many farmers, unable to

70. These were, reportedly, the main sources for frog legs in France prior to 2003, after which occurred a sharp increase in worldwide production from frog farms in Indonesia, China, Vietnam, and elsewhere. Source: UN Commodity Trade Statistics Database, reported in Brian Gratwicke, Mathew J. Evans, Peter T. Jenkins, Mirza D. Kusrini, Robin D. Moore, Jennifer Sevin, and David E. Wildt, "Is the International Frog Legs Trade a Potential Vector for Deadly Amphibian Pathogens?" *Frontiers in Ecology and the Environment*, 2009, doi:10.1890/090111; and see Noreen Parks, "Human Appetites Driving Frogs to Extinction?" *Frontiers in Ecology and the Environment*, Vol.7, No. 2 (Mar., 2009) p. 65.

71. H. P. Muth, *French Agriculture and the Political Integration of Western Europe* (Leyden: A. W. Sijthoff, 1970), p. 19.

72. According to Gordon Wright, the number of tractors in 1945 were just two thousand more than in 1938, and the number of harvesters increased by only fifty in this same period, thereby magnifying the massive increase in the 1950s even more. G. Wright, *Rural Revolution in France: The Peasantry in the Twentieth Century* (Stanford, CA: Stanford University Press, 1964), p. 146. And see J. Ardagh, *France in the 1980s* (New York: Penguin Books, 1982), p. 208.

73. J.T.S. Keeler, *The Politics of Neocorporatism in France: Farmers, the State, and Agricultural Policy-Making in the Fifth Republic* (New York: Oxford University Press, 1987), p. 94. According to Gordon Wright (*Rural Revolution in France*, p. 145) state subsidies of machin-

keep up the interest payments on their purchases, this first incursion into the market economy with its costings of labour, efficiency and debt repayments, proved to be their last."[74]

Accompanying the rapid diffusion of farm technologies was the spread of an ethos of productivism and enterprise that was a sharp break from the traditional orientation and outlook of the French peasant.[75] Supported by the FNSEA, the largest union of French farmers, and by a political class that dominated rural regions, there was increasing acceptance of the idea of long-term economic planning and of the notion of agriculture as a key component of the French national economy. According to Gordon Wright, through their participation in key national economic planning commissions, such groups "came to see the virtues of higher productivity and continued expansion, and the fearsome limits of the narrowly defensive Malthusian outlook that had dominated French agriculture in the past."[76]

Along with this material transformation of French agriculture was a veritable "symbolic revolution" in which urban ways of life were increasingly celebrated as being both superior and inevitable, adding to the degradation of the peasant, in terms of their position and their disposition. As Bourdieu noted:[77]

> The growing subordination of the peasant economy to the logic of the market would not have sufficed, in itself, to determine the profound transformations of which the rural world has been the site, starting with massive emigration, if this process had not itself been linked, in a relation of circular causality, to a unification of the market in symbolic goods which tends to induce the decline of the

---

ery cooperatives, instituted with strong pressure from the powerful farmer's union, FSNEA (Fédération Nationale des Syndicats d'Exploitans Agricoles) tended to limit some of the effects of peasant debt and the inefficient employment of machinery.

74. Cleary stresses the regional disparities in the structures of farming in France (p. 17) and notes that farm indebtedness increased "from 16.5 percent of added value in agriculture in the late 1930s to 140 percent in 1983" (p.16) in M. C. Cleary, *Peasants, Politicians, and Producers: The Organization of Agriculture in France since 1918* (Cambridge: Cambridge University Press, 1989).

75. The history of these changes has been characterized very differently by Henri Mendras in *The Vanishing Peasant: Innovation and Change in French Agriculture* (Cambridge, MA: MIT Press, 1970); and by Pierre Bourdieu in *The Bachelors' Ball: The Crisis of Peasant Society in Bearn* (Chicago: University of Chicago Press, 2008).

76. G. Wright, *Rural Revolution in France*, p. 144.

77. P. Bourdieu, *The Bachelors' Ball: The Crisis of Peasant Society in Bearn* (Chicago: University of Chicago Press, 2008), p. 177.

ethical autonomy of the peasants and, thereby, the withering away of their capacities for resistance and refusal.

In other words, one effect of the transformation in the countryside was the devaluation of rural life in relation to the city, with its higher incomes and standards of living, its modern ways and cosmopolitan orientation. The traditional provincial outlook that had sealed the peasant off from much of the rest of French society was lifting just as changes in village life were prompting peasants to question their way of living in comparison with others. As Bourdieu remarked, "the attractions of the urban way of life can only work on minds converted to its attractions."[78] This view adds new meaning to conventional perspectives on the "modernization" of the French peasantry, whereby the acquisition of modern appliances, like television, were treated as markers of cultural integration, in themselves, rather than as vehicles for introducing information about urban lifestyles and ways of living into village life. In other words, new means of communication were introduced into the context of a symbolic struggle over the peasant's place in the social world. So, for example, in Laurence Wylie's classic study, *Village in the Vaucluse* the increase in television ownership in his village of Peyrane denoted both prosperity and the increasing individuation of French rural life:[79]

> Television came to Peyrane in the late fifties, when a transmitter was erected on the Luberon Mountain in order to bring the Marseille programs to the communities of the valley around Apt. Emile bought a set at once, or rather he brought it home and paid for it on the installment plan over a period of twelve months. This sort of transaction was new to him and contrary to his family training and tradition, according to which one should never buy on credit. Now, however, he is convinced that he has been foolish all these years to stay out of debt. . . . Most of the television sets operating in Peyrane were bought on the installment plan. How many are there? In 1961 the postman, Francis Favre, did me the favor of counting them as he made his rounds. He reported twenty-three sets in the village and seventeen on the farms.

---

78. Bourdieu, *Bachelors' Ball*, p. 177.
79. L. Wylie, *Village in the Vaucluse*, 3rd ed. (Cambridge, MA: Harvard University Press, 1974), p. 347.

Instead of a narrow view of economic change as the fundamental driv-ing force of rural transformation in postwar France, Bourdieu put analyti-cal attention on the matrimonial market as the strategic nexus of economic activity. This was because it was specifically domestic labor that served as the characteristic form of labor power in agricultural labor markets, and so the reproduction of agricultural labor power depended on a viable mat-rimonial market to sustain it. The rural crisis of peasant exodus and farm closures was, for Bourdieu, a profound *social* crisis represented by the break-down of traditional rural matrimonial markets along with a corresponding proliferation of peasant bachelors, and combined with the increasing in-ability of peasants to induce their younger sons (and daughters) to maintain the peasant lifestyle in the face of its symbolic devaluation and the lures of urban life. In this context women and younger sons tended to serve as a "Trojan Horse," bringing "into the heart of the peasant world the urban gaze that devalues and disqualifies 'peasant qualities.'"[80]

This social crisis of the French peasantry in the 1950s and 1960s became the basis for a series of rural development strategies initiated over the course of the 1970s and 1980s, and beyond, that were intended to stimulate rural revival. Rural revival essentially meant economic revival, in a domain where traditional forms of agricultural labor had become increasingly redundant, where farms had been closing down, and where the younger generations were heading to cities for employment and education. Economic renewal would not be specifically or necessarily agricultural but would aim to sta-bilize, if not reverse, rural demographic trends through policies designed to realize no less than a symbolic reconstitution of the French countryside.[81] In her detailed study of three rural French territories, Jacinthe Bessière found this process well under way, identifying two principal strategies of rural development, both of which were fully implicated in the shifting gastro-nomic field.[82] The first strategy was designed to promote the development

---

80. P. Bourdieu, *The Bachelor's Ball*, p.178; and also see Patrick Champagne, *L'Héritage refusé: La crise de la reproduction sociale de la paysannerie française 1950–2000* (Paris: Éditions du Seuil, 2002).

81. In fact, as Bernard Kayser documented in *La Renaissance rurale* (Paris: Armand Colin, 1990), France actually saw a substantial rural revival in the 1970s and 1980s in the form of (a) the number of the post-1968 generation moving "back to the land"; (b) in the purchase of second homes in rural areas by large number of urban dwellers; and (c) through the "re-placement" of roughly the same proportion of people leaving agricultural occupations by cadres (lower and midlevel managers) and *employés* (white-collar workers) in at least some rural departments.

82. Jacinthe Bessière, *Valorisation du Patrimoine Gastronomique et Dynamiques de Développe-*

of the gastronomic patrimony in an effort to both exploit and construct the "heritage" of specific regions in an attempt to create sites of gastronomic tourism. The second strategy took the form of industrial development (or redevelopment) to encourage corporate investment in local infrastructure to produce and market local foods for an international market.

The first approach was based on the systematic social construction and advancement of the gastronomic patrimony of particular regions and villages, strongly associated with local peasant foodways, including recipes, customary foods, and traditional modes of preparation, a gastronomy of terroir.[83] "Terroir" is a term with no real English equivalent. It refers to that which is drawn from the earth (a particular earth or place) and made sublime by the application of human artistry through traditional techniques. Terroir, "the taste of place" as Amy Trubeck has put it, denotes the distinctiveness of a region or place, combined with the traditional (and distinctive) methods of fabrication brought to bear on the fruits of that place, and to thereby create a distinctive taste.[84] The concept of the terroir is not simply a vague cultural sensibility, to the extent that it is enforced by the French state in the form of the Appellation d'Origine Controlée (AOC), a legally sanctioned designation that delimits the precise territorial origin of products; determines the rules for their fabrication; and specifies the qualities (taste, color, texture) of the product. Initially instituted (in 1905) to defend against fraudulent claims concerning the origin of products, the AOC was later amended to designate particular regions for the distinctive qualities of their products, with the area of Champagne receiving the first of many "regional delimitations"; and by 1990 a new law was passed to allow AOC status for not just wines and cheeses but any agricultural product.[85] By the 1990s AOC governed the pro-

ment Territorial (Paris: L'Harmattan, 2001).

83. Bessière, Valorisation du patrimoine gastronomique, pp. 53–54.

84. Amy B. Trubeck, The Taste of Place: A Cultural Journey into Terroir (Berkeley: University of California Press, 2008). The term "terroir" is of ancient lineage, used to refer to the soil of an often imprecise sense of a region (pays) until the end of the thirteenth century, when a more precise meaning was applied to the qualities of soil in the production of grapes for wine, while after the sixteenth century it emerged in popular usage as different soils were linked to nuanced differences in the taste of wines. See Kolleen M. Guy, When Champagne Became French: Wine and the Making of a National Identity (Baltimore: Johns Hopkins University Press, 2005), pp. 41–42.

85. The law was amended in 1908 to delimit regions (and not just to prosecute fraudulent claims); and in 1919 "uniqueness" and "quality" became key elements of the law; while in 1935 the Institut National des Appellations d'Origine [INAO] was created to adjudicate claims for AOC status; and in 1990 a law was passed to extend AOC protections to all products. See Trubeck, Taste of Place, pp. 26–28; and see Guy, When Champagne Became French.

duction and sale of some 400 wines and waters, and over 30 cheeses, as well as such products as poultry (from Bresse), lentils (from Le Puy), and grapes (from Moissac).[86] As Letablier and Delfosse have noted, since 1990 the AOC designation has been granted not so much to protect against fraud but to promote the national heritage (in response to European integration and fears of the erosion of the national identity as well as to encourage rural regional development): "Increasingly, the official logic of appellations of origin is that of belonging to the national heritage and supporting rural development. It is no longer a matter of protecting products against fraud and counterfeiting, but of defending and protecting appellations of origin as long as they constitute a common good."[87] These authors make the case that not only does AOC status add significant value by reclassifying products "above their station" ("It is primarily a reclassification of products that are unsuitable for industrial quality criteria . . . rustic cheeses locally sourced to the status of high-end cheeses destined to a clientele that distinguishes itself from the average consumer by his taste, or even his 'good taste'") but once products are reclassified with AOC status so too are the companies and consumers who touch these products. Moreover, the AOC is seen as a key element in the process of rural development for its ability to contribute to the elevation of a region, as well as sanctifying the space where products are fabricated:[88]

> The appellation reclassifies territories and production spaces. It promotes an alternative mode of development which, by highlighting the gastronomic dimension of products, diffuses a model of promotion of the local. It proposes a form of valorization of spaces and production models that would otherwise be denounced as archaic in the name of progress confused with an industrial logic. Finally, it contributes to the preservation of know-how and the rehabilitation of flavors and their variety and is part of the gastronomic heritage.

---

86. See Jacinthe Bessière, "Local Development and Heritage: Traditional Food and Cuisine as Tourist Attractions in Rural Areas," *Sociologia Ruralis*, vol. 38, no. 1, 1998, pp. 21–34.

87. M. T. Letablier and C. Delfosse, "Genèse d'une convention de qualité: Cas des appellations d'origine fromagères," in *La Grande Transformation de l'Agriculture*, ed. G. Allaire and R. Boyer (Paris: Economica, 1995), p. 106. Michaela DeSoucey offers a persuasive argument against the common view of the homogenizing tendencies of not only the European Union but of "globalization" in general, in "Gastronationalism: Food Traditions and Authenticity Politics in the European Union," *American Sociological Review*, vol. 75, no. 3, June 2010, pp. 432–455.

88. Letablier and Delfosse, "Genèse d'une convention," pp. 117–118.

Beyond the AOC, the most well-known certification, there are other stamps that certify that foods meet basic national regulations, that guarantee the provenance and quality of products, and that serve to promote specific local products in the service of rural, regional development. For example, the *label rouge* lists over 250 food products, including meats, fruits, and vegetables (and includes some thirty thousand farmers and two thousand companies); the *label regional* confers the blessing of authenticity on products of specific regions that are seen to reflect the local (or regional) character; *L'Appellation Montaigne* does the same for designated mountain zones (for products like lamb, honey, and certain cheeses); and *label biologique* certifies organic products and methods of cultivation.[89]

In addition to these official and quasi-official mechanisms of certification, there has been a proliferation of museums, institutes, and monuments dedicated to the terroir and its fruits throughout the rural departments. From a Musée de l'Absinthe, to a Musée du Camembert, to the Maison de la Pomme (as well as the Maison de la Pomme et de la Poire) to the Caves de Roquefort Société, with dozens more museums devoted to cognac, wines, honey, mustard, olives, and so on.[90] These institutions highlight and celebrate foodstuffs cultivated in their respective regions and provide information on traditional methods of cultivation and preparation. However, the pride of place that they seek to cultivate seems less a valorization of the primordial than a recent effort at regional self-promotion. Thus, of those museums dedicated to the local terroir, most were established in the 1970s or later, and thus were a part of the wider initiative to enhance and create a local gastronomic patrimony.[91]

Some analysts have argued that a fetish for local gastronomic traditions has been a reaction or a resistance to the industrialization of foodways and the construction of a European identity. As Poulain has asserted: "In a circular causal relationship, the food crisis is associated with an ideological crisis, reinforced by the context of the European construction and the risk of dilution of France in a larger entity . . . In the turbulence of the crisis of the agricultural world, the Big Mac embodies the degree zero of gastronomic culture, the antithesis of French food, 'real food.'. . . Faced with Europe being established, raw milk cheese emerges as the symbol of

89. J. Bessière, "Local Development and Heritage," p. 25.

90. Jean-Paul Branlard, *Les 100 Meilleurs Musées gastronomiques de France* (Paris: Editions Grancher, 2001).

91. Of the eighty-two gastronomic museums whose founding dates are listed (in Branlard, *Les 100 Meilleurs Musées*) only five were founded prior to 1970.

an identity stake."[92] This is a view that seems consonant with the logic presented in this analysis of the gastronomic field, constructed relationally in the polarity between the artisanal and the industrial, and facing the erosion of its autonomy as a cultural field to the logic and practice of a more dominant economic field. The construction of the gastronomic patrimony that we have considered could very reasonably be viewed as a retreat into the gastronomic patrimony, or a burrowing into the folds of *la France profonde*, and this would certainly seem to represent a good part of its appeal. But we should not forget that it has proceeded as a systematic development strategy, largely driven by local and regional commercial interests seeking to develop new commercial possibilities for recreation, and especially for tourism (and specifically for "gastronomic tourism"). As Bessière noted:[93]

> The rising numbers of retired people, second homes, weekend and summer visitors testify to the recreational part played by rural areas. . . . Tourism in rural areas seems to be influenced and idealized today by the myth of nature, the quest for an original *communitas* . . . and is often related to the mental perception of the countryside. This tendency, characterized by a re-activation of well-established stereotypes about nature and purity, holds a remarkable appeal in the collective consciousness. . . . As a reaction to the complexity of the modern world in which social links either are falling apart or weakening, rural areas chosen as holiday destinations seem to offer the possibility for socializing or for finding a community identity. . . . Consequently, studying rural tourism and its heritage component—more specifically gastronomy—leads us to consider rural space as a place to find compensation for lost identity, and as a representation of "the good old days." Let us remember here the mythical countryman, whose image was for centuries negative if not derogatory, but who is now idealized.

This last point underscores the irony surrounding the mythical French peasant, who has become increasingly idealized in the valorization of an economy now turned toward the marketing of local products and regional

---

92. Jean-Pierre Poulain, "Goût du terroir et tourisme vert à l'heure de l'Europe," *Ethnologie Française*, vol. 27, no. 1, 1997, pp. 18–26.
93. J. Bessiere, "Local Development and Heritage: Traditional Food and Cuisine as a Tourist Attraction in Rural Areas," *Sociologica Ruralis*, vol. 38, no. 1, 1998, p. 22.

specialties to lure tourists. As one analyst has added: "The image of country people, deprecated for so long, has been completely reversed and has gradually gained in nostalgia as rural dwellers have left the countryside for urban centers. In this manner, peasant life has become the sanctuary of people's origins, their lost roots, and the source of an improbable authenticity."[94] In a similar way the orientation of the rural economy toward gastronomic tourism can be seen as having made the countryside into "more of a landscape than a place of production; stage management comes before the productive function in the general public's eye."[95]

How all of these various interests, initiatives, and groups have come together in the construction of a local gastronomic patrimony "on the ground" might be briefly outlined for the "Haut Plateau de l'Aubrac," a rural region in central France.[96] Early on (1961) the Appellation d'Origine Controlée (AOC) certified the local "Laguiole" cheese; and in 1991 a local flower, "la fleur d'Aubrac," was recognized by the Appellation Montaigne; then, after a long lobbying campaign by associations of local producers the cows of Aubrac were consecrated by the Label Rouge as "Boeuf fermier Aubrac" in 1999. A traditional dish emblematic of the region, Aligot, composed of potatoes, tome cheese, and crème fraiche blended all together, was promoted by various local trade associations and syndicats d'initiatives (chambers of commerce) as "Aubrac Aligot," who organized an annual *fête de l'Aligot*, presided over by the local celebrity chef, Michel Bras. *Aligot* is one of the specialties of Michel Bras, a chef/owner of a three-star restaurant located on the Plateau de l'Aubrac. In 1990, he famously endorsed a frozen version of Aubrac Aligot produced by a frozen food company. Together, these initiatives served to valorize the terroir and to construct the local gastronomic heritage in an effort to boost tourism in the region. In the process the region itself was promoted, along with its traditional foods and their recipes, its livestock, and its flora, in extended campaigns that sought to create an image of charming rustic authenticity to cover over an older image of peasant backwardness and rural decline. It was not something easily accepted by the peasants of l'Aubrac, for whom farming (mostly the raising of livestock) was experienced as a noble (and remunerative) activity,

94. Burguière et al. 1993, quoted in Bessière, "Local Development and Heritage," p. 23.
95. Hervieu and Viard (1996), quoted in Bessière, "Local Development and Heritage," p. 23.
96. The Haut Plateau de l'Aubrac is one of three cases analyzed by Bessière, *Valorisation du patrimoine gastronomique*, pp. 115–149. Additional materials have been drawn from a dossier compiled on the chef Michel Bras by the author.

and to have embraced tourism would have been a sign of failure in their agricultural activities.[97] As it was, in l'Aubrac other social forces were active in animating the development of the gastronomic patrimony. We thus begin to see how the symbolic consecration of *Terroir* has been incorporated into the field of gastronomic practices in France. Local social actors, both individual and institutional, have been drawn into a process by which the exchange of various forms of capital (primarily symbolic and economic) has served to sustain the increasingly precarious edifice of French gastronomy by extending its boundaries. See Figure 5.9.

The second strategy of rural development entailed the industrial development (or redevelopment) of traditional areas along with the industrialization of traditional production processes, which Bessière has examined in the case of "Roquefort country" (*Le Pays du Roquefort*) in the southern part of the Aveyron in South-Central France.[98] Rather than "inventing tradition" as in the social construction of a local gastronomic heritage, this strategy entailed the appropriation of existing traditions by industrial corporations.[99] Roquefort, both the cheese and the place, was already laden with tradition in the form of historical lore stretching back to the Middle Ages.[100] In 2001 seven firms were producing Roquefort cheese, five of which represented the industry of agro-alimentaire and two others operated as smaller artisanal operations. The largest of the producers, Roquefort Société, since 1992 a subsidiary of Lactalis, the multinational dairy products corporation, accounted for some 60 percent of Roquefort production, after having purchased several of the Mont Combalou caves in Roquefort-sur-Soulzon. These natural limestone caves are the traditional sites where the ripening of Roquefort cheese has occurred, and indeed, where it *must* occur or it cannot be sold as "Roquefort," according to the AOC designation that Roquefort received in 1925. The caves of Roquefort may have been owned by multinational corporations, but they attracted thousands of tourists each year and, accordingly, Roquefort could be seen as having possessed several key

97. Bessière, *Valorisation du patrimoine gastronomique*, p. 148.

98. Her second case study was titled "Gastronomic Heritage and Integrated Production Chain: The Development of the Agro-industrial System of Roquefort and Its Territorial Integration," in Bessière, *Valorisation du patrimoine gastronomique*, pp. 151–187.

99. Eric Hobsbawm and Terence Ranger, *The Invention of Tradition* (Cambridge: Cambridge University Press, 1983).

100. Empirical materials for this section are largely drawn from Bessière, *Valorisation du patrimoine gastronomique*, and from Susan Carol Rogers, *Shaping Modern Times in Rural France: The Transformation and Reproduction of an Aveyronnaise Community* (Princeton, NJ: Princeton University Press, 1991), p. 61.

French Representations

3 MICHELIN STARS

Ducasse   Escoffier
Troisgros **Bocuse** Guide Culinare

Restricted Market (Exclusive)
Sophistication
Complexity
Formality
Expensive
Low volume

Academie   Robuchon "Thuries" **Grands Bistrots &**   Maxim's (chain)
Culinaire de Blanc Magazine   **Brasseries**
France   Pacaud Vergé   (La Coupole, Lipp, Le Balzar)   Ducasse's "sandwicherie"

Claude Terrail La Taillevent Restaurant
(La Tour d'Argent **Loiseau** Legendre Senderens Lameloise   **Chain Restaurants**
Restaurant)   **Conseil National** Lorain PIC Boyer Guerard   **Bistrots**
Des Arts "Le Chef" **Foundation** Trama Savoy   (Hippo, Buffalo Grill) Groupe
Culinaires Magazine Brillat-Savarin   Rostang   Holder
MOF **Veyrat** Chapel   **Guide Michelin** **Gault-Millau**   Eliance Agapes Restaurants
    Magazine   Autoroute rest areas   Corthay
Les Trois Alsaciens Huguet Mazere Passard
Artisanal(Jung, Westermmann, Haeberlin) **Production**   Autogrill Groupe Flo   **Industrial**
(Long Time)   (Short Time)
(Tradition)   **INDEPENDENT RESTAURANTS** **SIRHA** Danone Eurodisney S.A. (Modern)
AOC **AND BISTROS**   **Fleury** **GRANDS GROUPES** **Sodexho**
        AGRO ALIMENTAIRE(Pierre Bellon)
Products of   Label Bio   Neo
"Le Terbir"   Restauration **Accor** **Carrefour**   **Kraft**
    Roquefort Label Rouge Magazine   Lactalis **SIAL** **Unilever**
Vins et viniculture   camembert   (Michel Besnier)   **Nestlé**
        Revue Technique
Curnosky   Museums of Gastronomy   Magazine   B. Trujillo French Fast Food
            La Croissanteries,
        FSNEA   **Cafeterias and Canteens** Pomme de Pain
    Jose Bové et la   E. Leclerc (Institutional)
    Confederation Paysanne   **Mass Market (Inclusive)**   Auchan Hamburgers
        Convenience   Casino Fast Food
        Simplicity   Cafeteria McDonald's
        Informality Compass   Ray Kroc
'Tante Marie'   Rural Tourism   Cheap Groupe Domino's
Cookbook   High Volume   Pizza Servair
        Inclusive

Consumption

American Representations

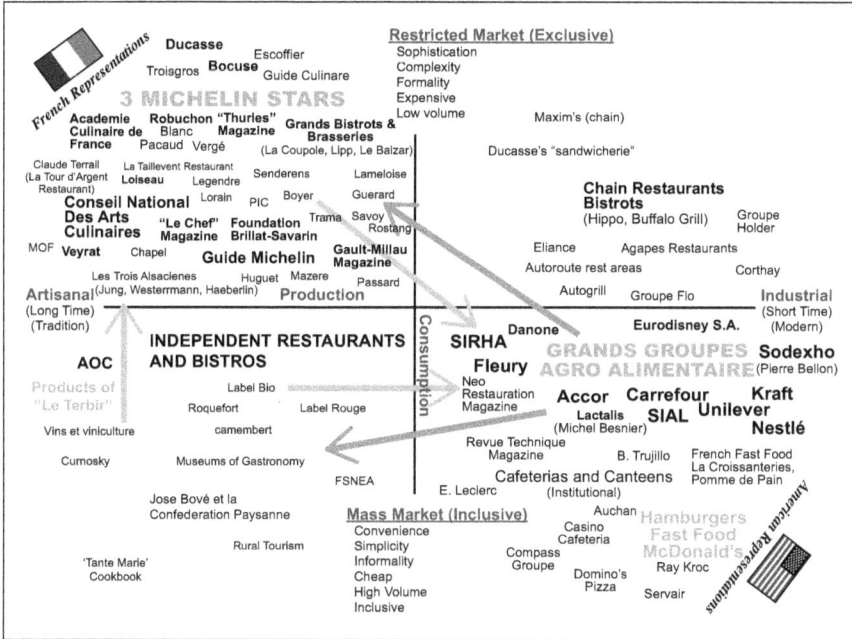

Figure 5.9 Direction of Capital Flows in the French Gastronomic Field

elements of the "symbolic infrastructure" that has been seen as central to the gastronomic heritage of a place.[101]

The volume of industrial production of Roquefort cheese has been significant enough, and for a long enough time, that it has sustained many of the surrounding villages in the Roquefort region, making them able to support a higher proportion of farmers, more farms, more schools, and more of a population than most other rural communities have been able to sustain. As Susan Carol Rogers noted in her ethnographic study of Ste Foy, a village in the Aveyron:[102]

It is largely thanks to Roquefort, they are quick to point out, that Ste Foy remains a vigorous community with almost as many inhabitants and farms as it ever had, and little need for its children to leave, unlike the severely depopulated communities elsewhere in the Aveyron. It was largely with Roquefort money that all Ste Foy farmers

101. That is, Roquefort already enjoyed a measure of historical lore, a gastronomic heritage, and an existing tourist industry.

102. Rogers, *Shaping Modern Times*, p. 64.

bought themselves tractors and other field equipment in the 1950s and with which almost all of them built new, well-equipped houses or renovated the old ones by the end of the 1960s. Roquefort money is what has made Ste Foy farmers prosperous enough to support the community's shops, cafes, and artisans, hold enough young families for the local primary schools to remain open, and to keep the church full enough to retain its own priests.

In addition to being able to furnish the industrial producers with their required ewe's milk, the base of Roquefort cheese, Aveyron farmers became France's leading producers of lamb, which has been an important secondary commodity. In certain ways the industrial exploitation of local foods and methods (and heritage) is a complex and even contradictory story, for it hinges local gastronomic traditions to a vertically integrated industrial model, governed by the imperatives of competition, efficiency, productivity, and profit maximization (as well as rural population revival). It makes it possible to produce goods not only for local residents and tourists but for an international market. Indeed, we might ask just how reasonable it is to maintain a distinction between the "local" and the "global" when the former is increasingly deployed by the latter on its own behalf.

In general, "global" and "globalization" are terms that seem euphemized or overly general, and seem too abstract to be particularly helpful in making sense of international exchange in relation to the gastronomic field. In seeking to understand the rise of a market for American-style fast food in France, for example (see Chapter 3), one dominant perspective saw the export of American fast food in France as little more than a benign reflection of the global circulation of culinary cultures, so that the popularity of hamburgers and Coca Cola in France was simply a particular manifestation of the same process of "transcultural fusion" and "alimentary cosmopolitanism" that made Italian pizza, Mexican tacos, and French croissants popular in the United States.[103] What made that seem problematic, as I indicated, was that U.S. corporations (and particularly in fast food) were involved in the export of "advanced" business practices (like computer applications in the cooking process; various labor market practices, including institutional antiunionism; as well as distinctive marketing practices) along with their characteristic foods. Drawing upon the concept of field, on the other hand,

---

103. Claude Fischler, *L'Homnivore: Le goût, la cuisine et le corps* (Paris: Editions Odile Jacob, 1990), p. 214; also see Goody, *Cooking, Cuisine, and Class.*

encouraged attention to the hierarchical structures of international circulation, of goods, of markets, and of institutions; and thus the relative power
and size of the McDonald's Corporation obviated the possibility of treating
it as just one player among equals, or viewing its actions as just one part of
a "global circulation of culinary cultures."

Symbolic power, or the "magic" of Americanism that we have referred
to, can be seen as a reflection of both the real position of American-based
corporations in certain (even many) international markets, including food
processing, and the symbolic "aura" that they have held in certain business
circles in France and internationally. That the American economic model
has enjoyed a significant amount of symbolic capital abroad should not be
at all surprising, since the very structures of the postwar economic system,
especially with regard to international trade policy and finance, were fash-
ioned by American-led initiatives and frameworks, from Bretton Woods, to
the liberalization of the World Trade Organization, to the forms of postwar
corporate governance, to the application of American legal culture in the formation of international commercial arbitration, so that many of the key rules
of the postwar world economy have, quite literally, been made in America.[104]
But it must be quickly added that this is not a simple matter of "American
imperialism" in which U.S. forms dominate by default, unchallenged, but an
international field of business practices in which American forms of practice
have certainly tended to be dominant, especially in the postwar decades and
across a number of industries, but which have been contested everywhere. As
Bourdieu has written with reference to the international legal field:[105]

> To speak of a global—or, better, international—legal field is imme-
> diately to escape the temptation to explain the processes of unifica-
> tion observed in very different domains of practices in one of two

---

104. Leo Panitch and Sam Gindin have produced the finest, most complete analysis of
American domination in the postwar world economy in *The Making of Global Capitalism:
The Political Economy of American Empire* (London: Verso, 2012); while the legal bases of U.S.
domination of international commerce is demonstrated by Yves Dezalay and Bryant G. Garth
in *Dealing in Virtue: International Commercial Arbitration and the Construction of a Transna-
tional Legal Order* (Chicago: University of Chicago Press, 1996). Kirshner has made a strong
case that what he calls the "triumph of globalism" is a reflection of U.S. trade policy that
has transmogrified into a "supranational regulatory authority for the management of trade
liberalization on a global basis" (p. 502) or American foreign trade policies "gone global." See
Orin Kirschner, "Triumph of Globalism: American Trade Politics," *Political Science Quarterly*,
vol. 120, no. 3, 2005, pp. 479–503.

105. Pierre Bourdieu, in the "Foreword" to Dezalay and Garth, *Dealing in Virtue*, p. vii.

ways: either as a quasi-mechanical effect of the intensification and acceleration of circulation and exchange, leading to an ecumenical reconciliation of all cultural traditions, or as an effect of imperialism exercised by a few great industrial powers capable of exporting and imposing, on a universal scale, not only their products but also their style of life. The notion of field (in the sense of fields of forces and fields of struggle to conserve and transform the relationship of forces) requires a position beyond the sophomoric alternatives of consensus and conflict, and thus permits us to understand and analyze the process of unification as a product of competition and conflict.

While the "magic" of American forms may highlight the symbolic power of American business practices for certain groups of French businessmen looking to modern, innovative techniques in relation to other groups in the economic domain, in the domain or field of cultural practices American styles tended to hold symbolic power for certain French youth who, in the 1980s, often treated American forms of dress, music, and cultural comportment as a stylistic "language of refusal" in relation to traditional French cultural styles.

The dichotomy between "local" and "global" in the French gastronomic field has generated a concern that when an industrial infrastructure is concealed behind a symbolic façade of artisanship, tradition, and le terroir, the business of gastronomic tourism may be facilitated, but what may be lost in the industrial process can be real and valuable qualities of perception, taste, and judgment. In his book on Camembert cheese, Pierre Boisard has described in fine, biotechnical detail what occurs when industrial methods are enacted in the cheese making process:[106]

Industrial fabrication begins by eradicating the original characteristics of the principal raw material, especially its inner life, its local and temporal qualities—in other words, anything that might recall the odor of the cow. The bacteria added to the milk to replace those killed by pasteurization are also closely monitored by industrial products. None are allowed into the factory unless their identities

---

106. Pierre Boisard, *Camembert: A National Myth* (Berkeley: University of California Press, 2003), p. 169. While raw milk cheeses are often considered superior to pasteurized cheeses for their ability to retain the taste of the land (grasses and herbs in the pastures), they constitute only 18 percent of cheese production in France, and have been under sustained regulatory pressure from the forces of industrial production via EU and U.S. lobbying efforts to forbid raw milk cheese production.

have been fixed and normalized. The industry creates a break in milk's spontaneous cycle of change, in order to inject its own norms. In this respect, the creation of Camembert is no different from that of any other industrial product.

Alongside this rendering has been the oddly confirming perspective of Michel Besnier, the "Emperor of Industrial Camembert," whose firm produced over 40 percent of all French Camembert cheeses in 2003 (and whose family owns the Lactalis Corporation, with its Roquefort holdings). For Besnier, his Camembert cheeses are "products that are uniform and better adapted to wide distribution. In supermarkets, our pasteurized-milk Camemberts stand up better in refrigerator sections. They change less after they have been packaged."[107]

Meanwhile, le terroir has become a central marketing device throughout the industrial region of the gastronomic field, from supermarket promotions paying homage to regional but industrially produced foods, to advertising campaigns by fast-food companies (including McDonald's) that highlight the local sourcing of their "natural ingredients," to the proliferation of product lines in French supermarkets that represent themselves as "*produits du terroir*," such as the Carrefour product label, "Reflections of France," in which "products reconnect with the recipes and know-how of each terroir that have made our country the symbol of good taste throughout the world" (and to which the grand chef Joël Robuchon has served as consultant).

The obvious paradox is that the appeal of le terroir in France has been as a refuge from the forces of standardization and homogenization, which has also meant from the pressures of European integration and the American economic model. But it has largely been the infrastructure of le terroir that has been maintained, when not produced, by these very institutions of standardization and homogenization, namely the industries of agro-alimentaire which are all, essentially, "Made in America" (no matter their actual national origin). So just as the autonomy of the gastronomic field has given way under the weight of the economic field, thereby increasing the porousness of barriers that traditionally separated the *grands chefs de cuisine* from the *grands chefs d'entreprise*, the myth of the "local" and of le terroir have increasingly concealed the industrial infrastructure that has sustained them on its own behalf.

---

107. Quoted in Boisard, *Camembert*, p. 173.

Index

Abbott, Andrew, 30n70
Académie culinaire de France, 29, 58, 69, 172
Accor, 156, 158
adolescents: American style and, 116, 122–124, 135; "fantasy of classlessness," and, 123; fast food in France and, 117–124
Adrouet, Pierre, 73
Agapes Restauration, 154, 154–156
agriculture, 91, 142; mechanization of, in France, 197–198
l'agro-alimentaire, 62–63, 95; American agribusiness, impact on, 144–145; farmers' cooperatives and, 143–144; French government initiatives in support of, 143; trade journals in, 147–148; traditional culinary practices, impact on, 142–143
Aldrich, Howard, 96n17
Almanach des gourmands (de la Reynière), 13
Amand, F., 141n42
American agribusiness, international dominance of, 144–145
American business model: as antithesis of artisan practices, 150; authority of, in France, 150–151; dissemination of, abroad, 133, 135–136; influence of, in France, 133–136, 142–145, 148–152, 158–160, 166; symbolic capital of, 151–152, 170, 209–210; American cultural practices; as cutting edge, in France, 109, 116, 122–124, 135; French youth and, 151–152, 210; symbolic capital of, 135, 210

Americanism: Europe as other, and, 24; fast food, association with, and, 118, 120–124; symbolic capital of, 135, 148–152; as transgressive, in France, 116, 119, 122
American managerial practices, adoption in France, 148–152
"American model" of food production, 24, 133, 166
"Americanophilia," 124
Anton, Frédéric, 56
Appellation d'Origine Controlée (AOC), 201–202
L'Appellation Montaigne, 203
Ardagh, John, 92, 134n22
art, 16
L'Art culinaire, 28–29
artisanal practices, 7, 168–173; breakdown of, 193–196; defenses of, 25, 30, 74; transfer from court to bourgeoisie, 10–11
artistic field, 38
Association of the Disciples of Paul Bocuse, 78–79, 81
Association Internationale de la Distribution des produits Alimentaires, 133

Baccalauréat Technologique Hôtellerie (BTH), 157
Balzac, Honoré, 14
banlieue, 130–131
Baudrillard, Jean, 109

Beatrice Foods, 145

Beauregard, Robert A., 131n12

Becker, Howard, 35n77

Beghin-Say, 144

Bel, 144

belief, production of, 33, 39, 171–173, 181; *concours* and, 63–69; consecration, and, 46–47, 60–61; food critics and, 54–57; gastronomic guides and, 41–54; mass-market magazines and, 57–59; professional magazines and, 59–62

Bellon, Pierre, 160, 178, 184–185

Benjamin, Walter, 39n4

Berger, Suzanne, 125n100

Berghahn, Volker R., 150n69

Bernachon, Maurice, 73

Bernard Loiseau S.A., 88

Besnier, Michel, 211

Bessière, Jacinthe, 200–201, 206

Bertron, Patrick, 191

big box stores, 139, 141. *See also* individual retailers

Blanc, Georges, 80, 179, 184

Boas, Max, 95n13

Bocuse, Paul, 2, 3, 51, 65, 67, 87; apprenticeship of, 76; food processing industry, partnership with, 175, 176–177, 185; legacy of, 78–80, 81; personification of French gastronomy, as, 176

Bohl, Charles C., 130n8

Boisard, Pierre, 210–211

Boltanski, Luc, 109, 110n60, 134n23

Bombal, Jacques, 95n12, 141n45, 147n61

Bonduelle Food Service, 63–64, 182

Bonanno, Alessandro, 95n12

Bottin Gourmand, 81, 87, 179

Bouchet, Dominique, 56

Boulud, Daniel, 78

Bourdieu, Pierre, 16n36, 17, 35; cultural production, and, 37–39; fashion world, on the, 181; fields as sites of struggle, and, 22, 210; international legal field, on, 209–210; magic, on, 37, 151; peasants, degradation of, on, 198–199, 200

Bovais, H., 106n44, 108n54, 121n87

Bové, José, 91, 129

Boyer, Gérard, 179

Boyer, Jean-Claude, 132n14

Branlard, Jean-Paul, 203n90

Branson, Richard, 139

Bras, Michel, 177, 187

Brazier, Eugénie "Mère," 32, 76, 79, 176

Bretton Woods, 209

brigade system, 69–72

Brillat-Savarin, Jean-Anthelme, 13–15, 16, 22, 25–26

La Brioche Dorée, 159

Brown, Derek, 3

BSN-Gervais-Danone, 144, 145

Bucher, Jean-Paul, 157

Buffalo Grill, 154

Buller, Michael, 65n58

Burger King, 126

Busch, Lawrence, 95n12

Calmin, Phillippe, 95n12, 141n45, 147n61

Camembert cheese, 210–211

Capatti, Alberto, 25n59

Caraux, Laurent, 93n9, 115n73

Cardin, Pierre, 179

Carême, Antonin, 12, 14, 16, 22

Carew, Anthony, 133n19, 150n67

Caroli, Eve, 138n34, 163n97

Carrefour, 133, 211

Casino Group, 156

catering. *See* institutional catering

Cayeaux, Pascal, 81

Centers of Apprenticeship Training, 76

chain restaurants: cooks in, 161–165; family ties of, 163–164; Parisian bistros, purchase of, 178–179; Président directeur-générals (p-dgs) in, 157–160; profitability, importance of, in, 156, 164; quantitative measures, importance of, in, 154–155. *See also* fast food; McDonald's Corporation; restaurants

Chain, Steve, 95n13

chain stores, 129–130

Chambre Nationale de la Restauration et de l'Hôtellerie, 93

Chambre Syndicale de la haute cuisine française, 2, 68, 124

Chambru, Sébastien, 81

Champ d'Oiseaux, 11

Champoiseau, 11

Chapel, Alain, 65, 78

Le Chef, 59–62, 67, 87; grand chefs' partnerships with industrial food, and, 177, 182–184

chef profession, 25; apprenticeship and, 76–78, 162; artisanship, and, 27–28; CAP/BEP diploma, 76–77, 85, 161–162; celebrity, and, 89–90; chefs de cuisine, 157; chefs d'entreprise, 157; consecration, and, 8, 32n75, 46; culinary journals, and, 28–30; cult of lineage in, 75, 77–82; elevation of, 27, 28–32; family dynasties in, 80, 184; gender, and, 27–28; jurisdiction, achievement of, 29, 30n70; *Michelin Guide*, and, 46–47. Meilleur Ouvrier de France and (MOF) and, 65–69, 74, 79, 176; "nostalgic syndrome," and, 164; profit-making, and, 89; restaurant proprietorship, and, 51–52; salaries of,

162–163; social capital, and, 77–82; stardom, and, 32, 52; succession, and, 81, 184; symbolic status of, 34, 162, 163, 171, 177; training in, 31, 74–82; unions and, 25. *See also* grand chefs
Chelminski, Rudolph, 193n59
Chemical Corn Exchange, 158
Chibois, Jacques, 177
Chirac, Jacques, 67
Cleary, Mark C., 198n74
Collonges au Mont-D'Or, 176
commercial culture, 137
commercial revolution, 133–140; conceptual vocabulary of, 140–141; convenience, and, 145–146; resistance to, 138–139
commercial strips, 128–129. *See also* périurbain fringe
Compass Group France, 160
Confédération Paysanne, 91–92
Conforama, 139
Conseil National des arts culinaires, 69
La Conserve alimentaire: Traité practique de fabrication (Corthay), 25–26
consumer society, 150–151
cookery books, 9–10
Le Cordon bleu, 28
Corthay, Auguste, 25–27
la Côte de'Or, 2, 4, 86, 87, 88, 189, 190–191
Creton, L., 15n35
Cross, Gary, 151n71
Crozier, Michel, 92
Csergo, Julia, 19, 20n47, 21n48
Culinary Institute of America, 70n67
cult of lineage, 77. *See also* under chef profession
Curnonsky, 20–22, 41
Le Cuisinier François (La Varenne), 9
culinary concours, 64–65, 68–69, 74. *See also* Meilleur Ouvrier de France (MOF); and under belief, production of
culinary journals, 28–30
culinary nationalism, 17–20
culinary patrimony, 18n42; preservation of, 124–125
culinary populism, 21
cultural field, 16, 23, 168–169; intrusion by economic field, and, 196; mass markets vs. restricted markets, and, 90; mutual recognition, and, 27, 57–59; producers, role in, 37–38
cultural production, 37–39
Darégal, 182
Dayan, Raymond, 96, 99–100
Debray, Regis, 124n95
décalage, 115
Dèchaux, Jean-Hughes, 132n17
Delfosse, C., 202n87

Delobez, Annie, 136n27, 138n35
d'Estaing, V. Giscard, 138
de la Reynière, Alexandre-Balthazar-Laurent Grimod, 13, 14, 16, 18n42
Delsaut, Yvette, 38n1
Dereau, Sylvain, 81
DeSoucey, Michaela, 202n87
Desquand, Louis-André, 58, 59
Dezalay, Yves, 209n104
Dézert, Bernard, 131n11
DiMaggio, Paul, 96n17, 134n23
Dior, House of, 37
Disney Corporation, 176
Disney Store, 139
Djelic, Marie-Laure, 149n64
domestic cuisine, 27–28
Dornenburg, Andrew, 31n71
Le Drugstore, 109
Dubois, Urbain, 12
Dubrule, Paul, 158
Ducasse, Alain, 78, 87, 179–180, 182, 183, 194
Duchamp, Marcel, 38
Dufour, François, 91n1
Dugléré, Adolphe, 12
Dumaine, Alexandre, 32, 86
Dupuis, Alain, 160n89
Durand, Rodolphe, 51n31, 86n101
Dutournier, Alain, 60–61
Duval, Jean-Baptiste, 134n22

Echikson, William, 1n1, 2n3, 4n11, 5n16, 44n13, 46n19, 50n30, 55, 76n77, 86, 88
l'école des Hautes Études Commerciales (HEC), 160
Elitair industrial group, 126
Escoffier, Auguste, 12, 27, 29, 30–32, 41
Evans, Archibald, 95n11
extraordinaires, 12

Fantasia, Rick, 105n39, 106n46
farmers' cooperatives, 143–144
fast food: advertising and, 99–100; American model of, 92, 96–97, 98–100, 108; antiunionism, and, 106–107; atmosphere in, 121–122; café's, contrast with, 120; "cheap commercialism," as, 124–125; consumer markets in France, creation of, 94–95; consumers of, in France, 110–114; "exoticism of the hamburger," and, 96–97; franchise system, and, 103–104; French companies and McDonald's formula, 96–97; French gastronomy, as inverse of, 92, 98; French government, response to, 124–25; French youth and, 113, 116–123; gender and, in France, 111–112; marketing strategies, in

France, 115; new bourgeois lifestyles, and, 109–110; part-time labor, and, 108; service experience, and, 105, 117–119; technological rationality in, 105–106; television advertising, and, 90, 100, 119; transgressive, as, 115, 117–118, 119; viennoiseries in France, 101, 113–114
faubourg, 129
Fauchon, 179–180
Ferguson, Priscilla, 12n26, 14–15, 17n40, 18n41, 20, 22, 31n72, 51
Feutre, M. Alain-Philippe, 93n8
Le Figaro, 2, 45, 54
fields: belief, and, 38–39; concept, analytical value of, 167–168, 209; cultural (*see* cultural field); definition of, 7, 167–168; gastronomic (*see* gastronomic field); hierarchy and, 16
Findus Restauration, 174
Fischler, Claude, 94n11, 208n103
Flandrin, Jean-Louis, 10n20, 11n24, 17n37, 142n47
Fondation Brillat-Savarin, 69
food processing industry: American model of, 24, 148–149; France, development of, in, 24, 25. *See also* l'agro-alimentaire; industrial cuisine under gastronomic field
Fourastié, Jean, 141n43
Forsè, Michel, 108n52, 132n17
Fourier, Charles, 14
Frambourt, Jean, 73n72
La France gastronomique (Curnonsky), 20
France Quick SAS, 154
Freeman, Charles E., 148n63
French Communist Party, 132n14
French cultural exception, 90
French eating practices after World War II, 94–95
French economic planning: American influence on, 148–152; postwar programs for, 148–150; rural redevelopment, and (*see* rural development); socialist models and, 149
French nobility, cooking practices of, 9–10
France Restauration, 175–176
French Revolution: haute cuisine, and, 10; Paris, authority of, and, 20; restaurants, relationship to, 10–12
French Socialist Party, 124, 125
Friedland, William H., 95n12
Gaborieau, Stéphane, 81
Gagnaire, Pierre, 190
Galliano, D., 144n55
Garson, Barbara, 105n41
Garth, Bryant G., 209n104
gastronome: author, as, 14; function of, 13–14; gourmand, distinction from, 13, 17; taste-maker, as, 14

gastronomic field: artisanal/industrial divide, 23–30, 168–173; autonomy of, 14–16, 23, 30, 80–81, 172–173; boundaries of, 35, 168–173; chefs in (*see* chef profession; grand chefs); consecration and, 33, 41, 46, 90; consolidation of, 22–23; consumption practices in, 168–173; emergence of, 9–11; erosion of, 184–196; enticement for French youth, as, 164; firewall in, 172–173, 175; fissures in, 7, 25; haute cuisine (*see* haute cuisine); hotels and, 31, 32, 33; industrial cuisine, and, 62–64, 168–170 (*see also* fast food; chain restaurants; institutional catering); industrialization in, 126 (*see also* fast food); industrial modernity, and, 23–26; legacy in, 78–80; literature and, 9–10, 14–16, 17–19; mass markets vs. restricted markets in, 168–173; mutual self-promotion in, 60–62; nationalism and, 17–20; neoliberalism, impact on, 105, 196; production practices in, 168–173 (*see also* artisanal practices; food production industry); regional cuisine and, 18–22, 201–206; social capital and, 77
gastronomic guides, influence of, 2, 44n12. See also *Gault&Millau*; *Michelin Guide*
gastronomic maps, 18
gastronomy: definition of, 13; field, as a, 7; mass market rules, introduction in, 146–148
Gault, Henri, 47, 52
Gault&Millau, 2, 21, 47–54, 62, 86n101, 87, 179; advertising in, 49; Michel Guérard's work for Nestlé, on, 174; nouvelle cuisine, and, 50–52, 174; ratings, influence of, 3–4; scoring system of, 48, 53
Gautie, Jerome, 138n34, 163n97
Générale de Restauration, 160
General Mills Europe, 160
genetically modified organisms (GTOs), 91
Gillingham, John, 148n63
Gindin, Sam, 166n103, 209n104
globalization, 208–210
Goody, Jack, 28n65, 171n6
Le Gourmet, 28
Gouveia, Lourdes, 95n12
grand chefs: l'annexité, and, 179, 186; artists, as, 27–32; celebrities, as, 179, 182–194; changing role of, 193–194; consecration and, 8, 32n75, 46; economic ambition of, 185; industrial field, entrance into, 173–196; justifications for industrial partnerships, 186–187; myth and, 85; symbolic capital of, 175–177, 179, 182, 185. *See also* chef profession; belief, production of; names of individual chefs
La Grande Cuisine Minceur (Guérard), 173
Le Grande Véfour, 82

Grand Prix National des Métiers d'Art, 58
La Grande Encyclopédie, 58
Le Grand Dictionnaire du XIXème siècle, 59
Greenfield, Liah, 19n46
Greenhouse, Steven, 92n4, 119nn83–84
Groupe Bertrand, 178
Groupe Elior, 160
Group Fabien SAAL, 126
Groupe Flo, 157, 178
Groupe Holder, 126
Groupe LeDuff, 158
Guérard, Michel, 78, 173–174
Guichard, Benoît, 56, 194
Le Guide culinaire (Escoffier), 27, 31
guild system, 10–11
Guiomarc'h, 175
Guy, Kolleen M., 201n85

Haeberlin, Marc, 80
Haeberlin, Paul, 80
hamburgers: exoticism of, in France, 96–97; as novelty in France, 108–109
Hara, Terushi, 150n66
Hatchette Guide, 87
haute couture, 37–38, 180–181
haute cuisine: art, association with, and, 52, 88, 90; belief in, production of (*see* belief, production of); codification of, 29–31; differentiation of, 28–30; family ties in, 79–80; food quality, 192–193; French Revolution and, 10; gastronomic field, role in, 34–36, 170–173; gender and, 28; industrial catering, *rapprochement* with, 178; industrial food practices, conflicts with, 188–196; international cultural hegemony of, 31–32, 55, 180; *Michelin Guide,* and (*see Michelin Guide; Michelin* star system); nouvelle cuisine, and, 50–52, 85, 173; profit margins and, 189–192; regional cuisine and, 21–22; restricted markets, and, 90; role players in, 72–74; symbolic importance, in gastronomic field, 35, 57, 170
Hechter, Daniel, 109
Heller, Chaia, 91n2
Hobsbawm, Eric, 206n99
Horowitz, Daniel, 151n71
L'Hôtellerie, 59, 184–185
Hotel Ritz, 31
hypermarché, 133, 135–136; clientele of, 136–137; customer experiences in, 137; resistance to, 138–140 (*see also* Royer Law). *See also* Carrefour; supermarkets

IBM Europe, 158, 160

IKEA, 139
industrial cuisine, 165–66; grand chefs, hiring of, 173–196. *See also* chain restaurants; fast food; institutional catering
industrial practices, 7, 168–173
l'Institute des Hautes Études Commerciales, 158
institutional catering (*restauration collective*), 153; cooks in, 161–165; family-ties and, 165–166; grand chefs' partnership with, 177; industrial methods in, 159–160; leadership in, 159–160; profitability, importance of, 164; workforce in, 161. *See also* Sodexho
International Herald Tribune, 5, 55, 56

Jackson, Kenneth T., 131n12
Jacobs, Jane, 130n8
Jacques Borel International, 158
Jaloux, Roger, 79n86, 81
James, B., 123n94
Jaslin, Jean-Pierre, 132n17

Katsumi, 81
Katz, Peter, 130n8
Kayser, Bernard, 200n81
Keeler, J.T.S., 197n73
Kirschner, Orin, 209n104
kitchens, organization of. *See* brigade system
Klinenberg, Eric, 6n17
Koop, M.-C. Weidmann, 123n94
Kottak, Conrad P., 92n3
Kowinski, William S., 130n8
Kroc, Ray, 102–103, 122, 166n104
Kuisel, Richard, 130n7, 148n62

label biologique, 203
label rouge, 203
label regional, 203
Lacombe, Jean-Paul, 179n29
Lactalis Corporation, 206, 211
Laguzet, C., 141n42
Lamont, Michèle, 172n7
Landes, David, 148n62
Lang, Jack, 124, 125
Larousse, Pierre, 59
Lazareff, Alexandre, 90n109, 171n5, 196n69
Learning from Las Vegas (Venturi, Brown and Izenour), 122
Ledoyen, 82
LeDuff, Louis, 158–159
legal field, 209–210
Legay, Guy, 65
Legendre, Philippe, 66
Legoupil, D., 119n84

Leidner, Robin, 105n42, 120n86
Lemel, Yannick, 132n17
Lenôtre, Gaston, 73
Le Point, Ferdinand, 32
Lerger, Claude, 85
Leroy Merlin, 139
Letablier, M. T., 202n87
Levenstein, Harvey, 110n62
L'Express, 55
Libby's Corporation, 144
libre-service, 133
"the local," 9, 19, 201–208
Loiseau, Bernard, 55, 82, 179, 189–190, 196; apprenticeship of, 76, 83–84; celebrity of, 87–90; childhood, 82–83; death of, 1–6; financial strategies of, 190–191; food processing industry, partnership with, 175, 185; military service of, 85
Loiseau, Dominique, 5
Lorain, Jean-Michel, 80, 177, 184, 189
Lorain, Michel, 80, 184
Love, John, 105n40
Lucas Carton, 175
Lundestad, Geir, 150n69

Magazine LSA (Libre Service Actualités), 147
magic: Americanism, of, 135, 151–152, 209–210; cultural production, and, 37–39; social phenomenon, as a, 135
Les Maîtres Cuisiniers de France, 68
Malapris, Michel, 58, 98n7
Markus, Francis, 160
Marshall Plan, 133, 136, 150
Martin, Guy, 175
Massachusetts Institute of Technology, 158
Mauss, Marcel, 61n50, 135, 151
Maxim's, 178
McDonald's Corporation, 91–92, 154, 209: company formula, 96–97; expansion in France, 101–104, 128; French unions and, 106–107; introduction to France, 96; suburbs, in France, and, 128–129; successes in France, 94
McMillan, Tracie, 134n21
Medal of National Merit, 88
Meilleur Ouvrier de France (MOF), 65–69, 74, 79, 176
Mendras, Henri, 132n17, 198n75
Mennell, Stephen, 10, 21, 51, 85n99
Meriot, Sylvie-Anne, 77n80, 83n95, 153n75, 161n90, 164
Mermet, Gérard, 132n13
Merriman, John, 131n9
Mesplède, Jean-François, 32n75, 42n9, 47n20, 50n29, 84n98, 85n101, 180n30

Métiers de Bouche, 65
Metton, Alain, 131n11, 136
Meunier, Sophie, 90n109
Michelin Guide, 2, 40–47, 52–54, 62, 71–72, 84, 87, 179; ratings, influence of, 3–5, 43, 190
Michelin star system, 42–44; anonymity, and, 44; consecration and, 32n75, 46, 84, 154; disinterestedness, and, 45–46; secrecy, 44–45; stability of, 53; timelessness of, 46
Michelin Tire Corporation, 41, 46, 53n38, 82
Mikogel, 182
Millau, Christian, 47, 49, 52
Miller, Bryan, 53n39
Mingione, Enzo, 95n12
Mirretti, Marc, 78
Mitterand, François, 88
Môet-Hennessy, 144
Le Monde, 45, 54
Mondial Moquette, 139
Monin, Phillippe, 51n31, 86n101
Monnet, Jean, 149–150
Montanari, Massimo, 10n20, 11n24, 17n37, 142n47
Muth, Hanns Peter, 197n71

National Cash Register Company, 133
National Council of Culinary Arts, 124
National des Meilleurs Ouvriers de France, 58
National Union of Hotel, Restaurant, and Café Operators, 194–195
neoliberalism. See gastronomic field
Néoerestauration magazine, 44–45, 62–64, 147, 158–159, 175; grand chefs' "annexes," on, 186; Michel Guérard's work for Nestlé, on, 174, 175; promotion of fast food, and, 97–102
Nestlé International, 173, 174
New York Times, 4
Noël, Philippe, 66n60
nomos, 41, 170n3, 171
Northcutt, Wayne, 91n2
nouvelle cuisine, 50–52, 85, 173
Novotel, 158
Nutri Pack Company, 64

Orsi, Laurent, 81
Orsi, Pierre, 81

Page, Karen, 31n71
Panitch, Leo, 166n103, 209n104
Paris, 12, 18
Paris Match, 4
Parsons, Talcott, 123n92
Passard, Alain, 177, 187

Pasteur, Louis, 24
pastry chef profession, 73
peasants, 19, 198–199, 200; gastronomic patrimony, and, 201–206
Pedrocco, Giorgio, 23n55, 142n47
Pélisson, Gérard, 158
Perez, Roland, 146n60
périurbain fringe, 130–131, 132, 133
Perrier, 144
Physiologie du gout, (Brillat-Savarin), 13–15
Piault, Fabrice, 94n11
Pic, André, 32, 80, 184
Pic, Anne-Sophie, 184, 188
Pic, Jacques, 188
Picard, 195
Piketty, Thomas, 141n43
Pinto, Diana, 124n96, 125n98
Pitte, Jean-Robert, 10n20, 11n21
Poilane, Lionel, 73
Point, Fernand, 51, 76, 79, 176
Le Pot au feu, 28
Poulaine, Jean-Pierre, 204n92
Pourcel, Laurent, 80
Pourcel, Jacques, 2, 80
Poussier, Olivier, 73n72
Powell, Walter, 96n17
La Prés d'Eugénie, 173
Prévos, A.J.M., 123n94
professional kitchen, organization of, 31–32
Prix Taittinger, 68
Pynson, Pascale, 94n11

Ranger, Terence, 206n99
Rao, Hayagreeva, 51n31, 86n101
regionalism. *See* regional cuisine under gastronomic field; *le terroir*
Regourd, Serge, 90n109
Rémy, Pascal, 41n8
restaurants (*restauration commercial*), 152–153; commercialization of, in France, 125–126; dissemination of throughout France, 12; functions of, 13; invention of, 10–11; menus of, 12; *Michelin*-starred, 154; ritualized behavior in, 116–117; salaries in, 72; structure of authority in, 71–72; workforce in, 161. *See also* chain restaurants; fast food
Restaurel, 159
La Revue de l'industrie agro-alimantaire, 147
Ribaut, Jean-Claude, 54, 171n6
Riding, Alan, 125n99
Rigalleau, Michelle, 94n10
Rigby, Brian, 124n96
Ritz, César, 31

Ritz Hotel, 64
Robuchon, Joël, 55–57, 66, 87; chefs' practical sense, on, 75; food processing industry, partnership with, 175, 189
Roellinger, Olivier, 177
Rogers, Susan Carol, 206n100, 207–208
Rolancy, Jacques, 81
Roosevelt, Franklin Delano, 149
Roquefort cheese, 206–208
Rosenblum, Mort, 92n3
Ross, Kristin, 132n15
Rostang, Michel, 179n29
Rouff, Marcel, 20
Rousselot, 144
Royer, Jean, 138
Royer Law, 138
Royle, Tony, 104n38
rural redevelopment, 200–208
rural life; devaluation of, 198–199; nostalgia for, 19

Sailland, Maurice-Edmond. *See* Curnonsky
Salon International de l'Alimentation (SIAL), 182
d'St. Martin, M., 110n60
Saint-Maclou, 139
Sampson, Anthony, 92n3
Sarran, Michel, 78
Sasser, W. E., 101n32
Saunier, P., 142n46
Savoy, Guy, 179, 185, 187
Savoy Hotel, 31
Schaller, B., 142n46
Schehr, Lawrence R., 12n26
scientific management, 69n66
Senderens, Alain, 175–176
Sennett, Richard, 89
Simon, François, 2, 54
social autopsy, 6
social capital, 77. *See also* under chef profession
Socopa France, 144
SODIMA, 144
Société des cuisiniers français pour le Progrès de l'art culinaire, 29
Société des Meilleurs Ouvriers de France, 65, 68
Sodexho (Groupe Sodexho France; Sodexo), 159–160; grand chefs, hiring of, 177–178, 187
Solivérès, Alain, 78
sommelier profession, 72–73
Sopad-Nestlé, 144, 182
Spang, Rebecca, 11n22, 12, 13
standardization, 127–128
Steinberg, Jean, 131n11

Steinberger, Michael, 31n73, 94n10, 193n59
Stephenson, Peter, 117n78
Stoclet, Denis, 132n17
Stovall, Tyler, 131n10
Strasser, Susan, 116n76
Strauss, David, 124n95
supermarkets, 129. *See also* hypermarché
Swinbank, Vicki A., 28n64, 171n6
Swiss Bank Corporation, 158
symbolic capital: definition of, 151, 175n16; economic capital, conversion to, 177, 182, 188–189. *See also* magic; under American business practices; Americanism; American styles
Syndicat National de l'Alimentation et de la Restauration Rapide (SNARR), 106–107, 110, 172

Taillevent, 82
television, 199. *See also* television advertising under fast food
Terence, Isabelle, 34n76, 47n21, 52–53, 70n67, 80n87, 161n91, 191n54
Terrail, Claude, 184–185
Terrio, Susan J., 74
le terroir, 9; celebration of, by non-state institutions, 203; commercial interests and, 204–208, 210–211; consecration of, 200–206; definition of, 127, 201; enforcement of, by French state, 201–202 (*see also* AOC); international markets, and, 208; marketing device, as a, 211; resistance to industrialization, as, 203–204
Tholoniat, Étienne, 73
Thomas, Dana, 181n33
Thornton, Sarah, 123
Thuriès, 57–59
Thuriès, Yves, 57–58
La Tour d'Argent, 82, 184
traiteurs guild, 11
Trillin, Calvin, 110
Troisgros, Jean, 65, 80, 87, 184
Troisgros, Pierre, 83–84, 184
Trubeck, Amy, 25n58, 28, 201
Trujillo, Bernardo, 133–134, 158
Tunstall, J., 15n35

Union Laitière Normande, 144
unions, 25, 138–139
United States: consumer society, creation of, 150–151; embrace of "continental cuisine," 110; European cultural goods, appreciation for, 124; "New Urbanist" development, and, 130; suburbanization, 131

Van De Calseyde, Y., 106n44, 107n50
Venturi, Robert, 122, 129n6
Vergé, Roger, 66, 78
Verger, Claude, 85, 86
Versailles, 12
Veyrat, Marc, 177, 178, 190
viennoiseries. *See* fast food
Vignat, Gérard, 81
Village in the Vaucluse (Wylie), 199
Villermet, Jean-Marc, 133n20
Virgin Megastore, 139
Voss, Kim, 106n46

Wall, Irwin, 109n58
Waquant, Loïc, 22n54, 131n11, 167n1
Warde, Ibrahim, 134n23
Weber, Eugen, 19n46, 21n52
Weisman, Katie, 181n33
Weiss, Allen S., 12n26
Wells, Patricia, 5, 40, 54–57
Williams-Gascon, A., 123n94
World Trade Organization (WTO), 91, 209
Wright, Gordon, 197n72, 198n76
Wyckoff, D. D., 101n32
Wylie, Laurence, 199

youth. *See* adolescents; French youth under American cultural practices; French youth under fast food; French youth, enticement for, under gastronomic field

Zeitlin, Jonathan, 150
Zeldin, Theodore, 11n25, 22n52
Zolade, Robert, 160
zones commerciales. *See* commercial strips
Zukin, Sharon, 51, 134n23

Rick Fantasia is the *Barbara Richmond 1940 Professor in the Social Sciences* and Professor of Sociology at Smith College. He is the author of several books including *Cultures of Solidarity: Consciousness, Action and Contemporary American Workers* and (with Kim Voss) *Hard Work: Remaking the American Labor Movement.*

www.ingramcontent.com/pod-product-compliance
Lightning Source LLC
Chambersburg PA
CBHW040148270326
41929CB00025B/3426

* 9 7 8 1 4 3 9 9 1 2 3 0 0 *